Space and Place in the
Works of D.H. Lawrence

Space and Place in the Works of D.H. Lawrence

STEFANIA MICHELUCCI

Translated by Jill Franks

McFarland & Company, Inc., Publishers
Jefferson, North Carolina, and London

This book was originally published as *L'orizzonte mobile. Spazio e luoghi nella narrativa di D.H. Lawrence*, by Edizioni dell'Orso, 1998. It is here translated from the Italian by Jill Franks.

Translator's Note: A translation inevitably changes some meanings and shades of meaning, even when it involves nonfiction prose. In particular, translating from Italian to English involves the shortening of sentences, the rearrangement of syntax to change passive to active voice, and the omission of certain conversational, yet formal, conventions which Italian prose typically contains, but which English academic writing avoids. To summarize, the English academic voice is a bolder one, which is more likely to assert propositions as true rather than possible or apparent. Whenever I could achieve exact translation, even when it meant retaining long sentences with several appositives, I did so, as long as I believed it would not compromise clarity.—JF

Library of Congress Cataloguing-in-Publication Data

Michelucci, Stefania.
    Space and place in the works of D.H. Lawrence / Stefania Michelucci; translated by Jill Franks.
        p.   cm.
    Includes bibliographical references and index.
    ISBN 0-7864-1152-X (softcover binding : 50# alkaline paper) ∞
    1. Lawrence, D.H. (David Herbert), 1885–1930 — Criticism and interpretation.   2. Place (Philosophy) in literature.   3. Space and time in literature.   4. Personal space in literature.   I. Title.
PR6023.A93 Z68126   2002
823'.912 — dc21   2001056258

British Library cataloguing data are available

©2002 Stefania Michelucci. All rights reserved

No part of this book may be reproduced or transmitted in any form or by any means, electronic or mechanical, including photocopying or recording, or by any information storage and retrieval system, without permission in writing from the publisher.

On the front cover: Detail from Claude Monet's *Garden in Bloom at Sainte-Addresse*, 1866, oil on canvas.

Manufactured in the United States of America

McFarland & Company, Inc., Publishers
    Box 611, Jefferson, North Carolina 28640
        www.mcfarlandpub.com

To John Worthen

It appears, however, to be something overwhelming and hard to grasp, the topos — that is, space-place.
— Aristotle

Acknowledgments

I am grateful to Giovanni Cianci and Giuseppe Sertoli for their attentive supervision while I was doing my doctoral research on Lawrence. Their suggestions have proved invaluable. I am also indebted to Giovanni Cianci for having encouraged me to publish this book in English. His highly perceptive and sensitive comments, as well as his constant scholarly support, have been of great value to me and have made him a pleasure to work with.

A very special thank you to John Worthen, my "Lawrencean Virgil," who from the very beginning has guided me with contagious enthusiasm along the tortuous path of Lawrencean studies. He has been generous in his support for this project and I am extremely grateful to him for all that he has done to enable its realization. Without him this book would have never come into being.

I would like to thank Jill Franks for her kind offer to undertake the translation of the book. Not only am I indebted to her for the dedication with which she carried out the task, but also for the sensitivity, perceptiveness and clarity she displayed throughout.

I am also particularly grateful to David Ellis, Martin F. Kearney and Louise E. Wright for their constant encouragement and stimulating scholarly assistance and for their invaluable criticism of various sections of the manuscript.

I would also like to thank John Unrau, who very generously read the entire manuscript and made useful suggestions for its improvement.

My thanks must also extend to Seán and Jessica Lysaght, Raffaele Macchione, Mario Russo, Ronald Packham, and Paul Poplawski for their help in many different ways.

A few changes have been made from the Italian edition, principally concerning the notes and the bibliography, which have been updated. But any translation, although faithful, impeccable and scrupulous, constitutes a new book.

Copyright material is reproduced by kind permission of Laurence Pollinger Ltd and the Estate of Frieda Lawrence Ravagli, and of Lorenzo Massobrio (Edizioni dell'Orso).

Contents

Acknowledgments v
Abbreviations xi

Introduction
Space 1
Space and Place in Literature 3
Places in Lawrence's Works 4

1 — Places of Us and Places of Others: *The White Peacock*
The Garden and the Jungle 7
Strelley Mill 8
Sacred Spaces 9
The Other Places 10
Confrontation with Reality 12
The Dispersal 14

2 — The Pact with the *Genius Loci*: *The Prussian Officer* 18

3 — Capsized Island: *The Trespasser*
The Impossible Flight 24
The Spatial Dimension 25
The Island 28
Routes 29

4 — "Widening Circles": *Sons and Lovers*

The Fight for Territory	32
The Bottoms	35
The House and Its Inhabitants	36
The Internal/External Opposition	39
Willey Farm	43
Miriam's Places	46
Clara's Place: The City	49
The Void	52

5 — The Beginning of the Quest: *The Lost Girl* and *Aaron's Rod*

The Escape	55
The Expanding Horizon	57
Verticality	60
Super-Civilized and Super-Primitive	61

6 — Uprooting: *The Rainbow* and *Women in Love*

Circularity and Polarity	64
The Dialectic of Center and Margins	67
The Crisis of Home	71
The Widening of Space	74
Places of Threshold	80
The Line and the Circle	85

7 — The Spirit of Place: Return to Origins

The Flight from the West	88
The Journey: "The Woman Who Rode Away" and "The Princess"	91
The Plumed Serpent	95
A Different Departure	95
The New Home	97
Rebirth from the Low — the Church	100
The Play of Different Viewpoints	103

Conclusion   107

Notes	115
Bibliography	159
Index	173

Abbreviations

AR	*Aaron's Rod* (1922), ed. Mara Kalnins, CUP, Cambridge 1988.
BB	*The Boy in the Bush* [with Mollie L. Skinner] (1924), ed. Paul Eggert, CUP, Cambridge 1990.
FU	*Fantasia of the Unconscious* (1922), Penguin, Harmondsworth 1971.
Hardy	"Study of Thomas Hardy" (1936), in *Studies of Thomas Hardy and Other Essays*, ed. Bruce Steele, CUP, Cambridge 1985.
K	*Kangaroo* (1923), ed. Bruce Steele, CUP, Cambridge 1994.
LCL	*Lady Chatterley's Lover* (1928), ed. Michael Squires, CUP, Cambridge 1993.
Letters i.	*The Letters of D.H. Lawrence*, Vol. I (1901–1913), ed. James T. Boulton, CUP, Cambridge 1979.
Letters ii.	*The Letters of D.H. Lawrence*, Vol. II (1913–1916), ed. George J. Zytaruk and James T. Boulton, CUP, Cambridge 1982.
LG	*The Lost Girl* (1920), ed. John Worthen, CUP, Cambridge 1981.
MM	*Mornings in Mexico* (1927), Penguin, Harmondsworth 1986.
NMC	"Nottingham and the Mining Countryside" (1930), in *Phoenix: The Posthumous Papers of D.H. Lawrence*, ed. Edward D. McDonald, Viking, New York 1936.
PO	*The Prussian Officer and Other Stories* (1914), ed. John Worthen, CUP, Cambridge 1983.

Princess	"The Princess" (1925), in *St. Mawr and Other Stories*, ed. Brian H. Finney, CUP, Cambridge 1983.
PS	*The Plumed Serpent (Quetzalcoatl)* (1926), ed. L.D. Clark, CUP, Cambridge 1987.
R	*The Rainbow* (1915), ed. Mark Kinkead-Weekes, CUP, Cambridge 1989.
SCAL	*Studies in Classic American Literature* (1923), Penguin, Harmondsworth 1977.
SL	*Sons and Lovers* (1913), ed. Helen Baron and Carl Baron, CUP, Cambridge 1992.
SM	*St. Mawr* (1925), in *St. Mawr and Other Stories*, ed. Brian H. Finney, CUP, Cambridge 1983.
T	*The Trespasser* (1912), ed. Elizabeth Mansfield, CUP, Cambridge 1981.
TSM	*The Symbolic Meaning: The Uncollected Versions of "Studies in Classic American Literature"* (1961), ed. Armin Arnold, Viking, New York 1964.
WL	*Women in Love* (1920), ed. David Farmer, Lindeth Vasey and John Worthen, CUP, Cambridge 1987.
WP	*The White Peacock* (1911), ed. Andrew Robertson, CUP, Cambridge 1983.
WRA	"The Woman Who Rode Away" (1925), in *The Woman Who Rode Away and Other Stories*, ed. Dieter Mehl and Christa Jansohn, CUP, Cambridge 1995.

Introduction

> *Clearing-away is release of places.*
> — Martin Heidegger

Space

It is probably no exaggeration to say that all the artistic revolutions of the past century have involved a reflection on space and new methods of conceptualizing and utilizing space in art. The so-called "crisis of representation" considered space a central concern, not only in the visual arts, but also in literature. In reference to some of the most important literary works of the twentieth century, and especially Joyce's *Ulysses*, we speak of the use of "spatial form."[1]

There is no scarcity of studies on spatial structures in twentieth-century literature, and this is the case with D. H. Lawrence's works as well (limited though they are, however, to *The Rainbow* and *Women in Love*).[2] On the other hand, the study of the function of place, particularly in narrative, has been much less extensive. This study requires a particularized approach, insofar as the concept of place, even though not initially discernible from that of space (if it is true that every place occupies a physical space and is visually perceived and measured in spatial terms) is intrinsically different from it. Space is in fact a physical and philosophical category, while place is a cultural and anthropological category.[3] Even though humans use space to define place, in the sense of position, size, and distance from other places, at the moment in which we name a space, we make it a human, cultural reality.[4] On a map, places are represented by the marks—and names—which humans have put upon physical space. Culture inscribes itself upon surrounding space. By individuating places and assigning them specific functions essential for the survival of the community, culture spreads itself into surrounding space and, naming it, inscribes, cuts, separates, and differentiates.[5] Differentiating its own environment from the surroundings, a specific community or social group *carves out* and imposes its own identity.[6]

The categories "space" and "place" also share, however, an area of overlap, which depends on the way in which they are conceived.[7] Both concepts arise from the primary psychological function of distinguishing between "self" and "not-self," between the subject and the surrounding world, a distinction which entails a fundamental binary in the mental organization of space and, consequently, of place. From the opposition "self/world" originate other oppositions of a spatial nature (internal/external, near/far, finite/infinite, closed/open, immobility/mobility, empty/full), to which are attached yet others of a psychological stamp, such as known/unknown, friend/enemy, security/threat, and so on.

These categories also play a central part in the cultural organization of places. But the overlap of ways of thinking of place and space is limited: if, for instance, space can be described as an unspecific, absolute, infinite entity, then place is, on the contrary, a finite, definite entity, identified in relation to other places and diametrically opposite to the dimension of the unknown which stretches beyond its boundaries. "Place" is a term closely connected with human activity and, as such, with what can be defined as known, controllable, humanized, "culturalized," as the space of being and the site of community. As such, it is often used as a positive pole against which we contrast the negative pole of external space—unknown, uncontrollable.

One's relationship with this "not-self" (which can be the unknown, but also an "Other" place) varies in different cultural models, but it is always described as the necessary condition for the existence and identity of community, as it is the condition for place itself.[8] Furthermore, in every culture, within the site of social community, are created functional "under places": for example, places for communal life and social communication are distinguished from the seats of power and worship,[9] making it possible to discern anthropological/cultural categories (such as "places of us" and "places of others") applicable to place but not to space, which are the subject of recent research and to which we will return, given their relevance to this study.[10] At this point, however, it is essential to note that these categories assume an important epistemological function: cultural organization of place often signifies a model for interpretation of reality.[11] Constructing its own site in space, a community creates a microcosm, on the basis of which it is possible to explain and understand the rest of the world and to cohabit in a dialectical relation with it, reinforcing one's own sense of belonging to one's own place by virtue of consciousness of separation from the external and from other places.

Space and Place in Literature

On the basis of these considerations about the relation of space and place, it is possible to distinguish their principal applications to the study of literature. It is not the intention of this study to analyze the predominance of spatial form in twentieth-century literature, a topic covered by many existing studies.[12] The intention is to focus on the "geography" of the text, on the ways in which it (especially the novel) utilizes places for its own ends, not only to create the "field" of action and the background against which the activities of the characters take place, but also to give life to a system of functional relations carefully integrated into the structure of the work.[13]

At this point another premise must be introduced: that the abovementioned categorization of space and place in terms of binary opposition cannot be transferred *tout court* from psychological and anthropological fields to literary discourse, even though that would seem to be most desirable and helpful. Literature also defines spaces and places, and imbues them with relational meanings, so that we can say, at least in many cases, *the geography (or topography) of literary works constitutes a system of meaningful relationships*. In Saussurean terms, this system is called a *system of difference*, a *code*, a *langue*. The reference to Saussure becomes even more relevant when we consider that places communicate among themselves using definite means (routes), which allows us to think of them as a communications system, a spatial *langue*. This can become (especially in the novel) a structural element of the text which mirrors a cultural model of interpretation of the world.[14]

Such a model, which may reflect a certain epochal episteme, or a system of anthropological archetypes,[15] has a conventional character and because of this we have spoken of a spatial *langue* in literary works. To the extent that this spatial *langue* becomes the object of personal appropriation by the writer, it becomes a *parole*; but such a *parole* constitutes a *langue* for the characters, who base their cultural model upon it, whereupon it becomes, in turn, a *parole* according to the method in which each character uses it. The double function of place therefore relates to the opposition of *langue* and *parole*: places serve as objective reference points for all of the characters, but they are interpreted and represented in personal ways by each character. Individual "readings" of places reflect the psychological, ideological, and semantic investments (idealization, demonization, recognition, disorientation, etc.) which characters give them.

Place in Lawrence's Works

The function of place changes significantly in Lawrence's artistic evolution, yet in all of his works we see an opposition between places of nature and places of culture, a subject that has been amply treated by criticism. A related subject, which has been treated less thoroughly, is the way in which the metaphorical and axiological investments of place change over the course of his opus.

In all of the works of his early period, from the first (c. 1907) to the publication of *The Prussian Officer and Other Stories* (1914), we find a polarization between civilization and nature, which links Lawrence to the Romantic tradition. He does not veer from this tradition except in his ideological ambivalence towards nature, which originates in the opposition between a Darwinian and an aesthetic viewpoint.[16] The first leads him to regard nature as a destructive, brutal, amoral force, and the second, to accentuate the more poetic, softer aspect. But his attitude is also ambivalent in relation to culture, so that his early works see culture, on the one hand, as a means for intellectual and aesthetic development (access to a "superior" existence) and on the other hand, as a negation of all spontaneity of life, as the source of inauthenticity, artifice and corruption. Metaphorical objectification of these ambivalences in the dichotomy garden/jungle recurs insistently in the stories of *The Prussian Officer* and in the first two novels, *The White Peacock* and *The Trespasser*, suggesting also axiological investments of place. Such a dichotomy reflects the writer's difficulty in confronting reality, the yearning for escape to a world of "superior" experience, perceived, however, as fragile and even inauthentic. Proof of this can be seen in the feeble attempts of many Lawrencean characters to escape, to confront reality and to achieve an "authentic" existence. These attempts are often destined to failure, which, significantly, focalizes the spatial dimensions of these works, attached as they are to the passage from the known to the unknown, from "places of us" (the garden, the home) to hostile, threatening, disorienting "places of others" (school, work, the city).

Lawrence began to emerge from this impasse only when he learned to turn the polarity known/unknown on its head, finding the positive pole in the unknown, which he increasingly identified with the chronologically, spatially, and culturally remote. This existential realization involves the exploration of an "other" universe, carrying the conviction of the necessity of a polarity in relations between the sexes (which become more vital the more "distant" the partners), and generating a need to explore new geographical and cultural spaces (Sardinia, Australia, Mexico, the Etruscan world), a need which inevitably is shared by many of his characters who, after a certain point, become, like himself, indefatigable travelers. The need to travel produced in the opus an enlargement of horizons, which only came in a gradual and rather tormented way, and which did not always entail his characters' appropriation of new spaces. For example, in *The Lost Girl*, written just after World War I, the title itself suggests the incapacity of the protagonist to integrate into a new place, a southern Italian village, which she is incapable of "reading" and in which, subsequently, she "loses herself."

Whereas in *The Lost Girl*, the relation with the world of the "Other" essentially fails, in *The Rainbow* and *Women in Love*, such a relation is more fruitful, at least for some of the characters, and is vitally connected to the maturing process and to their self-fulfillment (which, however, is never total). In these novels we notice a close relationship between place and experience, each place being appointed for a particular experience and each experience allocated to a particular place. Characters are constructed along the chain of their movements from one place to the next, a chain from which arises the eminently spatial structure of the novels themselves.

Lawrence explicitly affirms the importance of place and of the interaction of inhabitants with place in the introduction to his *Studies in Classic American Literature*, where he formulates the concept of "spirit of place" in terms of a man/environment polarity. On the basis of this polarity, not only does a community settle and establish itself in a specific place, but it is also influenced by that place in the formation of its own identity, its customs and traditions. Such polarity is at the very basis of self-construction through cultural data and culture's corresponding influence on the environment and surrounding places, even if a specific culture's life is limited in time:

> Every continent has its own great spirit of place. Every people is polarized in some particular locality, which is home, the homeland. Different places on the face of the earth have different vital effluence, different vibration, different chemical exhalation, different polarity with different stars: call it what you like. But the spirit of place is a great reality ... . There was a tremendous polarity in Italy, in the city of Rome. And this seems to have died. For even places die [*SCAL* 12].

"The spirit of place" emerges especially in narratives of "exotic" environments, where the characters' attempts to relate to and understand the specificities of place are the source of profound tension. This tension clearly emerges in novels like *The Plumed Serpent* and in novellas like *The Virgin and the Gipsy,* "The Woman Who Rode Away," and "The Princess," in which it is possible to measure the characters' capacity for growth and self-realization by their success or failure in confronting a disturbing "Other" world.

1

Places of Us and Places of Others: *The White Peacock*

> *Such was that happy garden-state,*
> *While man there walk'd without a mate.*
> — Andrew Marvell

The Garden and the Jungle

Ingenuously decadent, *The White Peacock* belongs to the literature of the fin de siècle, especially that influenced by Pater. Like many other works of its time, its central theme is youth destroyed or lost. It is the story of a failed initiation into adult life, but (herein lies its novelty) it develops this theme in a polyphonous mode, that is, by examining the affairs of three couples, each of which is distinctively characterized by a procedure of stylization consistent with certain cultural clichés, such as the "Arcadian farmer," the "noble savage," and the *femme fatale*. Such stylization is also present in the rendering of scenes in the dialogue and in the narrative sequences, imposing a fundamentally non-realistic imprint on the work.[1]

Structural partitions of the novel give it a threefold rhythm, as the activities of these three young couples are interwoven.[2] The novel is divided into three parts, which can be called "idyll," "confrontation with reality," and "dispersal." The first introduces adolescent attitudes shared by all of the characters; the second, the elements which upset the idyll; the third, the dispersal of the characters who, after being psychologically separated, distance themselves physically, thrust by circumstances in very different directions. The subplot provides variations on the theme of life's cruelty and an ambiguous reflection on the main plot. This story-within-the-story concerns the gamekeeper Annable, who, betrayed and disillusioned by a sophisticated *femme fatale*, seeks refuge and consolation in the simple life. In certain respects, he is the double of the farmer George, refused by the frivolous Lettie (the "white peacock"), who prefers Leslie, an example of the empty, "well-mannered citizen." Each of *The White Peacock*'s three parts includes a topography, a thematic and structural map, which characterizes the novel, insofar as it is closely related to the identity of the characters and their interpersonal relationships.[3]

Strelley Mill

In the novel's first part, the center of activity is Strelley Mill, the usual site of the characters' walks and the home of George, the idealized farmer. His natural beauty attracts Lettie and also the story's narrator, Cyril, whose admiration for George is fed by an innocently homosexual disposition. Consistent with the conventions of Romantic/Aesthetic stylization, each idealized figure corresponds to an idealized scene. Even though it is a place of work, Strelley Mill is never described as such by the narrator, nor felt as such by the characters, who see only its idyllic, picturesque, Arcadian aspect, closing their eyes to the biological and economic activities carried out there.[4] Precisely because it is seen and experienced as Arcadia, Strelley Mill, though existing materially, is in effect a place of dreams. Lawrence's depiction of the farm follows various pictorial models, all with a Romantic/Aesthetic stamp (Greiffenhagen, Clausen, Millais, the Pre-Raphaelites).[5]

The adolescent, idealizing viewpoint from which all of the characters see Strelley Mill contributes to the creation of a consensus among them, as they temporarily rebel against the sociocultural barriers which tend to separate them. In other words, they can only *meet* (in a sense not merely physical) in a place removed from reality, by virtue of a common consensus about the semantic and axiological investment of place.[6] This investment can only come about by a deliberate veiling of reality, so that the Arcadia into which the characters transform the farm is fragile and insecure, as the developments of the second and the third parts make clear. Once the characters begin to lose their common ground, the farm, too, changes its meaning, and becomes another place.[7]

Throughout the first part of the novel, however, Strelley Mill remains for the three young couples a "place of us," in anthropological terms, and also an *object of appropriation* destined to last as long as the consensus among them does.[8] Wherever we find such an appropriation, we also find sovereignty, implying the existence of a sovereign. Lettie presides over external spaces, while Emily, George's sister, presides over internal spaces (the home), forming the type of gynocracy which characterizes all of Lawrence's early works, including *Sons and Lovers*, a novel which revolves around the formidable matriarch, Mrs. Morel. Even fields and forests are subject to the sovereignty, in this case masculine, of George and Annable, suggesting that men may preside only in places where less sophisticated or civilized activities take place.

The concept of sovereignty, which implies consensus around the figure exercising power, is thus a social category belonging to the cultural order. In the early Lawrence it is not clearly distinguishable from the category of territorialism, which has, by contrast, an individual character and belongs to the order of nature, implying the fight for the possession of territory. The dichotomy between sovereignty and territorialism corresponds, in his early works, to that of garden and jungle.

Sacred Spaces

The nature of the sovereignty that Lettie exercises over Strelley Mill is that of a sacerdotal priestess. She officiates at the activities of the farm, all characterized by a marked element of ritual, due not only to their repetitive nature but also to the need of the characters to crystallize in a "perfect" canonical form the habitual gestures which mark their encounters and, together, to sacralize them. Ritual, then, is part of that process of transfiguration of experience, of separating a place from its normal "reality," which is at the very heart of this first part of the novel.

Many of the rites taking place at Strelley Mill are configured as a celebration of "gentle" nature (identified with the vegetable kingdom and definitively excluding the animal), ingenuously modeled on literary or pictorial reminiscences: the characters adorn themselves with variously colored flowers, cover themselves with berries, or weave crowns of plants, seeking to exorcize the dark, brutal, violent aspect of nature.[9] At other times they seek, albeit timidly, a contact and intimate communion with generative forces, as happens for example in the episode where the two young couples contemplate snowdrops in an isolated place, with a mystical simplicity that leads Lettie to important observations:

> ...they are so still. Something out of an old religion, that we have lost.

They make me feel afraid … . They belong to some knowledge we have lost, that I have lost, and that I need. I feel afraid [*WP* 129].

While, in this moment, her religious terror of *natura naturans* provides a surprising anticipation of later Lawrence (in the poems of *Birds, Beasts and Flowers*), in other places, the contemplation of flowers catalyzes communion not with nature but between two souls which reflect and meet each other in poetic emotion, as will occur with great frequency in *Sons and Lovers*.

Along with these initiation rites, which belong specifically to the "us" of the three couples, there are others of a more conventional and public character, in a different communicative mode. Whereas the most emotionally intense relationships are achieved in the floral rites, moments of intellectual intimacy are possible in the course of another ritual, the walk,[10] and, to a lesser degree, in social occasions such as mealtime conversations and parties. These last, by virtue of their worldly character, are contrasted to the floral rites; they signal moments, not of union, but of division. It is probably for this reason that Lawrence uses them for threshold moments (for example, at the ends of the first two parts), which introduce decisive changes in the characters' lives.

The Other Places

The function of happy Arcadia exercised by Strelley Mill is largely due to its isolation (which Lawrence emphasizes at every possible opportunity), and to its construction as an island, archetypically the place of utopia and of dreams. Connected to the external world by a single road which passes through the woods, the farm is partly surrounded by woods on the north, which represent, on the one hand, a kind of protective membrane separating it from the world of mining and industry, and on the other hand, a metaphorical opposition of garden/jungle which is of crucial importance in the novel, since Lawrence uses this metaphor to express his own ambivalence about nature.

In *The White Peacock*, there is a tacit law by which every place can be occupied only by certain characters. Also each place plays a precise function within a topography in which nothing is left to chance; the distribution of the places gives rise to a geometry so strict that it recalls medieval allegories. For example, the three habitations among which the characters move, that is, the farm (Strelley Mill), the middle-class cottage (Woodside) and the rich gentleman's home (Highclose) are arranged along an axis, oriented from low to high, that corresponds to a social hierarchy.[11] If the mill by itself represents the island of dreams, in relation to the other two homes it represents the pole of life-according-to-nature (associated with those biological activities which Lawrence in this period still sees as "lower"), as opposed to high bourgeois sophistication, in a way which adumbrates the opposition of *soul* and *mind* in the later works. Woodside, home of the narrator, is in a middle position between the other two, its function to mediate between the characters and places of the novel.[12]

To these three symmetrically related homes it is possible to add, in the external position of the narrative horizon, a fourth, that of the gamekeeper, which we may define as *obscene*, not only in the etymological sense of the word (because it is placed practically outside the scene) but also because, in its brazenly flaunted naturalness (for example, the gamekeeper's wife nurses the newborn without covering her breast), the characters experience it as a sort of taboo, and for this reason it is not usually the object of their visits. The characters frequent the other places in a measure proportional to their emotional significance, which is naturally greatest for Strelley Mill (the gravitational center of the walks and the characters) and most minimal for Highclose.

It is interesting to note how such walks delineate a substantial circularity in the characters' movements inside their microcosm, a circularity which Lawrence seems to relate (albeit unclearly) to the principle of cyclicity that presides in the macrocosm.[13] The doom of Strelley Mill is related to this principle. The happy island has reached its own twilight insofar as a historical cycle is concluding, one in which humans were still able to live in harmony with nature. In melancholy reflection about the imminent condemnation of his Eden, which is threatened by wild rabbits, but also by the inevitable advance of industrialized society, the narrator Cyril opens the novel in a passage that illustrates the twilit *Stimmung* which informs *The White Peacock*:

> I stood watching the shadowy fish slide through the gloom of the millpond. They were grey descendants of the silvery things that had darted away from the monks, in the young days when the valley was lusty. The whole place was gathered in the musing of old age. The thick-piled trees on the far shore were too dark and sober to dally with the sun, the reeds stood crowded and motionless. Not even a little wind flickered the willows of the islets. The water lay softly, intensely still. Only the thin stream falling through the mill-race murmured to itself of the tumult of life which had once quickened the valley [*WP* 1].

The passage is of great importance because it illuminates, from the very beginning, "the other face" of Strelley Mill, which, in this place of dreams (insofar as it is an island removed from time and the bustle of others' activities), is not and cannot be real life, and so, is often obliquely associated with death. Along with the funereal atmosphere that increasingly looms over it as the story develops, Strelley Mill is associated with the world of the dead, and the "infernal gods," by its location (to reach it, it is necessary to descend) and by the name of the nearby lake, Nethermere. Strelley Mill's interior, beyond its charming and welcoming aspect, occasionally suggests funereal connotations: for example, the parlor in which Cyril and Lettie find Emily after the episode of cat killing seems to them "long and not very high; there ... were wild flowers and fresh leaves plentifully scattered" (*WP* 14) evoking, intentionally or not, the image of a coffin.

The insistent emphasis upon Strelley Mill's isolation in the early part of the novel focuses on the element of separation but also that of communication, which makes it a *threshold*, an element which should not be taken in a strictly spatial sense. The threshold is not only the boundary of the farm, but all the places where characters are forced to become conscious of the existence of an "other" world, one which is perturbing and distressing. Thresholds are found particularly in watery places, the marshes and ponds placed near the three homes: the water where "the shadowy fish" slide silently and mysteriously under the surface (also a threshold); that in which occurs the violent episode of cat killing (and later, the poetic burial); and finally, the fountain near which Lettie and George meet and argue during the tea party episode. The water that the girl pours into the elegant pitcher in order to offer drinks turns out to be full of mud and pulsating with organisms, so that the threshold here is the boundary between poetic and unpoetic, or between the culturalized Eros of worldly ritual and the corruption from which life springs. The real threshold, however, is that of sexuality, which covertly informs the episode and which is clearly implied when Cyril and George, faced with each other's nudity on the marsh shore, experience a moment of chaste but intense physical intimacy, without daring to venture beyond the threshold.[14]

> When he [George] had rubbed me all warm, he let me go, and we looked at each other with eyes of still laughter, and our love was perfect for a moment ... [*WP* 222–23].

Confrontation with Reality

The strongly ritualistic and choreographic nature of the novel's action, its precise rhythms and symbolic significance, are particularly noticeable in the end of the first part. The characters' gravitation towards the central home, Woodside, where they meet for the last time, contrasts with their progressively centrifugal movement in the second and third parts. While the snowstorm rages outside, leaving, at dawn, a silvery, surreal landscape, all of the principal characters come together to celebrate Lettie's birthday and her entry into adulthood. The party signals her passage from adolescence to adulthood as well as from freedom to responsibility because of her engagement to Leslie, and is therefore paradigmatic of the *threshold*. As the snowstorm suggests with obvious symbolism, beyond the threshold lies the hard world of reality, with its cruel struggles in society (the miners' strike) and in nature (the struggle for survival, the exclusion of those not "adapted"), a world which presses threateningly on the boundaries of the garden, as much in the form of the invasive wild rabbits as in the mechanization that inexorably advances.[15]

At the spatial level, this threat manifests itself in the transformation of the property boundaries into a frontier: at this point, the places around Highclose are studded with "no trespassing" signs, which signal the end of peaceful, harmonious coexistence, and the establishment of struggle between places of "us" and those of "others," or even between nature and law. The warning "no trespassing" clearly implies that to cross the threshold means to run the risk of never being permitted to return.

In the second part, the repositioning of the action from the center to the threshold brings an enlargement of horizons and the extension of the action to "Other" places, each of which imposes on the characters an embarrassing and painful contact with the "unpoetic." One of these places is the ex-farm Selsby, now overcome by wilderness, where the gamekeeper Annable tells Cyril the story of his own unhappy affair with a lady, which forced him to open his eyes to the other side of Eros, that which is corrupt, anarchic, and destructive. It is no accident that this revelation occurs in a devastated garden, transformed into a jungle: "'Just look!' he [Annable] said, 'the dirty devil's run her muck over that angel. A woman to the end ... all vanity and screech and defilement,'" (*WP* 149). A second place where a similar meeting occurs is Ram Inn, a once-flourishing residence which is now in decay, where people smoke, drink, and curse, in a situation of "low" conviviality which is contrasted to the meals at Strelley Mill. A third is the squalid house of the gamekeeper. A deliberate contrast is created between the three homes in the first part and the three hovels of the second.

This encounter with reality corresponds, on a narrative level, with a brusque acceleration of rhythm (in itself mimetic of the fervor of life outside the garden), which contrasts with a slowing down in the final chapter, significantly entitled "Pastorals and Peonies" and dedicated to the description of a tea party where the principal characters unite for the last time. The sophisticated literariness of the language brings an expectation of a return, however ephemeral, to a harmonious situation, but such is not the case. The party establishes an oppositional relationship, not only with preceding episodes, but also with the birthday party which closes the first part, contrasting the melancholy "accords" and the elegiac music created by the three young couples, with the dissonance provoked by the intruders (human counterpart to the wild rabbits). They violate the "garden," impeding the re-creation of the old harmony, particularly that between Lettie and George, who is now recast in the role of lout from which the "dance" of the adolescents had temporarily removed him.

The episode also marks the beginning of his slow process of self-destruction, which proceeds apace with the decline of Strelley Mill.[16] After the episode of the party, in fact, the mill is transformed completely, undergoing first another intrusion (when the house is opened for the meals of day-laborers) and then its final abandonment, due to the dispersal of those who had lived or visited there. Cyril and Emily's last walk in the "garden" serves only to verify melancholically its metamorphosis into an "other" place, ruled by new laws and logic.

Although structurally varied in tone and expressive registers, the second part of the novel remains quite static. Positioned between Lettie's engagement and her wedding (in the beginning of the third part), the characters are involved in circular, reiterative movements, in Hamlet-like situations of hesitation between thought and action, in repeated meetings and disagreements which take place usually at "thresholds" — spaces functioning as passages between the known and the unknown, between the "in" and the "out"[17] — or in niches used to delay their confrontation with reality.[18] Apart from the story of Annable, told on the grass-covered graves of his ancestors (also a threshold between life and death),[19] the second part presents only three salient episodes, consisting of as many meetings between George and Lettie. The first is the evening at the edge of the forest, when Lettie anticipates the inevitable abandonment of the valley of Nethermere; in the second, she tries to rebel at the prospect, but George does not accept her invitation to the fight; in the third, the two appear resigned, when they sanction their final separation by the last embrace in a niche created by tree branches. By now internally destroyed, George seeks refuge in another niche, the granary, an "under place" which, like the stalls, allows him to close the door on reality and withdraw into a space of solitude and meditation.

The Dispersal

The expansion of the narrative horizon is accented in the transition from the second to the third part, where the characters are dispersed in places far from Nethermere valley, site of their adolescent happiness. For each of them, the abandonment of known places gives rise not so much to growth as to an odyssey which will not end in a safe haven. After initial enthusiasm for her new environment, Emily defines it not as a home but as a lodging where she can stay for a bit, maybe a year, but no more. George tries in vain to transform himself from farmer to innkeeper and ends his existential adventure as an alcoholic in the house of his sister. Lettie wanders from house to house, while Cyril seeks to follow the others, collecting information about their lives even after their dispersal.[20]

Paradoxically finding themselves in new and unknown spaces does not constitute an experience of freedom for any of the characters, who instead find themselves continually having to face the danger of trespassing on a hostile, disorienting world which can offer occasional moments of discovery, but whose rules are unknown and which is full of deception.[21] In the episode of George's journey to Nottingham after his wedding to Meg, for example, the protagonist, totally lost, "could not get over the feeling that he was trespassing" (*WP* 246). In fact, he continually commits errors of behavior which betray his utter disorientation.

Presented in the first chapter, this episode is the prelude to an encounter with the metropolis, which all of the characters have to undergo in the last part of the novel, and which has upsetting effects, especially on a farmer like George. The immensity of the city, the sea of unfamiliar faces, the coming and going of the crowd, the poverty and degradation seen under Waterloo Bridge show George the unknown face of an incomprehensibly violent world, to which it is impossible to adapt:

> The unintelligibility of the vast city made him [George] apprehensive, and the crudity of its big, coarse contrasts wounded him unutterably [*WP* 286].

Cyril's situation is not very different; the city seems to him a kingdom of artificiality, where roses do not grow, but are sold at the edges of the streets, where the natural rhythm of night following day is disturbed by the constant presence of lights, where the sky, the roof of the world which marks the horizon, is replaced by the roof of the Crystal Palace, "great dilapidated palace..., fretting because of its own degradation and ruin" (*WP* 261). Nevertheless, he gradually adapts himself to the city, begins to appreciate its various aspects, the magic of the lights, the exciting kaleidoscope of sounds and colors, which he discovers to be the vertiginous flux of modern life:

> I loved the city intensely for its movement of men and women, the soft, fascinating flow of the limbs of men and women, and the sudden flash of eyes and lips as they pass [*WP* 264].

His attitude towards London reveals an attempt to read the city as if it were a reality not radically different from that of the Nethermere Valley.[22] His attention is constantly turned to the poetic aspect, to the presence of flowers and colors. The evaluative standards he uses are constantly related to past experience, as when the coming and going of people is compared to the buzzing of bees around flowers. Cyril's degree of integration into the city is directly proportional to his ability to compare it with the Nethermere Valley.

To this same valley all the characters return, after their centrifugal movement away from it, but as the narrator's words show, they find it altogether changed, so much so that the places seem unable to recognize their old inhabitants: "I wanted to be recognized by something ... . I was a stranger, an intruder" (*WP* 306). The principal homes, especially, undergo a real metamorphosis: Woodside, center of equilibrium between opposite poles, appears empty (as if it were uninhabited) already at the beginning of the third part, when Cyril and George toast their new venture into life: "The rooms were very still and empty, but the cool silence responded at once to the gaiety of our sunwarm entrance" (*WP* 239). On Cyril's return from France, the house is surrounded by a barbed wire fence which impedes access, while Strelley Mill is unrecognizable, occupied by strangers from the north, invaders and predators like the rabbits who had caused destruction. Annable's residence is also changed, from a place of vaunted naturalness to a respectable home whose artificiality is symbolized by the paper flowers which adorn it. Only Emily's house remains a place of idyllic serenity.[23] It is, however, completely isolated from the rest of the world, the last cradle of civilization for generations who lived in harmony with nature, far from progress and transformation, where Emily, after much seeking, seems finally to find an existential haven:

> Emily, in her full-blooded beauty, was at home. It is rare now to feel a kinship between a room and the one who inhabits it ... . Emily had at last found her place, and had escaped from the torture of strange, complex modern life [*WP* 319].

Cyril sees the farm, however, as a place immersed in a silence which resembles death ("the place was breathing silence," *WP* 318). Furthermore, such tranquility is felt only by Emily and the Renshaw family who, in the logic of the novel, are already like "les derniers fils d'une race épuisée" (*SL* 180) with whom Paul in *Sons and Lovers* identifies the inhabitants of Willey Farm.

But the transformation of places is explicable in another way: by the advancement and growth of the dark, threatening world of the mines, made visible by the towering, black smokestacks which loom over the row-houses and become audible as well. While in the early parts of the novel, the noise of the mines was heard only from afar, now it fills Cyril's ears and mind, rendering him acutely conscious of the fact that the end of adolescence coincides, for those who belong to his "us," with the end of an era.

2

The Pact with the *Genius Loci: The Prussian Officer*

> *The frontiers are not east or west, north or south, but whenever a man fronts a fact....*
> — Henry David Thoreau

The stories in *The Prussian Officer* surround, so to speak, Lawrence's two earliest novels, being written in a wide span of time (1907-14) which begins with *The White Peacock* and ends after *Sons and Lovers*. The stories, even more than the novels, constitute valuable evidence of the artistic and ideological evolution of the writer, which they allow us to follow step by step.[1]

The fact that the stories belong to different creative moments is reflected in a noticeable and inevitable heterogeneity of form, style, and content, even though there are also recurrent elements, especially the strong emphasis conferred upon places, which play a very important role. Compared to *The White Peacock*, Lawrence sometimes demonstrates a better knowledge of how to utilize place to catalyze reactions and revelatory behaviors of the characters, or to objectify the themes and paradigmatic oppositions present in the stories.

As in the first novel, in some of the stories of *The Prussian Officer*, the escape from the "jungle" and the consequent search for a "garden" carries

2. The Prussian Officer

with it the consecration of certain places and the introduction of ritualistic elements, which, however, are different from those in *The White Peacock*.[2] In that novel, as we have seen, places belong to two principal categories: those of "us," of similar souls who isolate themselves in a congenial environment, removed from life's necessities, and those of "others," whose rituals, such as parties, conform to the social code and are often utilized to illuminate distances and oppositions between characters. This distinction does not appear as clear-cut in *The Prussian Officer*, where, in the first place, moments of happy isolation in the "garden" are missing, and in the second place, the rites of conviviality, in general, are not occasions for getting together, but only catalysts for latent conflicts of thresholds and insurmountable boundaries, or evidence of the violence and brutality which the individual hides underneath a fragile surface of civility.

This is true of the title story, where the captain's meals are occasions for sadistic persecution of his own attendant, and abuses of power. Provocations for this persecution originate from a "hunger" which is never recognized, his obsessive physical desire for the young soldier. The soldier, in his turn, is entirely possessed by another passion, also largely unconscious: hatred of his persecutor which assumes an essentially physical character, becoming eventually an aversion not to the *person* but to the *flesh* of the captain, so that a paradoxical reciprocity is established in their relations.[3] The ritual of meals, rendered more rigid by the hierarchical relationship between the two men, for awhile "covers" and keeps under control the tension between them. But later it explodes into violence on a convivial occasion, which is, not coincidentally, celebrated in the woods. The attendant, who has stoically borne the physical violence of his captain, cannot resist the "desire" excited by the sight of the captain's throat while he is drinking a tankard of beer, and, taken over by an uncontainable ecstasy, jumps on the other, strangling him.[4] Once he has broken the rules of ritual, man turns into a beast.

Voracity is again associated with animality, though in a different manner, in "Goose Fair." In one of the central scenes, Lawrence uses the ritual of mealtime to contrast the figure of the irresponsible father (who feigns indifference about the fire which broke out at the family factory, indirectly attributing fault to the future son-in-law) to that of the daughter, serious, sensitive and determined to confront the situation. If the failure to eat together symbolizes the latent conflict between the two characters, the contents of their meal — the steak which the one greedily devours and the coffee which the other sips — indicate their respective natures.[5]

Unlike these two stories, wherein the consumption of food is used as evidence of the tensions between the two antagonists, in others, the meal is evidence, as in *The White Peacock*, of insuperable social and psychological distances. In "The Shades of Spring,"[6] Syson's arrival at the farm during the family dinner is seen as an intrusion, and he himself feels out of place in a spot where he had once belonged but from whence he estranged himself by frequenting others: "[the farmer] assumed that Syson was become too refined to eat so roughly" (*PO* 102). In order to safeguard family intimacy and appease the laws of hospitality, a compromise is reached — "We'll give Addy something when we've finished" (*PO* 102) — arising from the hybrid situation of once-belonging felt by the protagonist.

In other stories as well, Lawrence uses places to represent the extraneousness felt by a character in a social environment different from his own. In "Daughters of the Vicar," the bourgeois ritual of inviting visitors to supper becomes the source of interminable misery for the miner Alfred, who minds not so much the impossibility of dialogue with the vicar and his wife, as their subtle manifestations of hostility, their sense that their "territory" is being invaded by an intruder. He is an object of scorn for both of them; he is oppressed by a sense of being *out of place* which his hosts sadistically exacerbate.[7] He has such a total experience of disorientation that his union with Louisa (the vicar's daughter) would be impossible if she, vice-versa, did not manage to orient herself immediately in his territory — "their fixed routine of life .... It was all so common, so like herding. She lost her own distinctness" (*PO* 72) — and make herself friendly so that she can be welcomed by her future mother-in-law.

The use of social meals as a circumstance which mandates the observance of the rules of the "code" reaches its highest dramatic intensity in "The Christening," where Lawrence uses with consummate skill the potential inherent in a situation — baptism of an illegitimate son — which constitutes a kind of social paradox, inasmuch as it is the (obligatory) celebration of public shame. He lingers pitilessly on the minutiae of every gesture of preparation for the convivial ritual, a source of acute suffering for family members, and at the same time the litmus test of the veiled rancor and petty jealousies which separate them:[8]

> Miss Rowbotham kept a keen eye on everything: she felt the importance of the occasion. The young mother ... ate in sulky discomfort..., Bertha ... scorned her sister, treated her like dirt [*PO* 176].

The only cohesive factor in the family is the religiosity of the father, a kind of biblical patriarch who has sacrificed himself to reach a bourgeois social status (symbolized by the residence he constructed, Woodbine Cottage),[9] but who is not enslaved, in the circumstance, by bourgeois conventions:

An' let this young childt be like a willow tree beside the waters, with no father but Thee, oh God. Ay, an' I wish it had been so with my children, that they'd had no father but Thee [*PO* 178–79].

Instead of a contested birth, the ritual of social eating occurs in its opposite form, a death in the family, in the story "Odour of Chrysanthemums": here, the kitchen in which the mother and sons eat their meals is a place where they daily confirm their alliance against "the intruder," the father. His unusual lateness (this time due to his death in the mine) offers an occasion for the mother to vent her accumulated rancor—"it is a scandalous thing as a man can't even come in to his dinner .... Past his very door he goes to get to a public house, and here I sit with his dinner waiting for him" (*PO* 185)— rancor which gives way, when the corpse is brought to the house, to a feeling of quasi-religious respect for the flesh she once loved: "[she] put her face against his neck, and trembled and shuddered" (*PO* 197). Many effects of this story, like the previous one, arise from the introduction into the same place, a domestic interior,[10] of two opposites: everydayness and the near-religious solemnity of encounters with the two great "thresholds" of existence, birth and death.

Another element of difference between the stories and *The White Peacock* is the almost total absence in them of those genteel rites which in the novel called attention to the organic world, in particular, to its flowers. Even when present in *The Prussian Officer*, they are not agents of harmony between like souls or of communion with place, but contribute, as do mealtimes, to bring out elements of separation or lack of communication, or to evoke specters of the world of dreams belonging to a past by now irremediably buried.[11] In "The Shadow in the Rose Garden," the place of Poetry, laden with flowers and perfumes, produces the melancholy voluptuousness of the memory: "[she came] at last to a tiny terrace all full of roses .... She felt herself in a strange crowd. It exhilarated her, carried her out of herself. She flushed with excitement. The air was pure scent" (*PO* 125). The garden is soon transformed into a nightmarish place when she meets the man she had loved before her marriage, now pathetically demented:

> She could see his shape, the shape she had loved with all her passion: ... fixed, intent, but mad, drawing his face nearer hers. Her horror was too great. The powerful lunatic was coming too near to her [*PO* 127].

A variation on this theme appears in "The Shades of Spring," where the romantic rite of two ex-lovers walking in the woods does not revitalize the intimacy of the years past, but crudely emphasizes their present alienation. This modification of the sentimental situation also suggests a different relationship to the environment. The "expropriation" of the woods suffered by Syson[12] contrasts with Hilda's decisive "appropriation" of them ("she ... was always dominant, letting him see *her* wood," *PO* 105, emphasis mine) after being engaged to a gamekeeper.

Accompanying the gradual devaluation of floral rites in this collection is the gradual acceptance of the world of nature, blood and sex. In "The Shades of Spring," Hilda, after showing Syson "her" woods, leads him to the gamekeeper's cabin, scene of their intimate meetings, and, in this circumstance, of a double ritualistic ceremony. First, she confirms her complete union with nature by putting on "a cloak of rabbit-skin and of white fur" (*PO* 107), then sucks the bee poison out of her fiancé's arm, giving him, as she says, "the reddest kiss you'll ever have" (*PO* 111).

Another bloody rite occurs in "Second Best," where it assumes the character of a true initiation to the mysteries of nature. Here the protagonist Frances, forced to give up her bourgeois *dream* of marriage, accepts the *reality* of a farmer-suitor and confirms her decision to belong completely to him and his world through the offer of a defenseless mole which she kills to demonstrate an unconditional acceptance of the brutal "logic" of nature.[13] This bloody, pagan rite contrasts with the bourgeois one of engagement to her first lover who, opting for society instead of nature, makes an existential choice opposite to Frances'.

In tying herself to a farmer who is also tied to a certain place, Frances has crossed a threshold. In that act we find the crucial moment of this and other stories in which the most important developments of the plot call attention to movements from one place to another or the crossing of a certain boundary. Examples include the stream which separates the area where the two sisters live from the cultivated fields in "Second Best," the gate of the Quarry cottage and the ivy hedge which surrounds the property of the vicar in "Daughters of the Vicar," the institutionally closed threshold of the garden—"the garden isn't open to-day" (*PO* 124)—in "The Shadow in the Rose Garden" and the gate that blocks access to the road through the woods in "The Shades of Spring."

The boundaries around a given place signify the jurisdiction within which the laws of *that* place are valid, laws which can appear strict to the point of intolerance, especially when they involve military discipline and when they are imposed upon "naturally sensitive" people, as in the case of the two soldiers who appear in "The Thorn in the Flesh" and "The Prussian Officer." In both stories, the space where the protagonist is confined is completely separate from the outside world, perceived by him through olfactory, visual, and auditory sensations which generate a very acute desire for the "outside," and exacerbate the protagonist's intolerance of the absurd tests which the "code" (or the brutality of those who use it sadistically) imposes:

> Through the moving of his comrades' bodies, he could see the small vines dusty by the road-side, the poppies among the tares fluttering and blown to pieces, the distant spaces of sky and fields all free with air and sunshine. But he was bound in a very dark enclosure of anxiety within himself [*PO* 23].

The young soldier in "The Thorn in the Flesh" flees from the place of his shame and humiliation (he had wet his pants while climbing up a ladder on a dangerously high wall) to seek refuge in another (his fiancée's room) where he finds redemption as a man through sexual relations with her.[14] In "The Prussian Officer," the high, uncontaminated mountains sharpen the protagonist's desire for freedom and render the captain's vexations more intolerable. After killing the captain, his dominant impulse is to run towards the mountains: "straight in front of him, blue and cool and tender, the mountains ranged across the pale edge of the morning sky. He wanted them — he wanted them alone — he wanted to leave himself and be identified with them" (*PO* 20) — an impulse made unrealizable by his loss of consciousness and his disorientation in the woods, a place which, after having symbolized the uncontrollable world of instinct, now becomes a labyrinth without exit and therefore the objective correlative of the soldier's flight without hope.[15]

Although his wandering in the forest ends in death, in the gothic story "A Fragment of Stained Glass," the endless flight of the two lovers in the snow-covered forest signifies the positive result of contact and reciprocal knowledge. Nevertheless, the forest itself becomes a game of paradigmatic oppositions somewhat similar to that in "The Prussian Officer": the contrast of the dark green vegetation with the cold whiteness of snow, but especially with the decorated fragment of stained glass from the church, represents the conflict between the dark world of instinct and a vague yearning for transcendence or at least a "liberation," which, in the desperate situation of flight in both stories, becomes identified with death itself.[16]

In some sense these two stories are at the opposite extreme from *The White Peacock,* not only in that they offer the woods as a nightmarish "nocturnal" image, opposite to the idyllic image in the novel, but also and especially because they show "the other face" of isolation: the place of flight from the world becomes a labyrinth in which one gets lost and can even die. By cutting ties with the external world, one makes the irreversible choice to become an "outlaw." The "garden" of refuge can transform into a place of exile or a distressing prison, which is exactly the experience presented by *The Trespasser.*

3

Capsized Island: *The Trespasser*

> *Beyond good and evil we discovered our island.*
> *Our green fields. Only the two of us!*
> *For this we must love each other!*
> — Friedrich Nietzsche

The Impossible Flight

Lawrence's second novel, *The Trespasser,* was not judged benevolently by his critics, who disposed of it as a pretentious, immature work, evidence of a search for his artistic identity which was far from successful.[1] The writer's immaturity, which is the most noticeable common denominator of his first two novels, stems from the difficulty of ridding himself of an affectation of aestheticism which, later, he himself would recognize as their greatest defect.[2] Like *The White Peacock, The Trespasser* contains elements (the love triangle; the insoluble conflict between passion and ethical responsibility; the exalted, febrile atmosphere; the Wagnerian allusions) which are typical of the literature of the epoch.

The aesthetic element is not the only tie between the two novels; even though the atmosphere, setting, technique and style of *The Trespasser* are notably distant from *The White Peacock,* its themes and issues are very close to the first novel, with which it shares a relationship of substantial continuity. The fundamental opposition in both books is between aesthetic/

decadent and crudely anti-romantic viewpoints, or, more simply, between the world of dreams and the world of reality. In *The Trespasser*, such opposition reaches a climax, even to the point of breakage, so that the ideological and artistic change of direction in Lawrence's later works seems inevitable.

The extremity of this opposition (real/ideal) is manifested primarily through a change which focuses on place: the happy island is substituted for the *topos* of Edenic garden, implying an even greater separation from the world and, theoretically, an even greater protection from it.[3] This is exactly the opposite, however, of what happens in the novel, where the two clandestine lovers, Siegmund and Helena (he a middle-aged violinist and she a young student of his), are not able to find, on the island to which they escape, either the fulfillment of passion or a defense against the encroachments of reality. In *The Trespasser*, these encroachments no longer come from the outside, as in *The White Peacock*, but from inside the place of refuge, where nature and man are always to some degree hostile. Similarly, it is from within the relationship of the two lovers that the incapacity to reach real union and harmony arises.[4]

If the world of nature is not presented in a positive light, the world of culture is the object of condemnation which is none the less extreme by virtue of remaining merely implied. The intellectual "vice" of the protagonists prevents them from living their relationship with spontaneity and threatens the failure of their adventure from the very beginning. Their inauthenticity is incited by their efforts to conform to the grand myths of passion (most of all, Wagner's *Tristan*) which continually creates a barrier between them and reality, between them and nature itself, so that even the island is no longer seen by the lovers for what it really is. If the island does not offer them the expected liberation, it is because both are incapable of an appropriate "reading" of the place and of their interaction with it.[5]

The island, place of romantic mystifications, is contrasted to London, world of reality, in such a way that contrast becomes central to the structure of the novel. Set in the island and the metropolis, it is divided into two parts, so that here, as in *The White Peacock*, the topography of the novel is perfectly fitted to the idea which informs it. The fact that London wins in the "battle" between these two places, decrees, besides the tragic end of the protagonist (who commits suicide because he cannot face returning to his family), the "death" of two myths: that of the Happy Island and that of Absolute Love.

The Spatial Dimension

Even though it is definitely dated, the novel contains an original aspect in the way in which it relates its characters to the places and spaces in which they interact. This happens from the very beginning of the story, when the escape of the two protagonists is figured as the search for a place of "us," arising from their conviction of the impossibility of reaching the erotic Absolute in places which are all, in some way, the domain of "others"—those who live there, administer its laws and defend its boundaries—and in spaces experienced as a negation of their desired freedom.[6]

The sense of liberation which Siegmund looks forward to when planning their escape is rendered in spatial terms: "Siegmund had already left the city ... the sea and the sunlight opened great spaces, tomorrow" (*T* 49). The boundless stretch of the sea here symbolizes the absence of limits, absolute liberty, the fullness of life in an adventure lived to the maximum, in a risky, yet exalting challenge to the "code." It is precisely the spatial structure of the novel which renders the reader immediately aware that the Absolute to which Siegmund believes himself to be heading is illusory: after all, only a channel of the sea separates the Isle of Wight from *terra firma*; only one week is *scheduled* for the escape.[7] What compromises from the outset his "trespass" of bourgeois rules are the very bourgeois limits fixed upon an adventure which should have had an "absolute" dimension and which becomes instead a mere escapade. Nevertheless, no matter how limited in intention and unsatisfying in execution, the escapade renders the *nostos* equally untenable to Siegmund, who, during the return journey is oppressed by a growing sense of claustrophobia which makes even Helena's presence a nuisance. Upon his return home, he locks himself into the "little cubicle of darkness" of his room, from which he emerges only to kill himself (*T* 51).

In a sense, the novel presents his suicide as the result of a vital lack of space: if, before his escape, the house is Siegmund's prison, after his return it becomes a taboo place in which his family always makes him feel shameful and unwanted, a place from which he knows he will have to undertake a new escape, this time without return. Long-lasting alternatives to the domestic space cannot be found within Siegmund's horizons of petit-bourgeois existence; neither can he look for an escape from his impasse in an interior space, in the memory of the lovers' flight, since that had failed and since the island revealed itself, besides a "place of others," a place of *separation* rather than *union*.[8] If Siegmund and Helena failed to connect deeply, it was due in part to the impossibility of sharing their experience of the island, which each one lived separately and solipsistically, superimposing upon the image of the real place their mystifying, "poetic" images, something that exposed both, but especially Siegmund, to traumatic battles with reality. What he actually gained from his "contact" with the island was a wounded thigh and elbow (results of banging himself on sharp cliffs), as well as sunstroke, which gave him a high fever and was in part responsible for his ultimate desperate decision.

The two protagonists never managed to find the proper approach to the island, which first, from a distance, they had idealized excessively and which later they were unable to see realistically, as the language with which they render their experience reveals.[9] Their nebulous, misty, exalted language displays their lack of contact with reality[10] and contrasts diametrically with the precise, cold, factual language of the London episodes. The spatial opposition of the two places is related, not only to the paradigmatic opposition between reality and dream, but also to the opposition between two types of writing.

This problem of distance also occurs at the structural level. For the first and last time in his artistic career, Lawrence reverts to an old literary expedient, that of the "frame," which has no justification except in terms of a search for the most appropriate distance from which to narrate Siegmund and Helena's affair. The part of the novel set on the island coincides with the characters' greatest closeness to it, and therefore with their maximum emotional intensity, but also with a condition of "myopia" which renders a clear perception of reality impossible. On the other hand, the frame (which appears as an epilogue, presenting the situation of Helena a year after Siegmund's death) coincides with the maximum chronological and psychological distance from the event itself, a distance which totally reverses the meaning, even trivializing the tragic end of the protagonist. In the viewpoint created by such distancing, the experience of the two protagonists reveals its own inauthenticity, which makes it quite similar to the dramatic scripts of the era.

The word "script" is not chosen randomly: in the novel the theatrical metaphor is used frequently and is intimately connected to the inauthenticity with which the two lovers live their romantic interlude.[11] Not only do both always "act" (at least when they are together), conforming to cultural referents taken as their models, but they even perceive reality in terms of a "show." When, for example, he compares the fiery summer sunset to a Beethoven symphony and she compares it to the music of *Lohengrin*, they literally transform the island into a theatre or concert hall (that is, they transform nature into culture). Even nature becomes a "show" or theatrical event for Siegmund and Helena, confirming that the central issue of the novel is the unattainability of naturalness.

The narrative frame returns to this theatrical metaphor, functioning like a stage curtain and creating not only an effect of distance from that part of the story set on the Isle of Wight, but also making the island appear as a sort of stage and making the affair of the two lovers seem like a mere dramatic "play." This dramatic artifice and the interplay of theatrical perspectives is further complicated by the fact that inside the frame itself—consisting of two chapters (first and last) which present Helena in a relationship with a new suitor — are placed, like a frame within a frame, two other chapters dedicated to the activities of Siegmund's family after his suicide.

In the last chapter, this Chinese box structure is linked to another circular structure: almost a year after Siegmund's death, Helena gets involved in another relationship in which she repeats step by step the ritual of the walk which she had often taken with Siegmund on the Isle of Wight, leading Byrne (the new lover) to a sort of fictitious island on *terra firma*, the larch-wood. This occasions a brief dialogue, evidently finalizing the idea of the cyclicity of experience on the one hand: "'History repeats itself,' he [Byrne] remarked" — and on the other, suggesting the incapacity of humans to "read" it and to learn a lesson from the past: "'How? ... I see no repetition,' she added" (*T* 226).

The Island

The usage of different stylistic modes in different "layers" of the novel (the frame, the parts set in London, the adventure) make the passage from the most interior layer to the most exterior a progressive *distancing* from the experience lived on the island, as well as a progressive *cooling* of the emotional temperature. From this results the insistent attention to the atmospheric conditions — those of an unusually warm English summer — in which the experience takes place. The adventure comes to stand for a magma-like, incandescent nucleus, a "body" which chills and hardens progressively, when we proceed from the nucleus towards the "crust;" or it comes to stand for a kind of sun, around which the other places in the novel rotate like satellites, darkened and brightened by it. They too are characterized, not accidentally, by a circumscribed form which resembles an island.[12]

Insofar as the place is quite *circumscribed*, it calls to attention, to an extent even greater than the "garden" in *The White Peacock*, issues connected to *boundaries* and to *thresholds*. Finding themselves constantly on thresholds, in fact, forces the two protagonists into a continuous encounter with the unknown, generating in them both desire and fear of the venture, so that even in relation to space, they betray the fundamental contradictions of their love experience, their incapacity to reconcile the Absolute with boundaries.

This theme is closely connected to their encounter with the primary reality of nature, and more precisely with cosmogonic elements, two of which, the earth and the water, are separated at the "threshold" of the island by its shore. The lovers experience the threshold as a division between the finite and the infinite and therefore as an *impassable* limit.[13] This is also because spread out beyond it is an impracticable *non-place*, the sea, culturally indivisible, stripped (for them) of points of reference and of orientation.[14] If the island, as suggested, is often a "place of others," the sea, conversely, is an "other space," inaccessible not only because of its association with the infinite, but also for the fact of being *nature in its pure state*. It is therefore not surprising that neither has much familiarity with it ("He was a poor swimmer … . She was no swimmer," *T* 73, 137) and that they see it as a threatening and unfaithful "being." To "exorcise" it, they must revert to their habitual mystifying practices of disguising and refining it poetically. Siegmund compares Helena to a marine animal which — she adds — belongs to the sea and one day will return there, even if, in reality, Helena prefers a safe niche, the rock-pools in which she splashes, to the boundless breadth and depth of the sea.

The other cosmic elements are also essentially hostile to the protagonists: in water, Siegmund hurts himself; fire (the sun) gives him a terrible sunstroke[15]; sand (earth), in which he seeks relief from the heat of the sun, emanates a deathly coldness[16]; and air, in two crucial moments (right after his arrival, and upon their departure from the island), is uncomfortably humid and foggy.

Routes

Their encounters with the "threshold" and with the "primary" elements occur in the course of a series of walks which always have as destination the seashore and as point of departure a "center" constituted by the lodging house, a "place of others" run by a landlady who affects them differently and who helps catalyze their disharmony. Almost a "home" for Helena,[17] the cottage where they stay is the source of uneasiness and oppression for Siegmund, as seen when he huddles by the fire in the armchair and by his silence when the landlady is present.[18]

But if he is nervous and uneasy here, he is never serene and relaxed in other environments either. Since his uneasiness is shared by Helena, their walks assume the quality of neurotic restlessness which, except in rare moments, characterizes their entire adventure. Structurally, however, these incidents confirm Lawrence's propensity to organize narration in the reiterative form seen in *The White Peacock* and more skillfully executed in *Sons and Lovers*.

The reiterative situation in *The Trespasser* consists (as in the first novel) in the walks. Although on a first reading this renders the narration fragmentary and episodic, when examined from a holistic perspective, it seems to reflect an intentional, functional narrative strategy. The routes of these walks are occasions to introduce the protagonists to various spheres of experience and to reveal the diversity of their responses in a way which makes *The Trespasser* a forerunner to *The Rainbow* and *Women in Love*.

If we examine the sequence of these iterations, we notice a doubly contrastive logic: a) every walk they take is followed by a solo walk which serves to re-establish an inner equilibrium after a moment of rupture with the partner; and b) between walks, or often during the same walk, Lawrence creates strong, continuous *chiaroscuro* effects such as the contrast between the festive, colorful crowd which hails Siegmund on his departure from London and the fog which welcomes him on his arrival at the island, filling him with sadness and desolation. Other examples develop the contrast between the sense of well-being felt during his first immersion in sea water and the acute pain brought on by his fall on the cliff; between the little girl (the beginning) which the protagonists run into at the beach and the cemetery (the end) they arrive at shortly after.

By virtue of its function as a *memento mori*, the cemetery is involved also in a macro-contrast in which the principal role is played by the great cross on a hill which supplies the protagonists a point of reference, but which at the same time opposes their desire for happiness to a sort of Schopenhauerian warning of the inevitability of suffering.[19]

Even more important, in that it occurs in almost all of the walks, is the spatial opposition between high and low (or between above and below). The "aboves" are the heights from which the paths unwind to the sea, as well as the country places, domesticated nature, which are rife with recognizable and reassuring signs for the two protagonists. Their attitudes substantially reflect the author's, who grew up in the country and was profoundly familiar with it. The "world of below" includes the seashore where their walks invariably lead: a world dominated by water and fire (sun), that is, by the primary elements. *The Trespasser* abounds in the contrasts between wild nature and "gentle," domesticated nature which are so prominent in Lawrence's early works. The "world of below" is the point of confluence of all the primal elements, of the intensity and uncertainty of the night, of the moon's enchantment, of the water which gives life but which also hides dangers, of the sun which in its intensity obscures the senses. The "low" produces disturbing experiences because of its capacity to unite opposites: sky and sea, sun and moon, man and woman.[20] Glamorous, dangerous, uncontrollable, it ends up being, perhaps without the writer's full awareness, the objective correlative of passion. Conversely, the "world of above" is identified with a serene and innocent existence, or with the sphere of normalcy which the lovers have left. It is no accident that the scenes of pastoral life, which the adolescents of *The White Peacock* closely observe and participate in, can only be contemplated from a distance by Siegmund and Helena, as part of a world that is no longer approachable.[21] Hardly less strange or hostile is the bourgeois world represented by "Londoners on holiday" (*T* 116) and presented in images of placid, festive, family harmony, arousing a painful feeling of exclusion and tacit envy in Siegmund and Helena.

In combination with the method of repetition and contrasts, another paradigmatic element that links episodes is reflection. For example, the first walk occurs in the midst of an obfuscating fog which renders the surrounding sights and sounds indeterminate, whereas the last walk leads the protagonists to a beach where the sunlight is so brilliant and blinding as to prevent Siegmund from reading his watch. The relationship between the first and last moments of the affair is at once analogous and opposite.

Of the same kind, yet more complex, is the relationship between the attitudes of the protagonists on their first and last walks. On the first, Siegmund abandons himself to voluptuous immersion in the beauty of nature and would like to stay out longer to enjoy it, in contrast to Helena, who is impatient to return because she cannot stand the feeling of bare feet on cold earth. The same situation is repeated in the last walk, but this time, the befuddlement caused by the scalding sun makes Siegmund tarry and Helena want to leave.

The mechanism of repetition and reflection links the two "extreme" walks which Siegmund takes alone: in the first, he hurts his thigh just when he is beginning to feel like a marine creature, while on the last walk he painfully bangs his elbow on a rock which was apparently "smooth as his thighs." But it is in the central episode of the adventure that the paradigm of reflection emerges most evidently, the meeting of Siegmund and Hampson, described as a "queer — sort of Doppelgänger" (*T* 115), a meeting which makes Siegmund "look in the mirror" before committing the bitter act to escape from his desperate existential *impasse*.

In spite of the undeniable artificiality, sensationalism and "theatricality" which are the most obvious faults of Lawrence's early works, the episode in question supplies a further confirmation of the clever construction of this second, disconcerting novel, which, from the standpoint of structural engineering, represents a remarkable advance from *The White Peacock*, forecasting the skillful structuring of *Sons and Lovers*, *The Rainbow* and *Women in Love*.

4

"Widening Circles": *Sons and Lovers*

> *With the dwelling the latent birth of the world is produced.*
> — Emmanuel Lévinas

The Fight for Territory

The merits of *Sons and Lovers*, Lawrence's first masterpiece, were immediately recognized by critics, even though most of them continued to see it as the highest instance of his "traditional" style, attributing only to his later works, especially *The Rainbow* and *Women in Love*, a technically and structurally innovative quality. There were also certain limited readings which focused solely on autobiographical elements (especially of a psychoanalytical and Freudian nature, in the kind of interpretation vehemently contested by the author himself).[1] There is no doubt, however, that, independently of how much biographical material it contains,[2] the novel marks an essential stage in Lawrence's artistic career, ending his early phase[3] and marking his passage between two different styles, one romantic/aesthetic, the other what critics have defined as "modernist."[4] The novel reproduces the themes and problems of his younger phase, but in a way that proves Lawrence's complete emancipation from it. This emancipation begins to emerge from the very beginning of the novel where the realistic presentation of the environment reveals a Lawrence now cured of the "vices" of affected aestheticism and escapism.[5]

4. *Sons and Lovers*

Apart from its realistic quality, the initial description also conveys a Darwinian view of existence, implying not only the deterministic idea of environment's conditioning effect upon characters,[6] but also the acceptance of the "jungle," identified finally with the positive pole of existence, inasmuch as it is the field of necessary struggle for the individual's formation. It enables him to leave the "den" or domestic environment, and adventure into the unknown of the external world. Such a view applies also to the structural level, the novel's division into two parts, the first of which presents the construction of the family nucleus (the dominant influence in the initial phase of the protagonist's formation), its internal conflicts, and the protagonist's struggle to find his own "space," while the second part illustrates his process of growth in relation to the external world.[7]

Places play a primary role in *Sons and Lovers,* and are closely connected to the characters' experience. The writer uses places not only to put characters to tests which prove, Darwinian-style, whether they can adapt to various situations, but also to develop a complex set of correspondences — contrast, analogy, and repetition — which structure the novel. In the first part, as mentioned, the place is the home, vital center and locus of struggle for its inhabitants, site of a power hierarchy that is also an emotional hierarchy. In the second part, even though the house remains the reference point until the death of its "sovereign" Mrs. Morel, other places, each of which is connected to a certain character, enter the action. In relation to the protagonist and his home, places correspond as well to modes of being, types of sensibility, different languages and viewpoints.[8] For example, in the description of the Morels' domestic universe, Lawrence resorts to a naturalistic viewpoint, whereas later, when Willey Farm is introduced, he brings back to some extent the romantic/aesthetic style of *The White Peacock*, and in particular the motif of the "garden" as idyllic place. This style is in turn very different from that describing Clara's world, which is Lawrence's first entry into the primitive vitalism which colors his subsequent works.

In *Sons and Lovers,* the protagonist's formation occurs through frequently-repeated movements between places. Each place reveals its own function: as a test of the degree of maturity he has achieved, as a stage of life, as an occasion for ideological, existential and artistic choices, or encounters with different microcosms and models of life, represented by characters who reside (and consequently preside) at certain places.

Besides the environment of Paul's formation, the first part of the novel introduces, though sometimes indirectly, all of the places that will be used in the second, establishing a mirror relationship, and also one of circularity and likeness, among these places. The parents' conflicts in the first part (in the domestic universe) correspond in the second part to conflicts between Paul and Miriam, and between Paul and Clara (both related to the venture into the external world); to the death of the first-born William in London corresponds Mrs. Morel's death at home at the end of the book; the first part opens with a term, "the Bottoms," which introduces the miners' habitations, relating them semantically to a place tied to the soil and the underground, and ends with a semantically analogous topographical reference, the cemetery. The dilemma of choice between death and life, already apparent at the end of the first part in relation to both Mrs. Morel and Paul, recurs, with the same outcome, at the end of the novel, when the protagonist, needing to choose between the temptation of the void and the persistent will to survive, leaves the darkness of the country behind to walk towards the city lights, opting for the unknown life which they represent.

The ending brings out the tension between the "center" (the Morel house) and the "extremity" (the city), tension which is a measure of the character's vitality and the source of his devastating interior conflicts. The progressive distancing of William as he goes towards unknown horizons, as far as "remote" London, would seem at first to signify his "victory," but in effect causes a progressive disorientation (rendering him incapable of choosing between home and city) and is ultimately the cause of his death.[9] In the second part this motif is more tenuous (Paul, who is more timid and cautious, does not venture beyond nearby Nottingham), and eventually reverses the meaning of "city," since to him it does not offer death, but restores him to life.

The opposition home/city, which represents the extremes of the domestic universe and the external world, relates to the oppositions nature/culture, country/city, and garden/jungle, which become particularly important in relation to Lawrence's artistic change of direction. In *Sons and Lovers*, these oppositions are presented in a way not substantially different from those in *The White Peacock* (where "garden" is associated with flower imagery and "jungle" with animal imagery) and the country is moreover a place of poetry and meditation, but it is also increasingly identified with an existence lived only by half, dedicated to poetry and contemplation and therefore essentially sterile. Reluctant to leave the garden to face the jungle, Paul manages to find in the city tranquil gardens and islands of meditation, but eventually becomes more conscious, as the end of the novel shows, that real life teems in the streets, where one must resolutely face the unpoetic and violent reality of existence. *Sons and Lovers* concludes Lawrence's early phase inasmuch as it, unlike the preceding novels, ends, not with a failed return to the center, but with the protagonist's search for an encounter with an "other" place. The tenuously positive note on which it closes is connected to the fact that Paul, through great effort, leaves the place of beginning and all it represents, and although directing himself towards the place of civilization, undergoes in actuality a "journey" towards nature.[10]

The Bottoms

The importance that places will assume in the novel is already obvious from the panoramic offering, through an almost cinematic method, of the opening pages in which the narrator begins with a "long shot" which embraces all of the scene and then, with a zoom effect, gradually restricts the field of vision to a typical Bestwood miner's house, preparatory to introducing the Morels and their home.[11]

On the spatial axis, the narrator constructs the scene, whereas on the temporal axis, he reconstructs history, illustrating the land-use effects of industrialization on the environment: "There lived the colliers who worked in the little gin-pits two fields away" (*SL* 9). Notwithstanding the objective, detached tone, several strongly negative connotations emerge from the historical and topographical data, beginning with the two place names, "Hell Row" and "the Bottoms," which through their connotations of depth, both evoke the mines that disfigure the landscape and erode the nucleus of rural life ("the … odd farms," *SL* 9) down to unimportant, forgotten islands.[12] Lawrence focuses on essential features in the miners' village, emphasizing the alienating effects produced by industrialization, which filled the place with houses planned by others, all the same, all impersonal, "to accommodate the regiments of miners" (*SL* 10). Lawrence uses the topography of the novel to underline the element of alienation present in the environment in which the protagonist and the other main characters grow up.

From the row of habitations, the visual field narrows to one of the houses and its internal structure, details of which demonstrate the process of depersonalization caused by industrialization's penetration of the inhabitants' privacy, its conditioning of their rhythms and ways of life.[13] If the cottages are given an element of bourgeois respectability by their "little front gardens with auriculas and saxifrage in the shadow of the bottom block, sweet williams and pinks, in the sunny top-block," the view is enjoyable, ironically, only from the "uninhabited parlours of all the colliers' wives" (*SL* 10). No less ironically, the "heart" of domestic life is the kitchen, an unhealthy, oppressive environment ("people must live in the kitchen, and the kitchens opened onto that nasty alley of ash-pits," *SL* 10), which encourages them in the tendency not to "live" at home, but to escape it, whenever weather permits ("every inhabitant remaining was out of doors"

SL 30) to seek refuge elsewhere, in the external world,[14] which is also made squalid and depressing by the dirtiness of the mines, or in places which become a surrogate for family intimacy such as the pub, also seen by Lawrence as a by-product of industrialization.[15]

In the opening description, the author emphasizes that the house is structured hierarchically, so that every place or "sub-place" inside the house corresponds with a specific function recognized by the entire community. Its center is the hearth, interior around which domestic activities occur; it is, however, ideally subordinated to the parlor with the view of the garden, the only concession to bourgeois decorum in the workers' houses, which is perceived as a foreign space and is almost always unused. In contrast to the parlor, the scullery represents (because of its rear position next to the ash-pit) the place of low activities (especially washing) and is in some sense a private environment, since strangers are not usually admitted there; it is less private, however, than bedrooms, whose thresholds are more difficult to cross (Mrs. Morel does not tolerate the presence of her husband in her bedroom after childbirth and while she is sick, she admits only her children).[16]

The House and Its Inhabitants

Even though uninviting, the house in *Sons and Lovers* is for its inhabitants a possession to defend or conquer with relentless battles, a true territory whose borders are jealously guarded from possible invaders from the outside and in the interior of which the inhabitants put up a mute fight for privileged spaces. In particular, the center (kitchen) is prime territory, since whoever manages to conquer it acquires sovereignty in the house and imposes a code of order, deciding who to admit and who to exclude from the house. Whoever is excluded must find other domestic space and prepare to defend it from possible attacks by other family members. The house, then, as is repeatedly shown in the early parts of the novel, is a place, not of peaceful cohabitation, but of tension and struggle. The family coalesces to defend it, but it never really becomes, for all of its inhabitants, a "place of us" because of the antagonistic relationships that exist between them.[17]

Whoever holds sovereignty also has the right to the nearest seat to the hearth, which becomes a throne from which is administered the whole universe of domestic life. Once she has won the war against her husband, Mrs. Morel takes possession of this throne, wielding her power in a despotic fashion and conceding favors in a manner no less despotic, so that a spatial hierarchy comes to correspond with an affective one.

4. Sons and Lovers

The first part of the novel is principally devoted to the illustration of the spouses' battle ("there began a battle between the husband and wife, a fearful, bloody battle that ended only with the death of one," *SL* 22), and of their fights, sometimes physical, in which they use domestic weapons (such as the drawer in Chapter II). Part One ends with Mrs. Morel's decisive victory, recognized by the entire family who doggedly take her part. As for the husband, once he has lost his sovereignty and with it the possibility of imposing patriarchal order upon the domestic universe, his presence is decreasingly tolerated, even if it is recognized as necessary because of his role as breadwinner, and his viewpoint is more and more resolutely refused, based as it is upon the values of the working class and more generally of nature, as will emerge towards the end of the novel.[18] For his values, Mrs. Morel substitutes those of the bourgeoisie and of culture, seeking to save her sons from the fate of working in the mines, to secure them a better future, a more decorous existence. "He [William] is *not* going in the pit" (*SL* 70) is in fact her firm response to her husband, regarding the poor earnings of the son's first job.

The war of the spouses is strongly "spatialized" by the writer: every fight produces not only a growing separation between them, but also the departure of the losing party (Mrs. Morel locked out of the house at the end of the first major fight; Morel slamming the door on the way to the pub). Corresponding to the gradual defeat of the husband is a reversal in the narrative viewpoint: in the initial pages of the novel, the narrator recognizes that it is the mother who destroys Morel's vigorous quality, his human warmth, the spontaneity originally attributed to him: "in seeking to make him nobler than he could be, she destroyed him" (*SL* 25). As Morel gradually loses power, he is seen more from the viewpoint of Mrs. Morel and her children, which emphasizes his brutal, violent aspects, his moral and physical degeneration.

Morel's defeat also occasions his family's ostracism and condemnation of him to the role of outcast, which forces him to seek spaces outside the domestic universe, to find substitute places, such as the pub, the scullery and even the garden. For him, these last two are both places of work, of physical activity often noisily accompanied by "his whistling ringing out as he sawed and hammered away" (*SL* 27). For Mrs. Morel, on the other hand, the garden is a place of poetry, meditation and escape from ugly reality. Her stillness in the garden, where she contemplates the flowers and gets drunk on their perfume, contrasts with the noisy restlessness of the husband. He can retake possession of the "center," the kitchen and hearth, only when the others are absent, which is to say in those hours when they are sleeping upstairs.[19] Once they have finished with conversations and confrontations, love and hate, the two spouses find a *modus vivendi* based in part on the fact that each is necessary to the other (consider Mrs. Morel's fear when her husband threatens to leave and Morel's sense of loss when his wife is sick at Annie's house) and in part by avoiding being in the same space. Generally, the presence of one spouse means the removal of the other, since being together in the same space inevitably causes tension and conflict.

Among the several episodes in which Lawrence shows the process of the conjugal war, one in particular merits attention, when Mrs. Morel is kicked out of the house and locked in the garden, at the end of Chapter I. On the one hand, it marks a conditional success in Morel's struggle to impose patriarchal order within the house; on the other hand, it emphasizes how being shut out of the house causes Mrs. Morel to feel a loss of security and power: "In the mysterious out-of-doors she felt forlorn .... Her heart began to burn to be indoors" (*SL* 35). At the same time, it illustrates the significance the garden has for her as a mirror of her emotions, as a refuge from harsh domestic battle, as a place of poetry and creativity, of joyous transports in the contemplation of blooming flowers, transports which she shares exclusively with her "lover" Paul. But in this nocturnal episode, the garden also represents a threshold from which she establishes a relationship with the unknown, with forces of nature which intoxicate and disturb at the same time.

Having won the marital battle, Mrs. Morel becomes not only sovereign but also, in a Darwinian sense, the coveted female object of all of the male children, who fight fiercely to gain her favor. To that end, they ritually resort to propitiatory offers, which, unlike Morel's, are always well received and imply the recognition of the mother's authority as well as their willingness to serve her. This willingness she less and less frequently demonstrates towards her husband, a fact which fills him with ineffectual rage. Mrs. Morel's favors are first given to her eldest, William, the object of an almost passionate love, which, in the first part of the novel, causes her to spend most of her time with him and to give him all her energy and hope.[20] Once William disappears,[21] his place is taken by Paul, who, aware and satisfied that he is "the man in the house," (*SL* 113) will hold that place definitely (and too long), defending it from the third son's advances. Mrs. Morel's sovereignty is expressed by her jealous guarding of the house from "intruders," especially from those whom she judges to be a potential threat to the social ascent of her sons (she pushes away William's girlfriends and opposes Miriam even more strongly). The only visitor to enjoy full rights of access to the house is the Non-Conformist clergyman, incarnation of the bourgeois respectability to which she aspires (her aspiration is symbolized by establishing her family in the last house on the row, which has a larger strip of garden).[22] For this very reason, Morel sees him, as an intruder and threatens him with overt hostility when, one day, coming home from work earlier than usual, he surprises his wife, who is in conversation with the clergyman. Struck not so much in his sense of honor as in his class-consciousness, and resenting the pastor for what feels like a violation of the intimacy of his territory, Morel aggressively opposes his wife's exhibition of bourgeois decorum by deliberately resting his dirty arms on the bleached white tablecloth and inviting the reluctant, reserved clergyman to touch his workman's sweat: "It's a bit dry now, but it's wet as a clout with sweat even yet. Feel it" (*SL* 46).

The Internal/External Opposition

The fact that Mr. Heaton represents to Mrs. Morel the world of her upbringing, the bourgeois one which is also her natural habitat, makes this moment seem like her husband's intrusion, rather than her guest's, while it is, naturally, the opposite for Morel. The episode illustrates the supporting structure of the novel, the opposition between the internal and external, the familiar and the strange, correlated with social climbing and falling, which underlies Mrs. Morel's situation.[23] Going to live at the Bottoms, she at the same time distanced and lowered herself from her origins. She stooped to live in an environment which she does not accept from the very beginning, as shown in the early episode in which, while waiting for her husband and becoming tired, she "went into the front garden, feeling too heavy to take herself out, yet unable to stay indoors" (*SL* 13-14), only to return inside almost immediately, oppressed by the depressing atmosphere experienced outdoors and by the sight of a group of miners returning home, who stumble and curse because they are drunk. Mrs. Morel's anxiety and dissatisfaction are symptomatic of the unsatisfying results of her transition towards the "lower" working class, a transition which Lawrence presents as a fundamental demonstration of her energies and vital resources, her capacity to confront the world when resolutely leaving her cocoon.

Choosing the miner Morel after having refused the bourgeois suitor Mr. Field (who was incapable of energetically confronting the world and rebelling against his father, who wanted to make him a businessman), Mrs. Morel chooses that Otherness necessary to her self-realization, the perfect complement to the Puritan strictness and bourgeois ambitions which she inherited from her father. Because of the necessity of sharing space, however, the spouses alienate each other, each trying to impose his or her own code of living upon the other. Mrs. Morel realizes the impossibility of completely absorbing her husband into her world ("it was not enough for him just to be near her," *SL* 19); he needs outside environments such as the pub, where he finds the complete acceptance which is denied him at home and where he is able to be himself. After their first months of passion, both spouses are exhausted, as they are too faithful to their own codes and unable to reach any compromise with their partner in the domestic universe, which becomes a territory of struggle and confrontation and the source of reciprocal alienation.[24] Mrs. Morel's life course is presented, first, as a descent towards the lower class (to appropriate some of the vital energies which it contains in the person of her husband), then as a gradual elevation to an equal or even higher position than her family of origin. As for Morel, he remains consistently (but also statically) faithful to principles inherited from his working class world, of which he has accepted the laws and attitudes, even though, restless by nature, he moves physically from one place to another inside his limited horizons (the fields, the pubs, the mine).[25]

The spouses' fight for possession of the home, their efforts to impose their own laws upon it, ends in a *modus vivendi* which makes Mrs. Morel the queen of the house and Morel the ruler outside or in the "lower places" of the house. Nevertheless, the woman, even though tightly bound to the home (she is the last to bank the fire and go to bed, even when William is there with his fiancée), is at the same time capable of going away, covering distances which the husband never does, whether compelled by domestic duties (visiting her husband in the hospital, attempting to get Arthur out of the military, and going alone to the disorienting London during William's sickness), or by her social aspirations (vacations at the seaside, trip with Paul to Nottingham for his first job, to Lincoln, and also to Willey Farm). When the children are grown, she manages to find other external spaces, such as the church and "the Women's Guild ... on Monday nights" (*SL* 69), in which she realizes, at least in part, her social and cultural aspirations.

The parents finally make their own choices with respect to the external world and see their home as the reference point of their own existence: Mrs. Morel, trapped by her illness at Annie's house, wants to return home as soon as possible,[26] while Morel, disoriented by the death of his wife, goes to live with a Nottingham family. The children live the internal/external opposition in both similar and different ways from their parents. On the one hand, for all of them the house represents, in a Darwinian sense, a cocoon, a refuge in which they are protected from the menace and accumulated tensions of the external world: William comes home exhausted from the fair; Paul and Arthur return hungry and fatigued from their exhausting search for wild berries. On the other hand, the home becomes a source of anxiety because of the daily conflicts which occur there and which profoundly implicate the children. Their rare moments of serenity, in the early phases of their lives, coincide almost always with the absence of one of the parents, especially the father, with whom communication diminishes to the point of complete estrangement and with whom dramatic conflicts develop. In the attempt to defend their mother, both William and Paul have violent physical encounters with him; Paul comes to the point of substituting for his father as man of the house ("I'm the man in the house now," SL 113), assuming even the economic responsibility of the family ("you can have my money—let him go to Hell," SL 239).

The house's double function for the children in the first phase of their lives is perfectly symbolized by the second residence which, while it marks a step forward in the social ascent of the family, also brings, in its relative isolation, an entry into the vast unknown of the external world. The ash tree, whose nocturnal rustling in the wind becomes for the children the voice of a cosmic conflict, warns them of the troubling presence of both the external and domestic universes[27]:

> Having such a great space in front of the house gave the children a feeling of night, of vastness, and of terror. This terror came in from the shrieking of the tree and the anguish of the home discord [SL 84].

The tensions and insecurity which the children experience inside the house undermine their capacity to confront the world. In a Darwinian sense, their growth means leaving the cocoon and confronting the "jungle," but this confrontation produces evidence of the fundamental weakness latent in each of them, rather than their great potential, though it is different for William and Paul, as Lawrence suggests by the juxtaposition of their gradual attempts at emancipation from the domestic environment. William's emancipation is much faster and more certain (even though he, like Paul, fails in the end), as shown by a series of tests which are undergone in the same order by his younger brother. From infancy, the firstborn is extremely attracted by the stimuli of the outside world, which he encounters in spaces progressively further from home (his job in the local cooperative, then the job at Nottingham, and finally in London), corresponding to an ascent on the social ladder (measured economically by the continual increase in his salary, up to the "fabulous sum" earned in London). His "aggression" in the external world applies not only in the study and work spheres, but also in those of play, entertainment and Eros. His quick maturation and sudden success, however, are in reality deeply fragile because he has inherited the conflict between his parents. This fragility manifests itself fully when he seeks to reconcile the place of his origins with the place in which he is, with apparent success, transplanted: two places presided over by two contrasting female figures, the sober, severe mother and the frivolous fiancée Lily, incarnation of the enchanting enticements of the city. The conflict begins when Lily is introduced to the intimacy of the miner's house, evoking a visceral hostility in Mrs. Morel and a complete disorientation of the girl, who is incapable of understanding the rules of such a different habitat. Lily's incompatibility with the Morels' domestic environment renders William conscious of the impossibility of reconciling the two worlds of his life, provoking an interior battle which somatically results in his fatal illness. His decline is as sudden as his earlier ascent.[28]

While William desires adventure from infancy onward, and is anxious to discover the world (which he always encounters alone), Paul is shy about every encounter with reality and extremely fragile and anxious even in the interior universe of home, where he requires his mother's constant attention. In the beginning of the novel, where the primary narrative focus is domestic conflict, Paul, indecisive and anxious, tormentedly matures, and seeks refuge in his mother, to the point of identifying himself as her shadow and hiding from every exposure to the world if he cannot experience it with her. The world of nature, which he always connects with his mother, attracts him. In it, he manages to orient himself quickly, whereas every public place is a source of interior wounding, which produces frequent physical illnesses. Recurring after every encounter with the external world (the return from school, and following his first trips to Nottingham to work in the surgical appliances factory), his sicknesses are cleverly used to attract his mother's attention. Paul's grave illness—after William's death and his mother's consequent apathy—and his subsequent recuperation conclude the novel's first part, which is dedicated to the family drama. They also open the second part, in which Paul's *Bildung* is the primary focus. In the domestic environment, Paul always seeks closeness with his mother to the point of seeing his father as a rival and detesting him ("Lord, let my father die," *SL* 85); his first public encounter with the mining environment and industrialization occasions psychic wounds cured only by his mother's intervention. She helps him to orient himself and confront the world, that jungle which for him is so insuperable and hostile. Symptomatic of this are the episode of fetching the father's pay, where Paul's inability to step forward is mocked by the miners, causing a profound hatred for their social environment, and the episode where he seeks a job by perusing newspaper advertisements in the library. If it were not for the stimulus and motivation provided by his mother, who, after William's death, begins to focus upon him her own hopes for social success, Paul would concentrate all of his energies in the domestic environment, from which he manages to detach himself only with great effort (even later his dream of the future is with his mother in a cottage). Only with her can he make his first difficult encounter with the city and the first introduction to the world of work.[29]

Willey Farm

While the first part of the novel revolves around the Morel house, in the second, the focus switches to the external world, of which Lawrence presents a wide range of aspects, all in some way related to fundamental moments of Paul's *Bildung*, such as his sentimental and sexual education, the experience of work, the assumption of new responsibilities, and his artistic formation.[30] In Part Two, the passing of time is measured in terms of exploration of spaces which become, in his formative process, temporary centers of gravity. On the level of narrative dynamics, this translates to a series of reiterative situations (mostly trips) which result in Paul's growing familiarity with certain places. His interest in these is based on the magnetism exerted by the person with whom the place is connected. The diminishment of that magnetism inevitably produces a progressive disinterest in the place itself and therefore the need to explore new spaces, which are also intimately connected to the power of attraction of a presiding female figure.[31] Each of these spaces is a microcosm intended to provide a certain type of experience related to other characters, who get in touch with the protagonist through a series of paradigmatic links through which the "world" of the novel is created. Once Paul has left the domestic realm, in accordance with the demands of his maturation process, he ventures upon Willey Farm and other places connected with Miriam, until, having exhausted that relationship's potential, even the farm loses all attraction for him. His next love relationship, with Clara, is accompanied by the discovery of and participation in a completely different world, the city, which is "low," unpoetic, and appropriate to the transition from mind to flesh, from mysticism to sensuality, which their relationship implies.

The radical diversity and complementarity of Willey Farm and the city positively configure this transition as a moment of growth insofar as both worlds have to be first explored, made his own, and then left behind so that his growth can continue. This process ends in failure because, instead of integrating the two worlds with his own, Paul refuses both and in such a way — once his mother is dead and his relationships with Miriam and Clara are over — that he seems to condemn himself to an existence where there is no longer any vital space, finding himself surrounded by a void. For this reason, at the conclusion of the novel, he confides to Baxter Dawes his intention to leave England and create a new life abroad.

The introduction of Willey Farm (near the end of the first part) undoubtedly marks an essential stage in Paul's growth — and also in the artistic capacity of the writer — even before he enters into Miriam's orbit. Just as it is the place of poetry and dreams, of the aesthetic/decadent transfiguration of reality present in the first two novels, *The White Peacock* and *The Trespasser*, Willey Farm represents a world of dreams in the protagonist's adolescence, the shattering of which corresponds with the end of the first phase of Lawrence's artistic career.

Paul's discovery of Willey Farm is an intoxicating experience which occurs when he has already had his first difficult contact with the external world, his job in the Nottingham factory. The harsh reality of the factory makes the country which Paul and his mother traverse to reach the farm seem like a place of dreams. He penetrates it with the amazement of one discovering a new, virginal world, as his words to Mrs. Morel suggest: "it's a wild road, mother … . Just like Canada" (*SL* 153). Certainly it is being with his mother — who in turn exclaims, "the world is a wonderful place" (*SL* 152) — which confers a particular enchantment to the contemplation of the spring landscape, depicted as an expansion and transfiguration of the narrow little garden at home and as an intensification of the intimate communion which mother and son often share while looking at flowers.[32]

A different experience occurs when the farm buildings emerge, as if out of nowhere, like an island separate from the world.[33] One must emphasize the recurrent process in Lawrence's works by which a certain place assumes distinct functions for different characters, who relate to it differently, according to their distinct interaction with it. Whereas for Paul, the arrival at the farm represents a prolonging of the experience of discovery and intoxication begun with the walk through the fields, for those who live there, naturally, it is entirely a different matter. For Miriam's mother, it is a place of sacrifice and humiliation which she bears "religiously"; for the girl, the reign of the "unpoetic" which she seeks to escape in a world of dreams colored by Walter Scott novels; for the men, Mr. Leivers and his sons, it is the place of "natural" life, hard but not unpleasant work, and contact with the realities of life and death of different generations, realistically and un-problematically accepted as facts. For the narrator, finally, Willey Farm is an island on the margins of progress, a border place which survives thanks to its marginality, to which it owes the peculiarity immediately perceived by Paul:

> The family was so cut off from the world, actually. They seemed somehow, like "les derniers fils d'une race épuisée" [*SL* 180].[34]

In a way which Lawrence seems to relate to archaic behavioral models, the domestic interior and the external world of fields and barns appear not simply as two worlds for strictly separate capabilities, domains respectively of female and male (it is always among males that biological activities are discussed, never inside the home), but are also factors of psychological separation. This separation favors the development of hypersensitivity and mystical self-containment in the women and deliberate roughness in the men.

Consequently, two battle-fronts emerge, destined to continually clash in everyday rituals. Thus, Miriam's scorn for her brothers' and sometimes her father's vulgarity is matched by their scorn for her ineptitude, resulting in continual arguments such as the one Paul witnesses at one of his first meals at Willey Farm, occasioned by Miriam's burnt potatoes. Strangely, Paul finds himself in the role of mediator between these two battle-fronts, due to the curiosity he feels about both sides.

Even though it is at the farm that Paul meets Miriam, the farm is not, in its entirety, Miriam's place, and, at least in a chronological sense, she is a later source of interest for the protagonist ("Miriam came later," *SL* 180). Indeed, Paul's curiosity arises in the first place with regard to the domestic realm which seems surprisingly different from his own and to which he reacts with interest and curiosity,[35] and in the second place, to the life of the fields, into which he is "initiated" by Miriam's brothers. Like Mrs. Morel, Miriam is intimately associated with the floral world, that is, the garden, place of poetry and delicate sentiments, even though, as we shall see, *her* gardens present different connotations in comparison with Mrs. Morel's. They are "corners" of a "world" (Willey Farm and its environs) which Paul invests with an experience of discovery which transcends them, inasmuch as it extends to multiple aspects of the country—the orchard, fields, woods and meadows—and is gradually stripped of that intellectualizing and almost pedantic element which initially causes him to try to classify and name all the flowers he sees. This discovery experience also becomes, for awhile, one of emancipation from his mother: although she is present during his first visit to Willey Farm, he later opens himself up to this new experience without her. The farm becomes an opportunity for Paul's growth, for the acquisition of new acquaintances, for the different experiences of a farmer's family. This is an encounter which occasions the family members' growth, as well, as they have the opportunity to open themselves up to the external world. His warm friendship with the brothers gives Paul the opportunity to find new self-esteem through manual activity and "initiation" tests of courage and strength. At the same time, he provides them with external stimuli, with news of the city and his working environment. His interaction with the female world is also fertile, leading him to discover Miriam's and Mrs. Leviers' world of mysticism and intense religiosity and allowing him to set Miriam on the road to her own intellectual education.

Miriam's Places

The events of Miriam's life[36] provide a second proof that, in *Sons and Lovers,* Lawrence conceives of character growth in terms of taking possession of places and spaces: when such appropriation does not occur, as in Paul's case, the *Bildung* process fails. Miriam, who at the end finds that the church is the only place where she truly belongs,[37] fails to mature as well. In her case, however, the difficulty stems less from the home and farm in which she grew up (in contrast to Paul, she has not put down roots in her own home), since the only world she will recognize is the world of dreams and romance: a "better, superior" world. To this world she wishes to "ascend," in what Paul calls her "verticality," contrasting it to his own presumed "horizontality" (concreteness, adherence to reality) which is, in effect, the world of Mrs. Morel.[38]

Her tendency to verticality brings Miriam to two places which allow her to abstract herself from reality: the garden (which however does not exist in "institutional" form at Willey Farm, so that she must "invent" her secret gardens, discovering them in corners of the farm or its surroundings) and the church, which she religiously attends and toward which she experiences a sense of belonging. It constitutes the only public place in which she feels at home and it will become her link between city and country, between adolescence and adulthood. As mentioned, it is in a Nottingham church that Paul meets her at the end of the novel, when their relationship has terminated, in an episode in which he notices the absence of change in her character, as though she had suddenly passed from initial blooming to aging ("she seemed old to him, older than Clara," *SL* 460).

Miriam's propensity to mysticism combines with another type of verticality (which indirectly associates her with and opposes her to Mrs. Morel), that implied by the aspiration to culture, seen as a means of access to a "superior" existence and liberation from her own low social condition.[39] This double propensity to verticality makes Paul a double center of attraction for her, a reason to accept him into her secret world, in which he becomes (at least initially) identified with the figure of the romantic knight à la Walter Scott, able to discover the princess hidden beneath the "swine girl" but also, in concrete terms, he becomes the bourgeois instructor, capable of guiding her in her own intellectual development.

For her, the relation with Paul involves the search for "places of us" which are, on the one hand, the world of romance, and on the other, as isolated as possible. Anyone else must be rigorously excluded because Miriam is never able to get along with others (excluding her mother and Paul) and even her rapport with Paul is only harmonious when they are alone; invariably, the presence of a third separates them.

Miriam's places are on the margin, isolated from the rest of the world, and, on walks which lead to them — invariably culminating in the rite of contemplating flowers— Paul and Miriam develop an adolescent love. It is always by the celebration of this rite that they reach their moments of spiritual communion, the first of which occurs, not coincidentally, deep in the woods, on the threshold which separates Willey Farm from the open environment of the mines. Here Miriam, on her return from the library, invites Paul to admire a bright bush she had discovered the day before which shines in the semi-darkness of dusk and which really comes to life for her only after she has bared to Paul the innermost recesses of her soul in that *secret* place. After the celebration of this mystery, Miriam is filled with satisfaction: "It was the communion she wanted" (*SL* 196).[40] For his own part, Paul experiences a discovery so intoxicating that he feels enchanted, as if he were under a spell; somehow, it is he who is "possessed" in this episode, in which Miriam assumes traits not only of the Pre-Raphaelite *demoiselle élue* but also of the Keatsian *belle dame sans merci* who tears the knight from his duties (in this case the duty not to get home too late), generating in him a vague uneasiness and sense of guilt ("something made him feel anxious and imprisoned," *SL* 196).[41]

Paul's and Miriam's later moments of communion occur not in the woods, place of mystery, but at ruins and medieval monuments—where she can pretend to be a princess and he a knight—and thus, in the world of dreams. Miriam and Paul go there with a group of friends and even on this occasion the girl does not feel part of the group, finding her satisfaction only when Paul invites her to contemplate, from the height of Hemlock Stone, "a quiet garden" (*SL* 200), an island of "us" separated from the world of "others." The epitome of this immersion in dreams occurs during the second trip, that to Wingfield Manor, where Paul's and Miriam's communion occurs in another romantic place, laden with historical suggestions: the tower in which Mary Queen of Scots was imprisoned. Like a perfect knight, Paul offers Miriam a floral bouquet, after having contemplated with her white lilies in a Gothic chapel.[42]

While Miriam gathers Paul into her own "garden," he, for his part, introduces her to his own intellectual world with algebra and French lessons. These lessons take place in their homes, which thus become places of intellectual communication, but not of intimate communion. On the contrary, from these lessons emerge tensions accumulated in the relationship over the passage of years.

These tensions are also partly connected to place: when Paul, as William had done with Lily, seeks to introduce Miriam to his "center," the interior of his own home, Mrs. Morel is hostile to the "intruder." He is *not able* to integrate the girl into his domestic realm, while she, in turn, *does not want* to (or cannot) integrate him into her own, where she does not feel rooted. Moments in which Paul manages to reconcile the two centers of his life are rare. One of them is when he participates at religious functions, during which the antagonism between Mrs. Morel and Miriam is momentarily suspended and he can maintain the illusion of peaceful coexistence with both of them. Another is shortly before the seaside vacation, an evening on which, in the presence of Miriam and in front of his whole family, he reads poetry, becoming for a moment the center of attention and harmony between irreconcilable poles. The vacation itself, perhaps conceived as an opportunity of "familiarization" between mother and girl, reveals the illusory nature of this plan. Miriam isolates herself, as she always does in public, relating only to Paul. On the one hand, while the shared vacation with Paul's family does not improve her relations with them, being with him in a place which is different from the setting of their usual encounters instigates a change in their relationship, which has been threatened by the exhaustion of its adolescent phase. During a walk with Miriam to witness a seaside sunset, Paul feels his first impulse of physical desire for her, which he represses, blocking any verification of the change in their relationship which could bring them to a different, more "adult" type of communion. When he does take the initiative to realize this change, it is too late, because by then, Miriam's senses refuse to be awakened.

Whereas in the first phase of their relationship it is the girl who brings the protagonist to her places, in the circumstances of the new sexual relationship, it is Paul who, determined to discover the mysteries of her body after descending from the tree in which he picked cherries (the substitution of fruits for flowers seems to allude to the transformation which is about to happen in their relationship), invites Miriam to follow him into the woods. This establishes both a parallel and opposite relationship to the episode of the rose bush: here, the woods are anthropologically once more the place of initiation into mystery, which now is not of the spirit, but of the body. Further, while in the first episode, the satisfaction is mostly Miriam's, in the second, it is only Paul's. His sexual gratification gives rise to a profound sense of peace, a mystical communion with the cosmos, while Miriam feels like a sacrificial victim, incapable of reading his body and spirit: "she had been afraid before of the brute in him; now of the mystic" (*SL* 331).

The failure of the sexual initiation is followed by an experiment of conjugal living which takes place at her grandmother's house, an experiment interesting for the reactions which the place elicits in the two protagonists. Their cohabitation succeeds to the extent that Paul is able to identify the house with his own and Miriam with his mother, but this identification is possible only in that "sub-place," the kitchen, where the two bustle and chatter harmoniously, and not in that other, more crucial spot, the bedroom, where Miriam undergoes a new mortification of the flesh, and Paul bitterly witnesses the impossibility of union with her.

At this point, their relationship is irreversibly doomed, but in the logic of the novel, that must happen in ritual form as well, with an exorcism of Miriam's floral enchantments and Paul's liberation from the "prison" of her garden. This occurs in an episode which confirms the burial, not only of their relationship, but of a protracted adolescence (Paul is twenty-four years old), in a conversation between Paul and his mother in which he first chews a flower unconsciously and then throws the rest in the fireplace, thus communicating, as if by "burying her," his decision to leave Miriam.[43] After this episode, flowers assume a different role in Paul's relationships with other characters. Flowers become a means of contact with the body by ornamentation, rather than a means of sublimating Eros, as had already happened in the episode at the Morel house where, his mother safely upstairs, Paul sought to adorn Miriam's dress with flowers, as if to indicate his interest in the body which the dress covers.

Clara's Place: The City

In the process of Paul's development, the loss of positivity of a given place (in this case Willey Farm and surroundings) influences the change of the protagonist's center of gravity to another place and another character linked to a new phase in his formative process. Foreshadowing of this new phase (linked to the exploration of sexuality) is present in the preceding one, as is exemplified by his new interest in Miriam's body, in the episode of adorning her dress with flowers and the magnetism immediately exerted by Clara's physicality.[44] Lawrence introduces Clara, not in her own urban environment, but in Miriam's, at Willey Farm. It is her presence (she has been carelessly invited by Miriam), that destroys Miriam's own gardens. During their walk to Strelley Mill (an even more isolated, poetic and condemned place than Willey Farm), Clara's participation in the rite of flower gathering is disturbing and disenchanted, and her condemnation of the picking itself betrays an attitude of primitive vitalism which Paul will make his own. At the base of her attitude is an acceptance of nature's laws.[45] For her, the flowers are beautiful when they grow in soil; once cut, they are like dead bodies.

In Paul's ongoing development, Clara represents a moment of passage from romance to reality because she helps him discover the world of the senses and the world of productive and social activities linked to the city. Thus she helps him to overcome the condition of isolation linked to Willey Farm and specifically, to Miriam. It should be remembered, however, that the protagonist's first contact with urban reality precedes his meeting with Clara. It is Mrs. Morel who accompanies her shy, reluctant son to Jordan's factory in Nottingham, where he, not yet sixteen, has his first contact with the world of work. Work is a difficult, but not negative, experience, because fortunately he is able to accept and feel at home in the atmosphere of the small factory, making it almost a second home by virtue of the warm, tender, and subtly erotic relations he establishes with Jordan's female workers. Lawrence does not overemphasize the difficulty of factory work nor the degradation of urban reality but he does not ignore them either ("Paul ... followed his mother up the dirty steps to the dirty door" *SL* 119)[46]; yet he prefers to emphasize the stimulating, euphoric effect which the city has on both characters by its animation, its intricate, Babel-like reality, its kaleidoscope of lights and colors, and its role as object of ingenuous amazement for the two provincials, who are, predictably, snubbed by the waiter as soon as they venture into a restaurant.[47]

As for the factory, Paul's first impression is not favorable ("the place was like a pit," 118): the entrance appears like "the jaws of the dragon" (*SL* 118)[48] and he sees Mr. Jordan as an "ogre." Although the boss is really a benevolent figure, he treats Paul with showy roughness, puts him through a test (the translation of a French letter written in illegible handwriting) which humiliates him.[49] His impression of the working premises is no better, especially those in the lower places ("it was an insanitary ancient place ... the stack room in the basement [was a] cellar of gloom and desolation" *SL* 128, 134). These places, however, are also a source of amazement: "He wondered what the things were .... He gazed in wonder, never having seen a speaking tube before" (*SL* 119, 130). His timidity does not make it easy for Paul to get used to the factory, but with the passing of time, he gradually integrates himself into its community and finds social affirmation in a place where his qualities (including the artistic) find their first public recognition.

After the trip to Nottingham, the motif of mother-and-son travel is repeated several times, proving, on the one hand, his growth (especially socio-economic), and on the other, Mrs. Morel's decline. During their excursion to Lincoln Cathedral in Chapter IX, unlike in the preceding trip, this time it is he who assumes the role of guide to his parent who, with a weak heart, follows him wearily along the climb to the cathedral. This episode, unlike that of the factory, links her, not to expectations for the future, but to thoughts of her impending death.[50] Again it is he who, taking her to an expensive restaurant, flaunts his economic independence, "scandalizing" her with his prodigality: "'Don't imagine I like it,' she said .... 'Just *think* of your money wasted!'" (*SL* 281).

4. *Sons and Lovers*

Even in this instance there is evidence of Mrs. Morel's extraneousness in the city, which is, as Paul lucidly intuits, Clara's place:

> Miriam ... belonged to Bestwood and home and his youth. Clara ... belonged to Nottingham, to life, to the world [*SL* 319].

Even though she belongs to the city and is active in women's liberation meetings, Clara has an ambivalent relationship to it. Attracted by its diversity of life and cultural opportunities, like the cinema and the theater, she is oppressed and victimized by a boring and alienating job and the difficulty of rising above of her status as a manual worker.[51] It is she who introduces Paul to the social world, assuming the role of guide which his mother had assumed at Bestwood and Miriam at Willey Farm.

But Clara's places are especially those connected with sexual experience, concentrated in one or two chapters, as if to symbolize the impetuous, frenetic rhythm of their sexual rapport. Clara's association with the carnal sphere arises from Paul's first visit to her house which, while the writer uses it to realistically describe a squalid worker's dwelling,[52] becomes also the place for an exploration of intimacy with her (as Miriam's house had been, but in a different way) and at the same time proof of an essential absence: "A house o' women is as dead as a house wi' no fire" (*SL* 302). Paul liberates Clara from this environment (winning her mother's respect) by offering the possibility of work at Jordan's, which helps develop their relationship. While Paul assumes this role of leadership in the socio-economic field, she, older and more expert, assumes it in the sexual field.[53]

In accordance with the reiterative structure of the novel, Paul's advances to Clara are made during a reiterative situation, the walk, which occurs in this case, not in the country, but in the natural "islands" of the city, like the Castle's park, the canal, and the banks of the river. Particularly interesting are the walks in the Castle's park, which, other than providing an occasion for relative intimacy, introduce a new aspect of verticality, offering the characters a point from which to observe the city and its surroundings. Lawrence uses this to give expression to their respective relationships with urban reality: while for Clara, it is an alienating agglomerate, a labyrinth which reflects her social and existential situation, for Paul, it represents a challenge, a world to conquer, which he, in this phase, is determined to meet.[54]

The walks are the means for an increasing physical intimacy, which establishes an atmosphere, not of sunshine, but of darkness, and which reaches its consummation in a scene dominated by the river Trent at highwater, a clear symbol of their passion. On the river banks, they have their first sexual encounter. Lawrence emphasizes the muddiness of the winding path which leads them to their precarious hide-away among the trees, and the fact that, to follow it, they must go lower, so that the moment of carnal knowledge seems to bring a sort of descent into hell correlated with Paul's penetration into the depth of her body and the sexual mystery which it reveals.[55] The experience itself is "lowering," suggested by the fact that Paul uses the "low" language of dialect when it is over.

"Low" describes another place in which the relationship with Clara develops, the factory basement, where she continually seeks to snare him for love-making, although impeded by the fact that it is a public place. The public/private opposition is insistent in their relationship, the public being where they must usually meet: for example, the theater, where Paul fervently desires Clara, who is seated next to him but inaccessible. The same situation recurs at her house, where he stays overnight, having missed the last train. By clever instinct, he manages to elude her mother's obstinate surveillance. Even in this circumstance, however, when he finds Clara in the kitchen, Paul must *descend*.[56]

The category of "low" is intimately connected to that of "darkness": it is in the darkness of the open country where the couple reach their fullest embrace, in the course of which, however, he becomes conscious of the impersonality of his relationship with the woman, a relationship which unites him to pulsating cosmic life more than to her, thus turning paradoxically into an experience of separation instead of union.[57] This consciousness becomes even stronger in the later episode of the seaside vacation, where Clara's image is presented under two contrasting and complementary aspects: she appears as insignificant as a grain of sand (as such she is still an element of cosmic Eros) while she swims far away in the waves, but also as the blooming, magnificent incarnation of the feminine while she dries herself nearby. In both cases, Paul cannot see her as a person. This foreshadows not only the end of their relationship but also his negation (his inner world) of all of the places associated with her.

The Void

The approach to the exhaustion-point of Paul's relationships with Miriam and Clara occurs at "threshold places" (especially the seashore, border between finite and infinite), in each of which he realizes *the boundary* of the relation between them and the impossibility of going *beyond*, while in other risky places (such as the park's edge, where it is possible to hear the voices of passers-by, or the river shore, a step away from turbulent waters) he tries to shatter the boundary itself, in order to revitalize a relationship in crisis.

The exploration of boundaries foreshadows the abandonment of a given place and the person to whom it is linked, and as the novel draws to a close, this happens at a faster pace: while his visits to Willey Farm lasted nearly seven years, visits to Clara's place, the city, did not last more than a number of months. An even shorter time is spent at those masculine places which he explores in desperation, since even his home, because of his mother's sickness, is an anxious place. Baxter Dawes plays an important role in Paul's initiation into the masculine realm. His relationship with Baxter is shown in two altercations (one verbal, the other physical), the second of which suggests the creation of a *Blutbrüderschaft* between the two men, a carnal intimacy which will eventually result in a psychological intimacy. The intensity is explained by the fact that in Dawes, Paul sees almost a double of his own father (vigorous, active, simple, instinctive), and the source of a profound sense of guilt which fuels an equally profound need for expiation.[58] This need explains, first, his visit to the hospital where Baxter is recovering (which contrasts with the visit he did *not* make to his injured father in the first part), and second, the fact that not only does he help Baxter come out of his apathy but also encourages him towards reconciliation with his wife.

Their friendship motivates Paul to seek other male companionship ("usually he was with men," *SL* 430) in the pub, and even to take a beach vacation with one, Newton,[59] in an attempt to escape, by simple rapport and thoughtless camaraderie, from the torturing complexity of his relationships in the feminine realm and especially with the most intimate and painful of these, with his mother, in whose sick room he is spending more and more time as Mrs. Morel's illness worsens.

Her approaching death causes a drastic simplification of spaces and places in the novel. After a certain point, there are only the inside and the outside, her room and what she can see from her window: first the sunflowers in the garden, symbol of her tenacious hold on life ("'they are my sunflowers!' she said," *SL* 422), then the cold, deathly whiteness of the snow, contrasted with the hearth which always burns in her room until her death. This focus is even narrower a little later, concentrating on the bed where agony consumes her.[60] The room is a claustrophobic space for Paul, yet one to which he feels magnetically drawn and from which, not able to accept the horror of the situation, he continually departs, only to return soon after, incapable of *any* rest in *any* place.

The mother's death, which empties the room and the house, gives Paul the tragic knowledge that he does not belong anywhere, and is surrounded by emptiness. This awareness intensifies, generating an always stronger sense of isolation, until he sees the void itself as the essence of reality ("there seemed no reason why these things should occupy the space instead of leaving it empty," *SL* 435).⁶¹ His own lodgings at Nottingham are also experienced as a void, as is the night world in which he wanders, desperately fighting the impulse of self-destruction, without finding valid reasons to fight it, yet irrationally refusing to yield and be swallowed by it. At the end of the novel, we see him turning towards the "fullness" of the city, which is no longer specifically identified as Nottingham, but as a new space in which to begin a new existential adventure.

5

The Beginning of the Quest: *The Lost Girl* and *Aaron's Rod*

> *Fuir! là-bas fuir! Je sens que des oiseaux sont ivres*
> *D'être parmi l'écume inconnue et les cieux!*
> — Stéphane Mallarmé

The Escape

Written in the years immediately following World War I, *The Lost Girl* (1920) and *Aaron's Rod* (1922) are not Lawrence's best novels, but they provide considerable interest in relation to his artistic evolution, due to the continuity and complementarity which links them to one another and to the preceding work, as well as to the new uses made of space and place, and specifically of the "spirit of place" which will inform the final phase of his fiction.

Relatively traditional in their writing, the novels are non-traditional both in the narrative voice — deliberately discontinuous and unified only by the recurrence of certain leitmotifs — and in the construction of the protagonists, Aaron and Alvina, who evolve, on the one hand, by alternating between centrifugal and centripetal motion and, on the other, by interacting with places always further and always more Other with respect to their point of departure. More than an interior evolution in the traditional sense, this produces a passage of the personality through various allotropic states, such that the study of the "physiology of matter," which reaches its highest point in *The Rainbow* and *Women in Love*, begins to replace psychological analysis.[1]

The mood of both *The Lost Girl* and *Aaron's Rod* reflects the disturbing experience of World War I, which, because it prompts the dissolution of an entire system of values, necessitates the search for new points of reference and helps motivate the quest toward the unknown that both of the protagonists undertake. Moreover, Lawrence sees the war as a threat to individual freedom, a threat inherent in the military's insistence that the individual wear a uniform and comply with regulations entirely alien to the vital necessities of life.

Thus, the war almost inevitably brings the persecution of *difference*, a theme which becomes evident toward the end of *The Lost Girl*, while in *Aaron's Rod*, which begins as soon as the war is over, a sense of loss and anxiety predominates throughout, the result of a situation which demands a radical and problematic reworking of the concept of civilization.[2] The autobiographical element, always strongly present in Lawrence's works, is also present in these two novels, which reflect the uneasiness that the author experienced in his native land during the war years as well as that resulting from his contact with the Continent.[3] For Lawrence, faced with the reality that was Italy, there was the sense of discovery, but also of disappointment and sometimes of rejection, as well as the slow, tiring attempt to adapt himself to foreign places.

In these years, however, Lawrence regarded the experience of the Other, be it a place or a person, as a vital necessity — no matter how difficult or problematic — for both himself and the protagonists of these two novels: it is no coincidence that of the various marriage proposals which Alvina receives, she chooses the most unthinkable one, uniting herself with Ciccio, an almost primitive being who takes her to live in a remote village of the Abruzzi, while Aaron, even though incapable of breaking the destructive tie which binds him to his wife, is attracted, however fleetingly, to women completely different from himself in origins and social class.

In any case, these women, Ciccio, and Italy, do not constitute the actual point of arrival of the quest undertaken by the protagonists, a quest motivated by a growing — and ultimately unbearable — intolerance for the region of their birth, the Midlands, to which they can never return, even though they have not actually put down roots elsewhere. Thus, both novels pick up where *Sons and Lovers* leaves off, with Paul turning instinctively, almost blindly, toward the "gold phosphorescence" (*SL* 464) of the city, thus initiating the quest of which *The Lost Girl* and *Aaron's Rod* dramatize the first phase, but a quest which never actually reaches a destination.

The only clear motivation for Paul, Aaron and Alvina, is to turn their backs on their own point of departure, a closed and suffocating world, in order to grope towards another, of which they know only that it must be the opposite of their familiar one. Consequently, the attraction which places and persons exerts upon them is directly proportional to their distance from the "center," and also directly proportional to the disorienting effect produced by the contact with the unknown. Alvina is attracted by characters completely foreign to Manchester House (an Australian doctor, a man who wants to emigrate to South Africa, an Italian vaudevillian) and foreign also to the model partner considered appropriate to her education and social status. Analogously, Aaron is attracted to foreign women, and even more to Lilly, the mouthpiece of an anti-bourgeois gospel which he would like to make his own; however, neither character finds existential self-realization in their encounter with the Other.[4]

The Expanding Horizon

The two novels share an analogous movement — the gravitation of the protagonists towards new vital centers in contrast with the magnetism exerted by their points of departure — with a difference. Whereas in *The Lost Girl*, Alvina oscillates between center and margin until her "final leap" to the Continent, in *Aaron's Rod*, a progressive displacement from center to center on a north-south axis occurs, a displacement determined by the dissolution of relationships which the protagonist has established around the pole of temporary gravity. For Aaron, the "center," the home, always remains a reference point of fundamental importance, a place to which he feels he belongs, but which rejects him (he returns only once, before finally leaving England) just as a part of him rejects it. Unlike *Sons and Lovers*, where home is a territory that must be conquered or defended, in these two novels it is, from the start, experienced as a suffocating prison, both by Aaron (whose wife and daughters appropriate every space that is "his own"), and by Alvina, who, despite her attachment to her family and her strong ties to her governess, Miss Frost, is absolutely convinced from the beginning of the novel of the necessity of leaving home in order to grow and be fulfilled.[5] Brought up as a "perfect lady" by Miss Frost, Alvina reveals from her early childhood a double nature ("there was an odd, derisive look at the back of her eyes, a look of old knowledge and deliberate derision," *LG* 21), something rebellious and indomitable which completely disorients those who know her and which is connected in some way to the duality of the place she calls home. Vast and labyrinthine, with doors and passages which separate its spacious living quarters from the work areas (which undergo frequent change as a result of the disastrous business activities of Alvina's father), Manchester House shelters those severe stalwarts of bourgeois conformity, Alvina's mother and Miss Frost. But it also houses Alvina's eccentric father, a businessman who fails precisely because he is incapable of fitting into the community in which he lives or sharing its *forma mentis*. The ambiguity of Manchester House is reflected in Alvina's deep-seated ambivalence toward it. Torn between the desire for the unknown and the sense of security and protection which the house offers, she returns to it after each disappointing experience in the outside world, finding there a refuge in which she contemplates the possibility of her next escape. Incapable of crossing the threshold of Eros with her first fiancé, the Australian doctor, she then passes through a constellation of "centers," in each of which she undergoes experiences of ritualistic initiation. These experiences constitute moments not so much of growth as of true metamorphosis, but they fail to integrate the two aspects of her personality or to make her "one," and this failure is suggested by the strange dichotomy which exists between the changes in her physical aspect and those in her character. Her first initiation takes place in Islington where she takes a course in obstetrics in order to become a "maternity nurse." The squalid atmosphere, even grayer and more vulgar than Woodhouse, attracts her precisely because of its vulgarity. She prefers it to the severe puritanism of Miss Frost. In the squalid halls and rooms of the hospital and in the poor hovels of the miners, Alvina completes her first steps towards "the low," educating not her mind (over which Miss Frost has tried so hard to gain control) but her body. She lowers herself to every physical and manual task, eats with the appetite of a common laborer (as a result of which she visibly puts on weight), and flirts with all the doctors, albeit without losing her virginity.

Having exhausted the potential of this experience, Alvina reverts to the pale, bashful creature that Miss Frost had fashioned in her own image, in order to raise Alvina's social position. Paradoxically, it is Alvina's own father (who has made her lower herself with him into the workaday world, into the mine and into the scullery when he thinks to transform Manchester House into a hotel) who provides the opportunities for her subsequent "descents." After ridding herself of a "good match," an Oxford student who is about to take a teaching post in Cape Town but who is completely alien to her, she becomes involved in her father's outlandish project of opening a theater, which, in addition to "lowering" her even further in the eyes of the townspeople (she plays the piano during shows), brings

5. *The Lost Girl* and *Aaron's Rod*

about her meeting with Ciccio, a meeting destined to become a journey without return. Composed of four young men of different nationalities,[6] Ciccio's theater company curiously reproduces the situation from which Alvina is trying to escape: the role which Miss Frost plays in Alvina's home is now performed by an imperious French woman, referred to as "Madame," the incarnation of an inflexible superego. All of the actors relinquish their will to her, as if by virtue of her rigid and inviolable rules (she decides when they can drink and chooses their foods), they are able to protect themselves from the threats and dangers of a foreign country, as well as to appease their jealousies and grudges.

Upon the death of her father, who was her strongest link to Woodhouse, Alvina makes up her mind, without telling anyone else, to abandon her hometown, to which, like Aaron, she will return only once.[7] The first radical change of her life occurs, in typically Lawrencean fashion, through a process of ritual initiation including formulas, chants, dances, even a change of name ("you will become one of the tribe of Natcha-Kee-Tawara, in the name Allaye ... . We are one tribe, one nation," *LG* 199). This ritual makes her part of the tribe, sister of all its members, and Ciccio's bride.[8] Following this social initiation on the same night, a profoundly traumatic, yet not dramatic, sexual one occurs. In the face of his passion, which "seemed to throw her down and suffocate her like a wave ... to make her his slave" (*LG* 202-3), she cannot resist, but neither can she abandon herself or lose herself in the other. A last tremor of her old identity causes her to accept a nursing post in Lancaster, that is, in a place far away (but not too far) from Manchester House. Apparently it is an attempt to lessen the tension between center and margin, a tension involving, as always, both people and places. At Lancaster, she is courted by a bachelor doctor who, inasmuch as he is a midway point between the known and the unknown, cannot constitute her destination. In light of this experience, she realizes that to achieve true fulfillment she must make a choice which implies a movement far beyond her initiation in the sphere of Eros, a choice between England's respectability and security (the known) and the dark glamor of Italy (the unknown). At this point, Alvina opts for the unknown.[9]

The same choice is made by Aaron, who leaves home on Christmas Eve, as if he wishes to celebrate the birth of a new man as he progressively distances himself from home.[10] Aaron's adventures differ from Alvina's in two ways: first, his relocations are not the result of conscious choices, but happen by chance or because of chance encounters. Second, whereas she, a girl of good family, moves towards "the low," the miner Aaron finds himself instead, in a completely unpremeditated way, progressively climbing the social scale, penetrating first the bohemian and intellectual circles, thanks to his musical instrument, the flute, which is a sign of his artistic vocation, and then being accepted even in aristocratic circles.[11]

In these environments, Aaron seems finally to find that space which the prison of his family precluded ("I wanted to have some free room round me — to loose myself — ... I wanted fresh air," *AR* 66), but he does not find roots, remaining always *disoriented*, deprived of sure points of reference. He cannot find them in art (even his involvement with the London orchestra is only "a job"), nor in personal relationships, about which he seems to have no clear ideas and which expose him to continual frustrations and disappointments.

It is thus no surprise that the city is for him not a place of exciting discovery and of life itself as in earlier novels, but a labyrinth ("in London he found himself at a loose end .... He wanted to disappear," *AR* 122) and a hell ("down there in the bowels of London, after midnight, everything seemed horrible and unnatural," *AR* 63). His sense of disorientation in the city causes him to lose himself in his relationship with Josephine and its failure results in a psychosomatic illness which Lilly cures. Aaron's physical intimacy with Lilly (when he rubs Aaron's body with a balsamic cream) causes a miraculous recovery.[12] Lilly, also a wanderer prone to isolation, afraid of promiscuity, mouthpiece for Nietzschean ethics, becomes the only sure reference point for Hamlet-like, Aaron, who makes Lilly the object of his own quest and his role model.

Oppressed by London, which seemed "to rub him the wrong way" (*AR* 130), Aaron tries to return home one last time before making his grand leap to the Continent, only to realize that the door is closed forever and his house is no longer his own.[13] Surprised at first by the garden cultivated by others, he then finds his wife incapable of forgiving him, more determined than ever to defend her throne, dominate him, and willing to take him back only in return for his total submission.

After this attempt to return, which emphasizes Aaron's complete existential disorientation, he blindly undertakes a journey-of-no-return, without a specific destination, towards the Continent.

Verticality

Aaron's movements on the high/low axis proceed in the opposite direction from Alvina's. After refusing to climb the social ladder (his mother wanted him to be a schoolteacher) and opting for the descent, in both senses, of mining work, he finds himself welcomed into the intellectual circles of the upper classes: the family that takes him in the first night that he leaves home, the world of the London opera and the high society people who invite him for frivolous evenings out, the elderly, aristocratic Englishman in Novara, and finally the Marquis Del Torre in Florence. He also frequents high places which serve as observation points (hotel rooms, the lodgings where his most important meetings and discussions occur, Argyle's room with its splendid view of Piazza Duomo in Florence).[14]

For Alvina, the reverse is true: cultural "high" places (Pisa, Florence and Rome) are passed through quickly in the course of her travels; "low" places include those she has frequented in England and, even more so, her destination, where, for the first time in Lawrence's fiction we feel the spirit of place ("she was ... startled, half-enraptured with the terrific beauty of the place ... the grand, pagan twilight of the valleys, savage, cold, with a sense of ancient gods who knew the right for human sacrifice," *LG* 314-15). Although beautiful, it is a lost and desolate spot, where the primeval reveals its menacing face, and where Alvina's habitation is anything but a home ("the house was quite large: but inhabitable," *LG* 317).[15] The small group of houses to which she is confined is hours from the nearest village, where there are only a post office and a few stores. The remoteness of the location overwhelms her with a sense of total disorientation ("she was lost — lost — lost utterly," *LG* 313), made all the worse by her awareness of the impossibility of return ("no one would ever find her. She had gone beyond the world into the pre-world" *LG* 316). Ironically, the only means of escape is the railway, the lone representative of the technological civilization she had abandoned.[16] But in reality, she knows that escape is an impracticable alternative, so she finally resigns herself to making her house livable and to finding a *modus vivendi* in a place which she can in no way see as the final resting place in her quest.[17]

Super-Civilized and Super-Primitive

Both protagonists' journeys to the Continent and their encounters with the new world of the South conform to the logic of complementarity and parallelism. For both, the journey is the source of fascinating discoveries as well as unpleasant experiences (especially for Alvina, in contact with the poverty, backwardness and ignorance of Ciccio's environment), but overall the experience is positive for both, if only because it makes them aware of the limitations and restrictions of the worlds from which they came.

While Aaron's itinerary is largely that of the classic British tourist (the only detour being Novara) with its final destination the not-to-be-missed Florence, Alvina catches only glimpses of the great artistic cities from the train, arriving in an Italy completely off the tourist track and almost outside of civilization.[18]

For both protagonists, art (if Aaron's humble talent can be so considered) occasions the journey to what is traditionally considered the land of art (as opposed to England, the land of technology and industry) and also to a different socio-cultural dimension, which for the miner Aaron is a move towards something higher and for the bourgeois Alvina, towards something lower.

Although contact with the "other" changes Aaron and Alvina, they in their turn have an effect on their environment, upsetting the order of the worlds which they enter. Aaron, a moody outsider who defies classification, disturbs both the family environment of Sir William, who is the quintessence of Old England, and the Marchioness' house, which is awakened by his instrument (the flute is also a phallic symbol) to new life, arising from the deathly feelings occasioned by the war.[19] A similar effect is produced by Alvina on the somnolent southern village where, because of her strangeness, she is nearly worshipped.[20]

In neither *Aaron's Rod* nor *The Lost Girl* are the effects of the encounter with the "other" limited to mutual enrichment. On the contrary, each suffers from an experience of loss, disorientation and diminution. Alvina becomes lost in the desolate Italian village in more than one sense: in the first place, due to the outbreak of war and Ciccio's departure, she finds it impossible to go home; in the second place, by virtue of her marriage, she has degraded and disgraced herself according to bourgeois standards; finally, her knowledge and culture are essentially useless (lost) in the out-of-the-way place that is Ciccio's home.

As for Aaron, he is lost because he lets the spirit of place permeate his own personality, already so unstable and ill-defined; because he lets himself be corrupted by the super-refined, but essentially ancient and diseased, cilivization of Florence, whose glamor is incarnated in the Marchioness with whom he has a rather sterile and useless affair.[21] For him, too, contact with the Other brings diminution, symbolically rendered by episodes like the one in which he is robbed and the one in which the bomb breaks his flute (a bomb and an explosion end the novel, creating a circular effect with the breaking of the Christmas ball in Chapter I and its explosion).[22] Aaron seeks to recover his loss in Lilly, the guide in whom he hopes to find an escape from his situation of personal confusion.[23]

In the final analysis, both protagonists are victims of a mirror-like illusion, produced in *The Lost Girl* by the fascination with the super-primitive and, in *Aaron's Rod*, by fascination with the super-civilized. This super-civilization is identified not with technology but with art; if northern cities hold Aaron's attention for only a brief period, it is because they

5. *The Lost Girl* and *Aaron's Rod*

remind him of England. Milan, full of frenetic life, seems to him a copy of London and only the Duomo attracts him, its gothic features not unlike Lincoln Cathedral, which inspired ecstatic raptures and dark terrors in *Sons and Lovers* and *The Rainbow*. Inside the cathedral, the sacred has given way to the unstoppable, frenetic uneasiness of modern life:

> And all the time, over the big-patterned marble floor, the faint click and rustle of feet coming and going, coming and going, like shallow uneasy water rustled back and forth in a trough [AR 182].

The encounter with something different does not occur until Florence, a city of human dimensions with a virile personality which gives Aaron the sense of having reached his destination:

> And he felt that here he was in one of the world's living centres, here, in the Piazza della Signoria. The sense of having arrived — of having reached a perfect centre of the human world: this he had [AR 212].[24]

The fascination of the super-primitive is exerted upon Alvina by a lonely and wild nature, by the beauty of steep mountains and flower-covered fields. It is a natural world as completely foreign to her as the splendor of Florence is to Aaron. Both works end with the paradox found in most of Lawrence's "travel novels" ("The Princess," "The Woman Who Rode Away," and *The Plumed Serpent*): that which represents a potential source of regeneration for individuals (because it irresistibly attracts them) ends by destroying them, inasmuch as they lack the personal resources to overcome the difficult challenge of contact with the Other.

6

Uprooting: *The Rainbow* and *Women in Love*

> *... when a certain type of home disappears,*
> *it means that a race is extinguished.*
> — Oswald Spengler

> *... the going round*
> *And round and round, the merely going round,*
> *Until merely going round is a final good ...*
> — Wallace Stevens

Circularity and Polarity

The composition of *The Rainbow* and *Women in Love* (with *Lady Chatterley's Lover*, the most problem-ridden in both composition and publishing history),[1] covers important years in the writer's artistic career, in which he also wrote the essays "Study of Thomas Hardy," "The Crown" and *Movements in European History*. While influencing the novels (especially *Women in Love*),[2] these essays also demonstrate increased personal suffering, rising not only from Lawrence's personal trials related to the choice (or condemnation) of self-exile, but also from the search for values which would enable the construction of a new world after the ruins of the war.

6. *The Rainbow* and *Women in Love*

The suffering of these years and the magnitude of these works help to explain the writer's difficulty in settling upon a definite title; those chosen and abandoned suggest his oscillation between two different, though essentially complementary, concepts of human experience, founded respectively on the principle of polarity (the prime example of which is sexual relations) and on that of circularity (applied especially to the progressive widening of experiential horizons). To the first category belongs "The Sisters," a dualistic title, and to the second the initial titles of the two works into which the first was divided, *The Rainbow* and "The Wedding Ring"; but when "The Wedding Ring" became *Women in Love*, circularity and polarity were balanced in the two titles.

A vast family saga which embraces several generations (which may be considered Lawrence's response to works like Thomas Mann's *Buddenbrooks*, Émile Zola's *Rougon-Macquart* and John Galsworthy's *The Forsyte Saga*), the twin novels, in typically Lawrencean style, focus on one or more couples in each generation, relating their psychological problems and their evolution to large epochal changes, to the social and cultural transformations taking place in England, to which the characters react sometimes as protagonists, sometimes as victims, and sometimes as both.

Only the first of the two novels appears in saga form: while *The Rainbow* ranges across three generations, *Women in Love* picks up the story of its protagonist (Ursula, whose arrival at the age of maturity concluded the first novel), interweaving it, in a fairly brief chronological range, with the activities of other characters (Birkin, Gerald, Hermione) who appear for the first time. In consequence of this shorter time span, *Women in Love* presents, with respect to *The Rainbow*, a structure in which the temporal category appears subordinate to the spatial one.[3] It is not by chance that *The Rainbow* opens with a detailed description of the setting, and a specific time:

> About 1840, a canal was constructed across the meadows of the Marsh Farm, connecting the newly opened collieries of the Erewash Valley .... So the Marsh was shut off from Ilkeston ... [R 13].

The specific time refers to a physical intervention in the topography of the place — the construction of a canal — which is a major factor in the changed existence of the Brangwens, "[who] had lived for generations on the Marsh Farm" (R 9). Thus begins a process of transformation which increasingly impinges on the existence of the characters and which, merely mentioned in the first part of *The Rainbow*, reaches a frenetic pace in *Women in Love*. The canal constitutes a physical sign in the landscape which, other than bringing water (the flow of which is symbolic of the passing of time, and therefore of history), opens a wound in the organic community of the Brangwen family. This wound is not entirely healed by the money earned from the expropriation of their land. From this moment on, the Brangwens will yearn, unsatisfied, for an unspecific "beyond," incapable of retrieving the ancient balance of earlier generations, who had harmonized their existence with cosmic rhythms and who were in visceral communion with the earth.[4]

As the novelistic structure changes from one novel to the next, so too does the characters' relationship with place. The fundamental element of *The Rainbow* is the presence of a distinct and definite center, represented by the home, around which revolve — like a planet around its orbit — the intimate relationships of the protagonists, a couple for each of the three generations. In *Women in Love,* on the other hand, it is the absence of a center and a home — those existing are precarious and provisory — which pushes the restless, disoriented characters into their anxious, frenetic quest.[5]

In *Women in Love* the lack of a home (a necessary element for a couple) transforms the characters' relationships, which become more unstable, reactive, and argumentative. These relationships evolve in a series of disagreements and encounters, mostly violent and unexpected, by which the two partners try to establish a more stable relationship upon which to base their own existence, and to find a place which might be appropriate for starting over.[6] Instead of the single couple symbolizing its generation, and the story of its settling down in an always more precarious balance, *Women in Love* moves the focal point to a complicated, changeable web of relationships between two couples which are related and opposed to one another in an innovative and structurally interesting way. In the beginning of the novel, the description of the Crich wedding offers Lawrence an occasion to introduce all of the principal characters, setting in motion a game of attractions and repulsions. None of the characters is established as "central," quite unlike those in the three sets which make up *The Rainbow* (Tom in the first, Anna in the second and Ursula in the third). In *Women in Love,* the couple is a gravitational force field on which precarious balances are struck based on the distance between the two characters. The ambivalence and dichotomy of their relationship depends on how much distance (and difference) there is between them. Distance creates, on the one hand, attraction and, on the other hand, friction and miscommunication. Even in its literal sense, distance influences the relationship: for example, Gerald needs Gudrun most after she leaves for London and Birkin gravitates towards Hermione (whose presence he can barely tolerate) only when she is absent.

All of this seeking and fleeing does not yield satisfying results; even though Birkin and Ursula manage to find themselves, they never succeed in freeing themselves completely from their sense of displacement or reaching a true *ubi consistam,* as is suggested by their inability to find a physical destination for their quest. The novel ends, analogously to *Aaron's Rod* and *The Lost Girl*, on a question which emphasizes the precariousness of the partners' relationship rather than the union they have reached.[7]

The open endings of *The Rainbow* and *Women in Love* also link them to *Sons and Lovers* (in the end, Paul walks towards the lights of the city) and to the protagonists' adventures into unknown territory in *Aaron's Rod* and *The Lost Girl*. There is also a reappearance of the binary oppositions between city and country, between the towns of the Midlands and London, and even, in the domestic realm, the fight for sovereignty in the home.

The strongest continuity, however, is in the characters' quests, which, for some, end, and, for others, begin at the point at which *Sons and Lovers* concludes. In the mountains, Gerald succumbs to the *cupio dissolvi* which Paul so strenuously overcame at the end of the novel, while Gudrun, instead of the promising "city's gold phosphorescence" (*SL* 464), foresees only a name, Dresden, which for her is closely connected to the corrupt figure of Loerke.[8]

Like all of the preceding novels (except perhaps *The Trespasser*), *The Rainbow* and *Women in Love* are stories of maturation and initiation. They represent a step forward both from *Sons and Lovers*, where Paul took his first steps into the world accompanied by his mother, and the type of experience undergone by Aaron and Alvina in *Aaron's Rod* and *The Lost Girl*, whose quest is presented here as having already been accomplished. In the two Italian novels, distance from England is felt to be a necessity, and the process of growth and discovery occurs on the Continent, while in *The Rainbow*, the path of discovery makes its way through a series of ever-widening concentric circles, and in *Women in Love*, the exploration of unknown spaces is incapable of producing regeneration or existential fulfillment. Gerald's search ends with his death in the mountains; Birkin and Ursula do not find the Continent stimulating enough, and decide to return to the mill where they began their courtship, in a type of *nostos* which anticipates the conclusion of *Lady Chatterley's Lover*, where the fulfillment of the quest is in a forest only a few minutes' walk from Connie's house.[9]

The Dialectic of Center and Margins

In their use of spatial structures, *The Rainbow* and *Women in Love* both resemble and develop beyond the immediately preceding novels, as is reflected in their narrative dynamics. As in *Sons and Lovers*, the Midlands are still the central point of reference; they are the heart of industrialized England from which all of the characters, in different ways and with different motivations, attempt to distance themselves. First, they go to London; then, they undertake voyages to the Continent (like Aaron and Alvina), which, however, do not provide satisfaction. Perhaps it is no coincidence that Gudrun and Gerald's journey finishes in the Alps, a threshold between north and south, whereas for Birkin and Ursula, traveling forward serves only to clinch their decision to return (even though the decision is not definite and certainly not satisfying).

The motivation for these travels is the exigency of exploration and conquest of new places, which Lawrence seems to see as an ethological drive — as a fundamental impulse of the animal (man) and an inevitable moment in his growth process. Travel is also motivated by the characters' intolerance of their home environment, which they perceive as no longer habitable. Travel is an attempt to escape the process of degradation in England, which characters see as a place of non-life, of empty shadows which move mechanically like "subdued beast[s] in sheep's clothing" (*R* 415), a place which, as Gudrun says upon her return from London, "is like a country in an underworld" (*WL* 11).[10] On the other hand, this process of corruption has by now pervaded all of Europe, whose cultural centers of London, Paris and Dresden are in decay and close to utter ruin. In the beginning of *The Rainbow*, the city is still, as in preceding novels, a place of discovery, affirmation, enrichment, or refuge from the hell of domestic strife. However, it progressively assumes more negative connotations in accordance with the culture/nature opposition upon which Lawrence founds his axiological system: it becomes a place of sterility and depravity. More precisely, it creates diseased individuals, prisoners of their own intellectualism, such as Halliday, Gudrun, Hermione and Loerke. The crossing of social boundaries which London appears to permit, especially in its bohemian, artistic circles, is deceptive, and the provincials who let themselves be deceived by the appearance of intellectual open-mindedness end up embittered and disillusioned.[11] Underneath the glitter of its undeniably attractive social life, the city hides its true jungle nature: a center fragmented into alienating microcosms, each regulated by rigid codes which, instead of offering liberty, imprison the individual, as in the Chapter "Crème de Menthe" and in Gudrun's story of her stay in Paris:

> Gudrun hated the Café [Pompadour], yet she always went back to it, as did most of the artists of her acquaintance .... It was as if she *had* to return to this small, slow, central whirlpool of disintegration and dissolution ... [*WL* 380].

If London is a hell which fills Birkin with desperation "as if it were the end of the world" (*WL* 61), then Paris, place of frivolous artists' parties, is no better. It supplies a place for temporary sojourn, as for Ursula at the end of *The Rainbow*, but is certainly not a final destination. Dresden is presented even more negatively, as the city which holds that grotesque caricature of an artist, Loerke, a character whose art Lawrence sees as a negation, rather than an expression, of life.

Just as city adventures are proven unsatisfying in *The Rainbow* and *Women in Love*, so too is the escape to the Continent, where, among other things, the romantic myth of Italy as the paradise of exiles which had brought Lawrence himself to this country, disintegrates. The liberating journey to the South is illusory; the Imperial Road which leads there is not. As Birkin says at the end of *Women in Love*, "a way out ... — It was only a way in again" (*WL* 478). Once he encounters a reality not so very different from what he found in his own country, he will return home.[12]

This does not mean, however, that the characters in either novel renounce their search for an Other place which is ethically and ideologically opposite to the arid, materialistic England which is at the root of their existential *Angst*. It does, however, change or problematize the site of this Other place, the discovery of which is from now on presented alternately as the result of greater enlargement of the characters' spatial horizons (as in the search for the extreme primitivism symbolized by Halliday's African statue which becomes the theme of the novels set in "exotic" places)[13] or by a return to the point of departure and a rediscovery of the uncontaminated corners of rural Old England. Overall, however, both novels unfold in a direction, not of positive outcomes, but of a decisive moment of crisis, and the closer the protagonist comes to such a moment, the further he or she is from the Brangwen farm which was the original setting of the story.

The farm does, however, contain the seeds of the crisis, because while it is, on the one hand, a happy island where people lead serene, almost idyllic lives in harmony with the surrounding natural environment, on the other hand, it is condemned to death by its very isolation, which explains the yearning of some of its inhabitants, especially the women, for contact with the outside world. Besides this anthropological reason, the novel suggests another, historical one: a different period — a time of progress, modernization, industry — is inexorably taking the place of those placid rhythms of an archaic existence regulated by the rotating seasons, which was completely satisfactory for preceding generations. In these "olden days," no member of the family felt the necessity, capacity or desire to move, but this is no longer the case for Tom.[14] The old, self-sufficient life (emphasized by the idiom "to live on" which indicates that the inhabited place also offers sustenance) begins to disturb Tom, who in some sense experiences any removal from the farm painfully, but who is also aware of the need to acquire a richer identity by interacting with the outside world. Initially satisfied with his farm work and home life, which is presided over by his mother, Tom feels an inexplicable restlessness and a need to enlarge his horizons after her death, which he indulges not so much by exploring other places as by meeting people who attract him by virtue of their Otherness. These individuals, rather than being rooted to the earth, are eternal wanderers, such as the foreigner whom he meets during his trip to Matlock; they carry within them something of the distant lands from which they come. Tom's yearning for the unknown finds its specific object in Lydia, a Polish widow who was exiled from her country for political reasons. She seems to Tom like an unknown country that he must explore with avid curiosity, but also with reserve and respect. By pairing the most rooted character, in a moment when his roots are weakening, with a foreigner (in every sense of the word), Lawrence is able to revitalize the center, reinforcing it by the sexual polarity that strongly attracts these two characters. Instead of jumping into the unknown, with the risk of failure which all of his earlier attempts had incurred, Tom attracts it to him with a centripetal movement; he brings the foreign into Marsh Farm, to which he is fiercely attached, reconciling the foreign with the familiar.[15] Thus, he establishes himself even more firmly on the farm (only for a moment is he attracted to his brother's lover and to a "higher" world of culture). Lydia, for her own part, finally finds in him an *ubi consistam* and a direction in her life, without having to renounce *her own* roots.[16]

The conciliation of opposites which enriches Tom and Lydia's relationship does not reappear in successive generations. On the contrary, in the passage from one generation to the next, conciliation lessens and there is rather a process of involution: between Anna and Will, polarity degenerates into a tiring conflict, and in the end, sterilizes the marriage, partly from a fear of the unknown which produces almost incestuous phenomena. Anna, who wishes, like her mother, to put down roots in one place, tries to strengthen her ties to her own roots by marrying another Brangwen, her cousin. Perhaps it is this very preference for the known over the unknown which makes her incapable of accepting the Otherness of her spouse. Lawrence frequently uses a spatial metaphor in *The Rainbow* (as he had already done in *Sons and Lovers*): Will, unlike Tom or Anna, is not oriented towards the horizontal (earth, calm, stasis) but towards the vertical, which implies climbing, effort, and the tension of change. Refusing to follow his vertical drive on a path that would lead her to pervert her true nature and renounce her identity, she tenaciously blocks him, trying (like Tom and Lydia, but without her father's respect for the Otherness of his wife) to contain him in her own center, mortifying his aspirations for social climbing and his religious tendencies.

In the third generation, this same fear of the Other influences Ursula's choice of Anton Skrebensky, a Pole like her grandmother, in whom she thinks she sees the man capable of reconciling her with her own remote origins and of reestablishing a vital tie with faraway lands and traditions. But this wish plunges her into a regression, with disastrous effects which threaten her very life; to avoid this, Ursula has to undergo a radical change, putting herself through many internal conflicts and denying parts of herself in order to construct a new existence.

Two processes of renewal fail at the end of *The Rainbow*: first, the cyclical/anthropological revitalization of the organic community, undone by the process of industrialization and the incestuous withering taking place within it; and second, the process of regeneration of male/female relationships, which is also thrown into crisis by "progress."

The Crisis of Home

The paradigmatic oppositions between rooting and uprooting established in the two novels are related to the above-described process of transformation. In *The Rainbow*, the characters, after the restless phase of adolescence, manage to put roots down in a place, usually making it a home, whereas in *Women in Love*, the absence and refusal of a home forces the characters, who suffer from a state of restlessness whose causes they cannot diagnose (when they do not outright refuse to admit its existence), to begin a quest which unfolds in a centrifugal direction, bringing them to a variety of places, but never to a definite haven.[17]

The concept of taking root, however, persists as a vague nostalgia for a past whose contours are hazy; and it persists only in characters who, like Ursula (but not Gudrun), maintain a tie, however fragile, to their own roots, as we see in the passage where Ursula departs for the unknown of the Continent with Birkin[18]:

> She thought of the Marsh, the old, intimate farm-life at Cossethay .... The great chasm of memory, from her childhood in the intimate country surroundings of Cossethay and the Marsh Farm ... and now, when she was travelling into the unknown with Birkin ... was so great, that it seemed she had no identity, that the child she had been, playing in Cossethay churchyard, was a little creature of history, not really herself [*WL* 390].

Most of the main characters in *Women in Love* feel a sense of loss of belonging to a place and community as well. While in *The Rainbow*, there is still a fairly precise demarcation between "places of us" and "places of others"—where "us" coincides with the house and its "under-places," which offer a refuge from external threats—in *Women in Love* there is little sense of any functional organization of space. In the destruction of this type of order, in this chaos, there emerges a state of crisis from which, as Birkin prophetically announces, it will be possible to exit only through a rebirth which requires, first of all, the destruction of the old order, not only in England, but in all of Europe.[19]

In these two novels, the crisis of home is also imputed to industrialization. Home is no longer seen as the place where an individual *lives*, organically belonging to an environment in a greater community, but as a mere lodging or dormitory.[20] The standardization of habitations, as the beginning of *Sons and Lovers* indicates, alienates their occupants. This situation becomes clearer at the end of *The Rainbow*, during Ursula's visit to her uncle Tom:

> The place had the strange desolation of a ruin. Colliers ... seemed not like living people, but like specters ... . The homogeneous amorphous sterility of the whole suggested death rather than life. There was no meeting place, no centre, no artery, no organic formation [R 320].

After her beloved uncle (in young Ursula's eyes a true hero) becomes director of a mine, his house seems cold and sterile, as lifeless as the surrounding environment. He himself seems to her to have lost the vitality he possessed when he was linked to the farm, thereby preparing us, through this negative transformation, for the introduction of Gerald. The two characters are linked as well by the fact that in both, their removal from their place of birth and their encounters with distant lands (America) paradoxically inhibits their capacity to accept the Other (as is witnessed by Gerald's sense of horror while looking at the African statue), rendering their faith in the processes of mechanization that much more fanatical, and contributing to their inner hardening.[21]

In the "crisis of home," as the two novels, and especially the second, make clear, are involved not only the working class habitations (in *Women in Love* the miner's villages appear as a sinister, hostile underworld), but also those of the bourgeoisie. The crisis is already foreshadowed or latent, however, in Marsh Farm, where the men are linked to the earth (horizontal dimension) and to the continuation of the existing order, while the women, not entirely satisfied with their own condition, turn their faces towards the "high," and a beyond which for the moment they identify with the highest point of the town, the church bell tower.

The decline of that world of which Marsh Farm is the symbol is implicated in its name: "marsh" evokes a fertile mix of earth and water, but also the idea of stagnation and decomposition. In its connection with water the name implies a relationship with both life and death: a flood sweeps over the farm and Tom's life is lost.[22] After this episode, Marsh Farm, by now deprived of its vital impetus, is virtually canceled from the scene; and when Ursula occasionally visits, it is not to re-establish her connection with the places of her youth, but to listen to her grandmother's stories of glamorous, faraway places. Fred, the farm's heir, never feels rooted there, but only accepts the farm as a life that was given him; he is constantly tormented by the necessity of measuring himself against other things ("He wanted change .... He would leave the Marsh," R 226).[23]

Parallel to the happenings at Marsh Farm are those at the upper class home of the Criches in *Women in Love*: its name, Shortlands, in apparent contradiction of the large estate, suggests a connection to processes of transformation, to the reduction of land and of livable space in industrialized England.[24] Here, too, water is the agent of death in a relationship which is both parallel and opposite to that in *The Rainbow*. Instead of a natural agent, the flood that took Tom's life, we have the still water of the artificial lake in which Gerald's sister drowns, together with the young doctor whom she strangles during his attempt to save her.[25] Analogously, the flood which signals Tom's death in *The Rainbow* occurs at the end of a party when he, like Gerald's sister, is drunk.[26] However, Tom almost enjoys this experience of discovery ("He *had* to go and look where it came from, though the ground was going from under his feet .... He rather enjoyed it," R 229), and his body is found when the waters recede in a natural way, whereas Gerald's sister's body is found only by artificial draining of the lake.

In the spatial structure of *Women in Love*, Shortlands is a central reference point for the characters' activities. In the beginning, it appears to be a place of life, because of the ritual event, Laura Crich's wedding, which is celebrated there. In reality, however, it is more connected than Marsh Farm to decadence and death, because it is more closely linked to industrialization. Its upper-class architecture, revealing signs of the past ("it has form ... it has a period" *WL* 48), does not conceal the ugliness of the nearby mines, just as the large trees of the park "did not quite hide the rising smoke" (*WL* 23) coming from that desolate, dirty, subterranean world which constitutes its *raison d'être*.[27]

At the same time, Shortlands demonstrates the passing from a humane industrialization (incarnated in the father who is generous and understanding to his dependents) to an inhumane one interested only in efficiency and productivity. Along with the disappearance of the cordial, paternalistic relationship of owner to workers comes the loss of the father's authority in the home. The father is old and weak in relation to his son, in whom he cannot stop the driving will to change, or the consequent decline of house and family into anarchy ("It was rather a resistance to authority, than liberty," *WL* 28).

The disappearance of the authority principle does not, however, bring a greater openness to the outside. In the Chapter "Water-Party," for instance, the annual Crich party should be a moment of interaction between different social classes, but instead, it reconfirms the existence of rigid social barriers and the latent antagonism between classes (the police guard the entrance and patrol those who enter). Breadalby, the other high-class residence of the novel, is no different. Tired of the city, Hermione retires there, but certainly not to immerse herself in nature: the landscape simply serves as an appropriate backdrop for the salons which she continues to conduct in the country. Of a purely aesthetic kind, her relationship with nature is sterile and inauthentic, as Birkin notices when he bridles at the little ceremonies she imposes on guests ("She intended them all to walk with her in the park," *WL* 87). He flees from her house to find relief from the claustrophobia she elicits, in a Pan-like, nude immersion in the vegetation; the episode marks the end of his attempt to find fulfillment in the urban world or in its rural extension at Breadalby.[28]

The Widening of Space

The decline of the grand, high-class homes is matched by the characters' inexorable process of uprooting from their place of origin. The existence of these older homes manifests the continuation of the generations and their common grounding in a specific place. Yet the new generation maturing during the era of World War I experiences the rituals associated with these environments as merely burdensome, empty forms. Their infrequent attempts to keep these forms alive fail. Hermione, the grand hostess, fails dramatically when she strikes Birkin on the head, simply because he dared to challenge her in front of her other, more obedient, guests. Her failure is due to her unadulterated intellectual snobbery.

Even more than in individuals, the process of uprooting takes place in couples, that starting point for nuclear families which, in *Women in Love*, never manage to be created (while those that do exist break down). The main couples, who have repudiated their homes of origin, either do not wish to create another home (in Ursula and Birkin's case) or cannot (in Gudrun and Gerald's) because that would mean rooting themselves in the old order, choosing the easier way and renouncing complete fulfillment of the self. Before leaving for the Continent, in the chapter significantly entitled "Marriage or Not," Birkin opposes Gerald's idea of getting married because he realizes that for him it would come not from the desire to establish a vital link with his partner, but simply to settle down. According to Birkin, this nesting instinct to avoid exposure to the external world is a lethal germ which is exterminating his generation:

> One should avoid this *home* instinct. It's not an instinct, it's a habit of cowardliness. One should never have a *home* [*WL* 352].

Convinced that married life would be a continuous argument and questioning of each other, a perpetual ending and starting over, for Birkin, the "place of us" of married life is "anywhere" that two people could open themselves simultaneously, but separately, to new experiences. To the lethal stability of home, he counter-proposes the fertile precariousness of homelessness.

Faced with this uncomfortable but vital idea, Gudrun draws back in discomfort. Despite her self-declared restlessness, she, like Gerald, is tormented by the desire to possess a place and to be possessed by it[29]:

> ... the wonderful stability of marriage. She did want it ... . The old idea of marriage was right even now — marriage and the home ... . She suddenly conjured up a rosy room, with herself in a beautiful gown, and a handsome man in evening dress who held her in his arms in the firelight, and kissed her [WL 376].

In the course of the two novels, the process which moves the characters from rootedness in an organic, self-sufficient home life to total uprooting, to finding a new place of belonging *only* through a harmonious relationship with their partner ("'It isn't really a locality, though,' he [Birkin] said. 'It's a perfected relation between you and me,'" WL 316) takes place in an alternation between centripetal and centrifugal movements, between the tendency to absorb external space into the home and the opposite tendency to expand the self in a space free of predetermined limits. After the equilibrium reached at Marsh Farm between Tom and Lydia, founded upon a division of space and labor (she presides over the house, he over the fields and barn), the closed spaces, instead of offering refuge, are loaded with negative connotations, and become prisons. Instead of continuing to be extensions of the self, privileged places in which loved persons gather (like the barn for Tom, who took refuge there with young Anna while awaiting Lydia's next child),[30] they become projections of an individual will which absorbs the space, cutting all contact with the external world and excluding others. This process of contracting space is accompanied by a deconsecration of places, which arises from the loss of values associated with human cohabitation. This process begins with Anna and Will's wedding and their move from Marsh Farm into a bourgeois cottage, a more sophisticated and higher class environment than the farm, signaling, in a socio-cultural sense, a step towards the "high." It is not, however, an enlargement of their horizons; on the contrary, since the cottage is situated opposite the church near the vicar's house where Tom proposed to Lydia, this move suggests a return to the point of departure and foreshadows a regression.

After their move to the cottage, a phenomenon apparently analogous to the one that affected the preceding generation occurs with Anna and Will, that is, an appropriation of complementary spaces on the part of the two partners. In actuality, however, things are quite different: Anna *shuts herself* into the domestic universe, appointing her bedroom as the center of the world, distancing herself more and more from her husband until she finally expels him from the love nest ("she would not sleep with him any more ... she drove him off ... . She made him a bed in the small room," R 174). The house's interior becomes a place of ferocious conflict and profound humiliation for the husband, who seeks compensation in the external world, especially in the church, in sacred art and music. Finally, he vindicates himself by having an affair with a working-class girl (which has parallels with but also contrasts with Tom's experience; Tom was attracted to a woman belonging to a "higher" class, his brother's lover). In other words, instead of the organic complementarity of places, reflecting a fertile polarity between the spouses, there is a complete unhinging between the domestic and external worlds, reflecting the division between Anna and Will. In this situation, Will is the loser: he is deprived of a place to call his own, uprooted, but not by his own will. As the title of Chapter VI emphasizes, Anna is "Victrix." During a pregnancy which makes her feel complete and self-sufficient, she celebrates her victory with a self-celebratory pagan dance, transforming her bedroom into a temple[31] (a metamorphosis which is not new in Lawrence's work). Obviously, she does not reach true fulfillment, but has only the satisfaction of being Anna Victrix, secure in her own nest, in which she imposes her despotic will not only on her husband but also upon her daughter Ursula. This situation, however, lasts only as long as her procreative power[32]: when her children are grown, she accepts the move to Beldover (which is due to her husband's job), to a house where her role is no longer central. On the contrary, from this moment forth her presence is relegated to the background, even after the last move (also occasioned by Will's work). By the end of the novel, the spouses have lived in three houses, but since their relationship is *empty*, all three homes are themselves *empty*, lifeless shells, and so it seems to Ursula and Gudrun when they return to retrieve their belongings:

> The whole place seemed to resound about them with a noise of hollow, empty futility ... . It was a void, with a meaninglessness that was almost dreadful [*WL* 373].

Ursula's heart-stopping observation in her parents' bedroom ("this room *couldn't* be sacred, could it?" *WL* 373) denies the process of consecration of her own room which Anna began with her propitiatory dance, relegating such sanctity to the past, of which no fragments remain, after just one generation. In part, Anna's dance was a response to the unease and impotence she felt during Will's ecstatic contemplation of Lincoln Cathedral, for him a condensation and synthesis of the entire world, "a reality, an order, an absolute, within a meaningless confusion" (*R* 191).[33]

Towards the end of *The Rainbow*, the home begins to reveal its fragility, and the isolation, rather than the harmony, of its inhabitants, whereas in *Women in Love*, the house decisively signifies a place of conflict, absence of communication, and mutual violence. Lawrence uses the parallel development of the couples' stories to confirm, by comparison and contrast, the by now ineluctable idea of *the impracticability of home*. The opposition of "closed/open" supports this conviction, and is correlated to the opposition between centripetal movements (tied to regressive processes) and centrifugal (linked to evolutionary processes).[34]

Ursula and Birkin move slowly towards acceptance and mutual respect, as each ceases to try to engulf the other in his/her own world, when each manages to create "star equilibrium" in their relationship, after a series of conflicts which, significantly, are always worse indoors. This process ultimately leads them to renounce the very concept of home and to choose a vagabond existence in which their residence is, as for Lawrence and Frieda, a changeable "anywhere." While they are outdoors, especially in unconfined places, they reach moments of identification, or at least of closeness. Islands, real or metaphorical, feel restrictive, such as the island in the pond of Willey Water, where they experience a discouraging separation and incommunicability not dissimilar to that experienced by Siegmund and Helena on the Isle of Wight, or Paul and Miriam in their unhappy experiment of wedded life in the isolated cottage in the woods:

> "Do let us go to the shore...," she [Ursula] said, afraid of being any longer imprisoned on the island [*WL* 131].

In *Women in Love*, the place *par excellence* of isolation is the home, especially when it is associated with a stable marital relationship, which is (for Lawrence) inert and static, as in the episode in which Birkin asks Ursula's father for her hand in marriage. The absence of communication between the two men parallels Birkin's profound and extreme sense of separation from Ursula, so strong that he nearly repudiates her sex. At least, this is what Birkin's impulsive visit to Gerald immediately after the visit to Ursula's father suggests, when Birkin and Gerald have an intense physical relationship (the Japanese wrestling match) which seems to imply a repudiation of the idea of star equilibrium between man and woman in favor of *Blutbrüderschaft* between man and man. Later developments in the novel suggest quite clearly, however, that in the interior environment of Gerald's house, no fertile or vital relationship is established.

On the contrary, the most intensely involving relationships always occur outdoors, and moreover, between characters in motion: for instance, the first moment of complete harmony between Ursula and Birkin occurs in the chapter entitled "Excurse," in which the two embark on an exploration of different places ("'where are we going?' 'Anywhere.' It was the answer she liked" [*WL* 303–04]) which foreshadows the discoveries offered by their erotic encounter. After arguing, they decide not to return to the mill, and they spend the night in Sherwood Forest. The experience constitutes a definite step forward in their relationship, allowing them not only to discover its potential but also to confirm their decision to open themselves to the outside world and to new life by burning their bridges to the previous one, that is, by leaving school and home.[35]

Unlike Birkin and Ursula, Gerald and Gudrun are involved in a centripetal relationship which is in some way connected to their desire to attract and enclose their partner in their own world, a desire that introduces an inevitable current of conflict. While the erotic initiation of Birkin and Ursula occurs at the same time as their gradual opening to nature's open spaces, Gudrun and Gerald's occurs in her closed bedroom, to which he brings a sense of death — symbolized by the soil on his shoes from his father's grave — and an obscure, destructive desire which he passes on to his lover ("She was exhausted, wearied .... There was something monstrous about him, about his juxtaposition against her," *WL* 346). This stolen intimacy with Gudrun (Gerald enters the cottage like a thief) results from a centripetal movement (his intention was to enclose her within his own space when he invited her to teach art to his younger sister Winifred), which, however, was not accompanied by a real welcoming of Gudrun into the house. She remains confined in the competing spaces of the estate ("the isolation of the studio," *WL* 335), spaces which, on the one hand, guarantee a sterile self-sufficiency, and on the other, favor the formation of a kind of homosexual relationship between her and Winifred which is parallel and complementary to the one that Ursula had with her own teacher (also named Winifred) in *The Rainbow*. Gudrun herself tends to transform every outdoor environment into a study, a place in which she can exercise her desire for control and power.[36] The episode of her ritualistic dancing in front of the cattle in "Water-Party," is similar to her mother's dance, but different in its significance. Anna's dance celebrated her fulfillment as a woman through pregnancy; Gudrun's is a hypnotic rite through which she demonstrates her desire to establish control over the animal world,[37] as Gerald had done with his horse in front of the passing train. Between the two wills, however, Gudrun's is weaker, as proven by the fact that her hypnotic power lessens upon Gerald's approach. So centripetal is their relationship — which demands a total assimilation of the external and the rejection of that which refuses to assimilate and cancel itself — that they manage to make even the immense stretch of snow in the Tyrol ("This is something I never expected ... . It is a different world, here" exclaims Ursula, *WL* 399) into a closed place, a prison which becomes, for Gerald, a tomb.[38] Even in this environment — which at the beginning promised freedom because of its difference ("One could never feel like this in England" *WL* 394) — Gudrun and Gerald experience an oppressive claustrophobia. Especially in the interiors of the chalet rooms, violent conflicts erupt ("finally, he might kill her," *WL* 445), linked especially to the violation of personal space which each feels they have suffered because of the other. Paradoxically, the conflict expands out into the ethereal, inhuman mountains, that literal and metaphorical blank space which catalyzes the freezing of their intimacy and highlights their incompatibility. The environment has opposite effects on Birkin and Ursula; it is actually the difference of the place, the unnaturalness of its whiteness, which forces them to find each other, contrasting the cold of the snow to the warmth of their love:

> I couldn't bear this cold, eternal place without you..., it would kill the quick of my life [*WL* 408].

On the other hand, Gudrun and Gerald find in this place of non-life their fitting reflection and therefore experience its glamour intensely, as when Gudrun is exalted by the magic of an alpine sunset ("It is the most beautiful thing I have ever seen in my life," *WL* 447). Because of this, they feel an intimate communion between them to be radically impossible and even undesirable. To the above-cited words, Gudrun immediately adds the icy phrase; "Don't try and come between it and me. Take yourself away, you are out of place —"(*WL* 447).

Between rare moments of ecstatic rapture come more frequent moments of disorientation and loss caused by finding herself so far from home and so close to the stars, surrounded by infinite, changeless forms:

> From high above, on either side, swept down the white fold of snow..., all strangely radiant and changeless and silent ... . It was a silence and a sheer whiteness exhilarating to madness [*WL* 398–99].

While Ursula and Birkin manage to break the deadly spell exerted by this environment ("Miracle of miracles! — this utterly silent, frozen world of the mountain-tops was not universal! One might leave it and have done with it. One might go away," WL 434), Gudrun and Gerald succumb to it, finding themselves incapable of leaving or returning, or escaping to salvation in another place.

Contact with a place in which the characters are subjected to extreme situations—the claustrophobic confinement in the chalet and getting lost in the endless expanse of the mountains—precipitates, in both positive and negative senses, the potentialities inherent in the couples' relationships[39]: in Gerald and Gudrun's case, it renders them more unstable and fragile, making the distance between them either excessive or insufficient, or in any event, lacking the necessary star equilibrium.[40]

The already-existing friction between Gudrun and Gerald is further aggravated by the intervention of Loerke, who creates a new center of gravity for Gudrun and, after Birkin and Ursula's departure, invades the space previously occupied by them. Thus an erotic triangle is formed, which, from a spatial viewpoint, pits Gudrun between the "high" represented by willful, ambitious Gerald, and the "low," incarnated in the slimy, corrupt, and sensual Loerke. He literally creeps on the ground after being struck by Gerald, who, in contrast, turns towards the "high" of the mountains after his attempt to strangle Gudrun. In his desperate search for escape from the total disorientation which solitude in the alpine "desert" only accentuates ("He had lost all his sense of place," WL 473), he exhibits a radical reversal of the dominating role he previously exercised over various environments.

For Birkin and Ursula, the contact with the mountains affords an opportunity to mature, increasing in both partners an awareness of their individual limits and those of their relationship. In contact with the icy snow, Birkin becomes fully aware that he cannot live without Ursula's warmth, and she in turn makes a decisive step forward in her existential quest when she fully frees herself from her origins—"she had no father, no mother, no anterior connections, she was herself, pure and silvery, she belonged only to the oneness with Birkin" (WL 409)—to give herself completely to her relationship with her partner.

Places of Threshold

The aforementioned opposition of closed/open focuses on the threshold, or line of demarcation between two different worlds and environments, the space of passage which, on the one hand, makes the process of growth possible, and on the other, because of the irreversibility of such process, inevitably blocks the possibility of return.

Sometimes, however, when the goal cannot be perceived, the road ahead is blocked. This is particularly true of Gerald, who, once he has left

England, becomes fixed in the ethereal whiteness of the Tyrolean snows, completely incapable of identifying a new destination. When Birkin, reporting his decision to leave, asks Gerald how long he will stay, Gerald's response reveals his sense of disorientation and a vague presentiment of his imminent death: "Oh, I don't know. We may never get back. I don't look before and after" (*WL* 439). While the thought of return inspires a sense of repulsion ("he shuddered with nausea at the thought of home" *WL* 460), he sees a circle around himself which, instead of getting wider, as the opening towards the Continent had seemed to promise, is closing tightly around him:

> ... he set himself to be free. He even prepared to go away .... But for the first time there was a flaw in his will. "Where shall I go?" he asked himself [*WL* 445].

In the final phase of the novel, thresholds, which in *The Rainbow* were clearly delineated, appear to be completely blurred. While in the first novel, the trespassing of a threshold brought a definite liberation from a given place — from Marsh Farm and from a patriarchal system of life for Anna (when she moved to Yew Cottage) as well as for Ursula, when the latter made inroads into the "man's world"— in *Women in Love*, thresholds are more and more indefinite, corresponding with the characters' difficulties in finding a true direction in life:

> Her [Gudrun's] tomorrow was perfectly vague before her .... And today was the white, snowy, iridescent *threshold* of all possibility [*WL* 467–68, emphasis mine].

This process develops in step with the characters' uprooting; it changes their center of gravity from the past to the future, and they lose stable reference points. In place of these, they find vague mirages—like the one Gerald sees in the snow — or mysterious, though possibly illusory, promises such as the vision of rebirth offered to Ursula at the end of *The Rainbow*.

As for the *Bildung* of Ursula, on the other hand, the thresholds between her various phases are clearly distinguishable, signaled by a series of passages which lead her to interact with places—school, university, and the ones where she explores Eros with Anton — each of which is connected with a phase of her development.

It is interesting to note that each of these passages—which keep widening the circle of experience, rendering her increasingly independent and mature, but also bringing contact, mostly violent and painful, with Otherness—refers to the paradigmatic *high/low* opposition. None of her adventures into the world is as "high" as she had expected. Like her father, she harbours expectations of an ideal world, even though in her there is also something of the horizontal earthiness of her mother, which gives rise to a recurrent contrast that is the leitmotif of the novel's second half. From childhood, Ursula's fantastic projections, which cause her to imagine herself the queen of a turreted castle, for instance (linking her to Miriam in *Sons and Lovers*), are threatened by the mother's invasiveness and especially by the lack of privacy from her noisy, demanding siblings ("Ursula! ... Open the door, our Ursula," R 247). But already during her early childhood, the imaginary experience of *descent* inherent in her every contact with reality, occurs in a premonitory episode of the type already found in *Sons and Lovers*: the visit to the amusement park with her father, initially experienced as discovery and complicity with her parent (as was the market for Anna and Tom), but later as a nightmare because of the irresistible will of her father to *push her higher*:

> He sent the swingboat sweeping through the air in a great semi-circle, till it jerked and swayed at the high horizontal .... The jerk at the top had almost shaken them both out [R 209–10].

The contrast between anticipation and experience, between the representation of reality and the experience of it, is often tied to that quintessential place of threshold, the window, which for Ursula signifies the boundary between reality and dream. At her room's window, she abandons herself to her imagination of journeys to distant lands, and from her grandmother's high window at Marsh Farm, listening to her memories of a fantastical time, Ursula dreams of putting together the pieces of a magical past, which she feels to be her rightful inheritance:

> ... the illusion of her grandmother, of realities so shadowy and far-off that they became as mystic symbols..., the multitude of illusions concerning herself, how she was truly a princess of Poland [R 249–50].

The decline of her ingenuous romantic fantasies linked to Poland occurs, appropriately, through her relationship with Anton Skrebensky, a Pole, and especially in the moment when he reveals himself far below *the height* of the image which Ursula had created. When the exaltation created by moonlight generates her irrepressible impulse to push beyond all boundaries, to discover the mysteries of Eros, he is overcome and nearly assaulted and raped by her passion[41]:

> She took him in the kiss, hard her kiss seized upon him, hard and fierce and burning corrosive as the moonlight. She seemed to be destroying him [R 299].

6. *The Rainbow* and *Women in Love*   83

Despite his aristocratic descent, which puts him high on the social scale, and his aspirations to a command in India, which would allow him to enjoy the comfortable superiority of someone belonging to the "governing class, *superimposed* upon an old civilisation" (R 411 emphasis mine), he is a flat, mediocre person, and therefore *below* Ursula's expectations. His function with respect to the protagonist is only to be a threshold for her adventure into the mysteries of sexuality and for an experience of self-discovery from which he remains excluded.[42] He is merely a spectator, not only during their embraces, in which she is always the active party, but also in the significant episode of their walk along the canal, during which she crosses the threshold of the boat on which a family lives, wishing to discover their intimacy, while Anton remains passive and observes from shore. On the one hand, this experience shows Ursula's separation from her companion; on the other, it anticipates, in the attraction that she feels towards this free-floating family, her later choice of a wandering existence with Birkin.

Ursula's homosexual experience with her teacher Winifred, in the chapter entitled "Shame," is a mark of her disappointment and her plunge into the "low." It takes place far from home, on the ambiguous threshold between earth and water (the swimming pool and the pond). Induced by the high ideals of women's liberation initially identified with her teacher, the affair leaves Ursula in a state of disgust and profound anxiety.[43]

Other painful "lowering" of her aspirations occurs in the world of institutional learning, where her dreams of teaching conflict with a rigid, obsolete behavioral code and obtuse didactic formulae which leave little to the imagination, to individuality or creativity:

> ... it was so inhuman. They were so many, that they were not children. They were a squadron..., a collective inhuman thing ... . The first great task was to reduce sixty children to one state of mind, or being [R 350, 355].

The school is a prison, betraying its true nature even in its exterior aspect:

> The whole place seemed to have a threatening expression, imitating the church's architecture for the purpose of domineering, like a gesture of vulgar authority [R 343].

The university, imagined as a temple of wisdom, is not much different:

> ... a little, slovenly laboratory for the factory ... . It pretended to exist by the religious virtue of knowledge. But the religious virtue of knowledge was become a flunkey to the god of material success [R 403].

It is worth noticing that both the school and the university are associated with religion, another of Ursula's *high* ideals, which crashes to earth through her dislike of the sterile formalism of Sunday rites, her growing awareness of the inapplicability of dogma to real life, and especially her Nietzschean rebellion against the Christian ethic of self-denial, sacrifice and privation: "she was *not* going to be as poor as the Wherrys, not for all the sayings on earth — the miserable squalid Wherrys" (*R* 258). Ursula fully realizes that this ethic creates the illusion of *ascent* towards a pure, high world of transcendence, but arrests every tendency towards full experience and the enlargement of one's horizons.

The gap between anticipation and experience occurs one last time — but with a reversal — when Ursula is surrounded by a herd of wild horses and, from the shock, aborts her child. In fact, what her imagination has perceived as negative is later perceived as positive. In the darkness of the woods, the horses seemed the incarnation of the demoniacal and destructive essence of nature, but once past the threshold of the field, they are innocuous and inoffensive:

> She could feel them there in their huddled group all the while she hastened across the bare field. They were almost pathetic, now [*R* 454].

Unlike the previous crisis caused by unexpected "descents," this encounter focuses not on the human world of culture, but on nature, and the experience is one not of conflict, but of reconciliation. More precisely, she experiences union in separation, foreshadowing, like the later apparition of the rainbow, the star equilibrium with Birkin that will be her existential destiny and which implies overcoming the sterile, self-destructive contradiction between ideal and real. As she affirms in a moment of intimacy with Birkin, "while we are only people, we've got to take the world that's given — because there isn't any other" (*WL* 315).

Ursula and Birkin's acceptance of reality contrasts with Gudrun and Gerald's rejection of it. Symptomatic of this rejection is their privileging of the artificial over the natural, of the empty, worldly rituals in which both of them indulge ("Gerald was dressed for dinner, as usual in the evening, although he was alone .... She stood before the mirror every night for some minutes, brushing her fine dark hair. It was part of the inevitable ritual of her life," *WL* 267, 414). Gerald's symbiotic relationship with machines and the worship of art is here clearly meant as a surrogate and negation of life.[44] The *vanity* inherent in such a choice (of the artificial) produces in turn an attraction to the *void*, the non-life, which Gerald feels when he meets his destiny and freezes in the snow:

He only wanted to go on, to go on whilst he could, to move, to keep going, that was all, to keep going, until it was finished [WL 473].

A consequence of this tendency to substitute the artificial for the natural — which also causes violence against nature, as with the rabbit in Chapter XVIII and the episode of Gerald with the horse (WL 110–12) — is a worship of the machine which links Gerald and Gudrun, culturally, to the Futurists, whose paintings, perhaps not coincidentally, resemble the Boccioni-like image of Gerald darting like a pure force of motion through the snow.[45]

The Line and the Circle

In the two novels, the dichotomy between anticipation and action is correlated with a prismatic exploration of the whole spectrum of crucial existential experience. In *The Rainbow*, however, such exploration occurs through a progressive enlargement of the characters' horizons (even if the promising "Widening Circle" ends by being always a "Narrowing Circle"),[46] while in *Women in Love*, it happens in a contrapuntal way, through parallelism between the activities of the two sisters, who confront analogous situations but react differently. For both, the series of formative experiences leads to a journey to the Continent, where, however, their paths diverge forever.

The journey itself happens in both complementary and opposite ways: while Birkin and Ursula follow the classic way of emigrants, undertaking a long trip in ships and trains across the Alps (similar to the one-way journey of Alvina in *The Lost Girl*), where the enchantment of anticipation is replaced with disappointment, discomfort and disorientation, Gerald and Gudrun pass through the large, frivolous European capitals and their trip is characterized by a succession of stops. While for Ursula and Birkin the experience of the Continent occurs in dynamic terms, for Gerald and Gudrun, it is in essentially static terms.

Throughout the two novels, the Continent itself represents the point of arrival of a centrifugal movement which has taken place parallel to the passing of the years and generations. From the "center" provided by the farm in *The Rainbow*, where the dominant element was the fertile marsh — earth mixed with water, generator of life — Tom Brangwen's descendants undertake a long road which goes from low to high, from the mud to the Tyrolean mountains. It is a road which undoubtedly brings intellectual refinement, but not a higher quality of life, at least not for Gudrun and Gerald, in whom the distance from fertile and vital mud creates an interior freezing and produces only the sterile, frozen perfection of ice crystals.[47]

The representation of the journey focuses on two perspectives—the historic and the mythical/anthropological—which interact constantly in both novels, and often in a nebulous way. In *The Rainbow*, they weave together continuously, bringing each character in contact with, on the one hand, progress and history, and on the other, with the great archetypes of experience. The interaction between the two produces, in correlation with the passage from one generation to the next, a progressive widening of the characters' horizons, but also, paradoxically, a narrowing of their living spaces, which in some cases leads them to the total loss of an *ubi consistam*. Tom adapts to the changes imposed by history, remaining harmoniously in his own space, but things change in the next generation, when Anna finds her own vital space in the claustrophobic, closed bedroom and Will finds his space in places that are a substitution for the house. In the last generation, we see a total distancing of characters from their roots, and consequently a frenetic race towards new spaces, which are soon abandoned because they are unsatisfying. Both novels present the race, rather vaguely, as the product of anxiety created by progress. This is particularly true of Ursula, whose maturation includes not only the rites of passage belonging to the anthropological dimension of the novel, but also, in a progressive enlargement of her life's horizons, the "crossing" of experiences—university, contact with cities, the discovery of new scientific theories, feminist ideas, etc.—which are essentially connected to modernity, and therefore to history. From a certain moment onward, the rituals of initiation which were surmounted by virtue of knowledge passed from generation to generation or through the wisdom of instinct, are followed by contact with a new type of the unknown, to confront which, Ursula, like Birkin and the others, must rely only on her own powers.

Lawrence uses different structural strategies to coordinate these two perspectives: in *The Rainbow*, the narration proceeds in a mostly linear fashion, unraveling over the course of three generations and exploring, on the one hand, all of the great spheres of experience (relationship with nature, work, Eros, family, religion, society, etc.) and on the other hand, a progressive enlargement of spatial horizons. In *Women in Love*—wherein the protagonists' growth is reduced to the experience of couples' relationships—the narrative is contrapuntal, presenting in tandem the evolutionary progression of two male/female relationships, neither of which achieves total fulfillment. That of Ursula and Birkin does not entirely reach beyond the *egoisme à deux* which Birkin so fears because it inevitably isolates the couple from the outside world, and yet their relationship appears condemned to a sort of perpetual instability from the modern condition of the two characters, for whom axiological, ideological and moral Absolutes no longer exist. But it is this very precariousness that constitutes the richness of the relationship, full of potential for discovery and development. Unharmonious, but dynamic, the relationship between Ursula and Birkin is the mirror of an epoch — the epoch surrounding World War I — fragmentary, chaotic, and even tragic, but not without potential for renewal. The individual faces a multitude of doors; many of them will open onto a void, others will reveal dazzling glimmers of light to whoever stops to contemplate the potentials of the threshold (as in the parable "Vor dem Gesetz" by Franz Kafka). On this threshold rest the two protagonists of the novels, a fact which, according to Giovanni Cianci, contributes to their modernistically open endings, which do not yield definition or synthesis.[48]

7

The Spirit of Place: Return to Origins

> *Every continent has its own great spirit of place...:*
> *call it what you like. But the spirit of place is a great reality*
> — D. H. Lawrence

The Flight from the West

The quests of the characters in *The Rainbow* and *Women in Love* stop before arriving at a destination, pausing in an uncertain border between north and south; the uprooting is not without its positive potential for Ursula and Birkin, but is completely negative for Gudrun and Gerald. The arrival in Italy of the protagonists of *The Lost Girl* and *Aaron's Rod* is no more satisfying; both are incapable, for different reasons, of fully integrating themselves into that Mediterranean world which the Romantic tradition advertises as "the paradise of exiles." The reasons Lawrence provides for the failure of their southern migration are neither very clear nor very coherent: in *The Rainbow* and *Women in Love,* the role of the external environment is limited to precipitating change in the couples' relationships. In the first of the Italian novels, Alvina cannot adapt to the primitivism of the Abruzzi village in which she finds herself; by contrast, Aaron is disappointed by Italy's rush to be acknowledged as one of the industrialized countries of Europe.

7. Return to Origins

As for Lawrence himself, it was above all this industrialization that pushed him away from England to a journey in space which was also a journey back in time. As he expresses at the end of *Twilight in Italy*, in the essay entitled "The Return Journey," during his approach to the south he felt as though he were followed by the process of increasing and spreading mechanization which he sought to escape by leaving England, a process which he bitterly observes while having a bitter Campari in Milan's Piazza Duomo. As a result, he redirects his quest at this point towards a "beyond" as far from Europe as possible.

From Lawrence's second migration arise all the works belonging to the third and final phase of his career, which — with the exception of some of the stories and to a certain extent of *Lady Chatterley's Lover*— are focused on the binaries Europe/New World, known/unknown, old/new, tradition/cultural virginity, and the dilemmas, ambivalence and dichotomies associated with them. Although on the one hand, the Otherness of places on the margins of the known world is attractive and offers the vague promise of a definite existential haven, this is always later revealed as a temporary illusion and a fragile goal.

Having burned their bridges to Europe, Lawrence's characters experience a return to origins, seeking remote, uncontaminated corners, in journeys which are, in a certain sense, opposite to those in *The Rainbow* and *Women in Love*, where the characters were projected towards modernity. It is this very condition which the characters seek to escape in the later works, through the search for "an Otherness," a remote spatial and temporal beyond, whether Mexico or the most inaccessible corners of North America (*St. Mawr*), or even "The uttermost ends of the earth" (*BB* 8) or "the youngest country on the globe" (*K* 19), that is, Australia.

With this flight from Europe — a place of departure which always remains a term of comparison and the object of occasional nostalgic longings— ends the *Bildung* of Lawrencean characters. From this point on, they confront the unknown as adults (they are all middle-aged characters), playing their final card in the search for existential self-realization.

The titles of the travel books allude to the illusion of discovery inherent in the destination of Other places, which are loaded with essentially false promises of regeneration. In the case of *Twilight in Italy*, a work replete with Spengler-like reflections on the destiny of Europe and western civilization, the title alludes to the decline of the west, whereas *Mornings in Mexico* suggests the promise of a new beginning, a promise which can find true fulfillment only at the cost of confrontation with a world that is challenging for western man to understand and accept. As Lawrence points out in the essay "Indians and Entertainment," interaction with the indigenous population inevitably causes "either sentimentality or dislike" (*MM* 52), based in both cases on ancient cultural prejudices and convenient simplifications. It is necessary to free ourselves from both and surrender to the uncomfortable awareness that between the two ways of being, of seeing, and of relating to reality, "there is no bridge, no canal of connexion" (*MM* 53), and to realize that the attempt to unify the two worlds would be fatal to both, but especially to the Indian one, which would be crushed and drained of its cultural identity. Respect for binary oppositions, upon which Lawrence bases his ethic of sexual relations is also, for him, essential for relations between cultures.

The idea that culture is formed by the interaction of inhabitants with place is explicitly stated by the writer in the introduction to his *Studies in Classic American Literature*, in the essay entitled "The Spirit of Place." His study of the New Continent and his apprehension of its intrinsic difference causes Lawrence to hypothesize the existence of a "spirit of place," defined in terms of the polarity of man/environment, which he identifies as a foundational structure in cultural heritage:

> Every people is polarised in some particular locality, some home or homeland. And every great era of civilisation seems to be the expression of a particular continent or continent region, as well as of the people concerned [*TSM* 20].

From this awareness arises the necessity of a different way of relating to other cultures, a way which entails the recognition and respect of reciprocal difference. Upon this recognition is founded the richness of the exchange and interaction between different peoples. Trying to identify the Other with ourselves means not only to violate them, but also to persevere in a way which is no longer practicable and which has irremediably destructive effects, as shown in *Sketches of Etruscan Places*[1]:

> We have thought and spoken till now in terms of likeness and oneness. Now we must learn to think in terms of difference and otherness ... . There is an unthinkable gulf between us and America, and across the space we see, not our own folk signalling to us, but strangers, incomprehensible beings, simulacra perhaps of ourselves, but *other*, creatures of an other-world [*TSM* 17].

In America, this Otherness is defined for the first time in terms of "spirit of place," that is, as a fascinating entity, but one with which it is difficult to interact, as evidenced by the structural difference between the two travel books dedicated to Italy and Mexico. Whereas *Twilight in Italy* documents, by means of a series of essays, Lawrence's gradual integration into the local community, and his progressive understanding of its most profound secrets (as in "The Theatre" and "San Gaudenzio"), in *Mornings in Mexico,* the difficulty of attaining an organic vision of the life of the Indios is suggested by the book's fragmentary nature. Every essay — whether Lawrence is describing exhausting trips to a nearby village or contemplating the bizarre, lunatic character of his *mozo*—constitutes a nucleus in itself, a slice of life. It is only when he tries to describe a local dance in detail that he has the impression of understanding the true "spirit of place," that intense, vital flow which runs through the nature and the people of this desolate, impervious, hostile place.[2] While attending this dance, in which Indians become one with the divinity which animates the entire universe, Lawrence gets in contact with the Otherness of a place where only extremes seem possible, whether in the climate — sweltering by day and freezing by night — or in the natives' temperament, passionate and reserved, curious and shy.[3] To this play of polarity, another one is added, that between life and death, which he feels more strongly here than in any other place. What strikes him most about Mexico is the strong sense of death, which he explains in part by the inhospitable environment ("Unable to wrest a positive significance for themselves from the vast, beautiful, but vindictive landscape they were born into, they [the Indians] turned on their own selves, and worshipped death through self-torture," *Princess* 168). He also attributes the sense of death to the fact that their religiosity and intimate interaction with the spirit of place are dying, being suffocated by the encroachment of progress, which, instead of heightening awareness and novelty, brings only destruction. This theme resounds with particular insistence in *The Plumed Serpent.*

The Journey: "The Woman Who Rode Away" and "The Princess"

Preparatory studies for *The Plumed Serpent,* the stories "The Woman Who Rode Away" and "The Princess" were written in the same period (1924–25). At the center of each, as in *The Plumed Serpent,* is a western woman who has arrived at middle age (Kate is celebrating her fortieth birthday, whereas the other two are thirty-three and thirty-eight years old) and at the threshold of change. All three have solid backgrounds and are "independent women" of the new generation. Of American origin, raised in the tolerant, progressive atmosphere of California, the protagonist of "The Woman Who Rode Away" has been living unhappily with her husband for some time, in a way which foreshadows *Lady Chatterley's Lover.* The husband owns a silver mine in Mexico. Oppressed by the claustrophobic environment of her house — where her spouse, like Sir Clifford, keeps her in a state of semi-isolation, considering her a possession — and by the desolation of the surrounding environment (the silver mines and the squalid, crowded miners' tenements are even more oppressive than those in England), she conceives the desire to escape, to find a "beyond" which she does not identify with any particular place, but which arises from her nearly unconscious desire to know the true nature of the place, the rhythms of the indigenous population.[4] Her desire is one which, once acted on, will forever prevent her return. She will die, sacrificed by the Indians to their gods in a rite intended to impede the extinction of their community by whites.

"The Princess" is similar yet different; it ends not with sacrifice, but with the protagonist's marriage to a much older man after she has had semi-consensual sexual relations with a man of mixed blood who accompanies her into the mountains and later dies after being shot by members of the Forest Service. In place of American innocence, the "princess" carries the burden of her European heredity (on her father's side, she is the last descendent of a fallen Scotch nobleman), a heredity inculcated in her by a parent who has protected her from the outside world and calls her "My Princess." This upbringing creates in her the conviction of her innate superiority to the rest of the world and a desire to dominate everybody and everything. Upon the death of her father, who had been the central reference point in her wandering life, which is divided between two continents and two houses (her American grandfather left her property on the condition that she spend half of each year in America),[5] she feels surrounded by a void, prey to a sense of loss similar to that felt by the protagonist of "The Woman Who Rode Away." Both seek to escape this feeling by taking a long trip, which is at the same time a flight from their present life and an unconscious quest for an entirely "other" dimension of life. Their ways of realizing this goal are, however, different: the willful element prevails in the protagonist of "The Princess," who is determined to undertake the journey into the Rocky Mountains — even though her guide, Domingo Romero, warns her of its dangers and difficulties ("nobody ever goes there. Too lonesome!" *Princess* 172) — whereas the characteristic trait of the protagonist of "The Woman Who Rode Away" is her absence of will. For her, the trip is the result of her abandonment to a vague but imperious impulse to undertake and continue it to the very end, even without knowing "where she was going, or what she was going for " (*WRA* 45).[6]

Similarities and differences exist also with respect to the women's identities. The first character has a triple identity (she is "the Princess" to her father, Dollie to her American grandparents, and Miss Urquhar to everybody else), whereas the second woman, as is suggested

7. Return to Origins

by the title, does not even have a name, and for the whole story is identified only as "she," or, when referring to her pre-married life, as "the Californian girl" (*WRA* 40). The redundant identity of the first character corresponds to a highly structured, strong personality, while the missing identity of the second corresponds to an extremely labile personality, but neither personality is able to withstand its contact with the unknown. For both women, however, the choice of adventure occurs in a furtive way: the destination is an undetermined "secret," and secret, too, is the moment of departure, which they perceive, like Kate in *The Plumed Serpent*, as cutting their ties with their old existence.[7]

For both, the journey constitutes an experience which is anything but gratifying: for the American it is "not safe, lawless and crude" (*WRA* 43), while the Scot finds the atmosphere "cold ... mysterious and fearful" (*Princess* 185). Both find themselves in the contradictory position of rejecting what they had longed for, which is contact with the Other — whether the indigenous community or the inhospitable heights. Each wants to assess the unknown by her own lights, yet the unknown is an entity which has both similar and opposite effects on the two women. The princess is possessed by an indomitable will to reach her destination. She reacts hysterically when Miss Cummins, her travel companion, is obliged to return home because of an injured horse, but the princess is almost happier continuing alone with the guide. As for the protagonist of "The Woman Who Rode Away," the journey has the effect of progressively stripping her of her will and reducing her to a state of extreme tiredness ("The woman was conscious only of her fatigue, her unspeakable fatigue," *WRA* 48), which causes near-inertia. The world which she seeks to enter, the unknown which earlier attracted her, creates a strange state of sensual paralysis, causing her to gradually lose her own identity. In the "princess" such a condition begins to show only when she arrives in the heart of the mountains and suddenly apprehends her own fragility and precariousness, causing an unexpected impulse to flee:

> She had not thought it could be so inhuman, so, as it were, anti-life. And yet now one of her desires was fulfilled. She had seen it, the massive, gruesome, repellent core of the Rockies .... And she wanted to go back [*Princess* 181].

For the protagonist of "The Woman Who Rode Away," on the other hand, fear is an entirely unknown emotion. The further she enters into the mountains, the more she undergoes a dehumanizing process, induced by the inhumanity of the landscape, losing first her power to feel, and then her power to desire ("if she had had any will of her own left, she would have turned back ... to be protected and sent home ... . But she had no will of her own," WRA 45) and finally the power to think, to use her inherited cultural patterns to defend herself against the wilderness. This process of losing her personality is not, however, complete at the moment she meets the Indian tribe she has been seeking (its members are similar to those who work for her husband, except for their very long hair) and it is they who help her finish the process.[8] They ignore her womanhood ("They could not see her as a woman at all. As if she *were* not a woman," WRA 49), relegating her to the margins of the community, where "not a soul was in sight ... all the doors were closed" (WRA 53) in a house where only the old sages once in a while came to visit her.

From this hut which, like all of the Indians', is without windows and in which the only source of light is the door,[9] she observes village life from a distance, watching the preparation for dances and even for her eventual sacrifice, to which she responds with an unconscious assent. It is this same loss of her old identity and absorption of the "feelings of the world," as well as the absorption of the Indians' sense of the supernatural, which renders her a nearly consensual victim of her own sacrifice ("The Indians, with their heavily religious natures, had made her succumb to their vision," WRA 64).[10] Her journey backwards towards the primitive ends in a physical death which is the inevitable consequence of the destruction of her self.

The failure of her journey (she ceases to be what she was but does not become anything else) contrasts with Dollie Urquhart's adventure, which is motivated not by a lack, but by an excess, of determination, which makes her see the adventure as a challenge from which to emerge the victor, imposing on everything and everyone, especially her male companion, her implacable will. She is not, however, capable of enacting this project, especially because of the inherent ambivalence of her relationship to him, socially beneath her, but, at an unconscious level, sexually desirable to her. Such ambivalence is only heightened by their entry into the wilderness where the social hierarchies of the civilized world lose significance and where Domingo Romero, less and less disposed to play the role of docile servant, gradually assumes the opposite role of masculine dominator, and tries to make a real woman of the princess, to awaken her to her female nature. She hurts his pride by denying that she feels pleasure in his embrace, and he reacts with destructive and self-destructive fury, holding her prisoner in the shack, then shooting at two whites who approach and finally causing them (perhaps intentionally on his part) to kill him. This story also ends with a death, which confirms the infeasibility of the attempt to journey back in time or perhaps the incapacity of both women (for opposite reasons) to undertake the journey in an appropriate way.

The Plumed Serpent

A Different Departure

The tragic endings of the two travelers in "The Woman Who Rode Away" and "The Princess" provide a term of comparison for evaluating the partial success of the protagonist in *The Plumed Serpent*, who begins with greater advantages than those of the two stories, being older and further along in her rejection of her own origins (she has already repudiated both her European and American cultural heritage).

This book delineates a return to origins with respect to the preceding novels, that is, a journey from city to country and to the heart of the nation. Disgusted by the westernized, chaotic inauthenticity of Mexico City, Kate begins her flight towards a "beyond" inspired by her intolerance for the bull fight (where the animals are slaughter victims, mere tools of man and of his vanity),[11] and by an article on the rebirth of ancient Aztec myth. She travels to Sayula Lake, the center of the revitalization of the ancient rites, sensing vaguely that the real Mexican life is completely submerged under a civilized surface, and lived by the masses of peasants who are only marginally touched by the civilization imposed by Spanish conquistadors and later by North Americans.

Unlike European cities, Mexico City elicits extreme reactions in Kate:

> Usually she was so good-tempered and easy. But something about this country irritated her and put her into such violent anger she felt she would die [*PS* 54].

However, it is the violently contradictory essence of the country ("Superficially, Mexico might be all right ... . Until you were alone with it ... . The spirit of place was cruel, down-dragging, destructive," *PS* 49-50) that exerts a powerful attraction: "amid all the bitterness that Mexico produced in her spirit, there was still a strange beam of wonder and mystery" (*PS* 58).

The protagonist's situation, a decisive existential turning-point, is in some respects analogous to the situation of Mexico itself, as it undergoes a revolution which upsets its political and social order. The revolution, however, changes only the surface of the country, without touching its soul. To change the soul of Mexico, only a rebirth arising from the heart of the country itself will suffice, which is just what the movement led by Don Ramón and Cipriano intends to do. Both Kate and Mexico are on a threshold of true, total metamorphosis and for this reason, it is extremely difficult to cross. In the country, the rebirth of ancient rituals is continually challenged by authority, whereas in Kate, the metamorphosis struggles to occur but does not entirely succeed at the end of the novel, when she contends that "she belonged too much to the old world of Europe, she could not, could not make herself over so quickly" (*PS* 421). Just as the new religious movement needs continual manifestations of the repudiation of the old order, so too the achievement of a new *ubi consistam* for Kate is possible only by the repudiation of her past. Just as the movement, expanding from small villages to the cities' cores, must defend its success with armies, so, too, must the protagonist, to renounce her old identity and achieve metamorphosis, overcome strong interior resistance and poignant nostalgia for her home country, which symbolizes stability, tradition, and security.

The political-religious level and the existential level, the process of transformation of the country and transformation of the protagonist are not only linked by similarities; they are also intertwined with the affairs of the three main characters, Kate, Cipriano and Don Ramón, on whom Lawrence focuses after the shift of setting from Mexico City in the initial chapters to the lake at Sayula in the subsequent ones.

These three form a triangle whose dynamics are interesting from the spatial viewpoint because of the play of polarity and gravitational forces among them. Physically and intellectually attracted to Don Ramón, Kate is seen by him mostly as an important member of the movement (he invites her to stay every time she hints of an impending departure) or as an advisor in difficult moments (after the visit of his sons, who scorn his activities and who partly renounce him as their father). Paradoxically, however, her relationship with Ramón is less intense than her relationship with Cipriano, who represents for her the irreconcilable poles of the soul and mystery of Mexico:

> It was curious, that though he spoke such English English, it seemed always foreign to her, more foreign than Doña Carlota's Spanish [*PS* 203].

As for Cipriano, he is attracted to Kate's difference, to her persona of emancipated, white woman, that makes her the only possible companion for him. Intensifying the relationship among the three are analogies created by their respective origins — since Ireland, like Mexico, is a country of ancient traditions, recently coming out of a war for independence (which killed Kate's dearly-loved second husband) — and also by a common situation of colonization which creates identity problems for all three: while the protagonist is Anglicized Irish, Cipriano has Indian blood but a European education and upbringing, and Don Ramón "is almost pure Spaniard, but most probably he has the blood of Tlaxcalan Indians in his veins as well" (*PS* 64).[12] This also contributes to the dynamic correspondence of the three characters, which those of *The Rainbow* and *Women in Love* were not able to establish. In *The Plumed Serpent,* this correspondence is realized not so much in male/female relationships, which are in continual upheaval (except for Ramón and Teresa's, which entails Teresa's total dedication and submission to her partner),[13] as in man-to-man relationships, in that bond of faith which links the two leaders, a bond which seems to Kate to arise from the very essence of the place:

> It seemed to Kate that the highest thing this country might produce would be some powerful relationship of man to man [*PS* 152].

Even such a bond, which reaches its maximum expression in the nocturnal communion when Don Ramón elects Cipriano to the office of "the Living Huitzilopochtli," the Aztec god of war and fire who accompanies Quetzalcoatl,[14] is much more vital when they are far apart. This distance is also a factor in their relationships with their respective female partners. While Ramón, after Carlota's death, chooses a woman who is completely dedicated to him and always present, Cipriano, of a more independent spirit, needs a woman like Kate, with whom to share intimate moments but also mutual respect for the freedom of each:

> ... when he had to go away, it did not matter so very much. His presence was something he left with her, and he took her presence along with him [*PS* 423].

The New Home

Although united by a common faith, by analogous situations concerning their personal histories, and deep interpersonal bonds, the three protagonists are profoundly different psychologically, and establish different relationships with places in terms of absence/presence. While Kate and Ramón both remain rooted to the village at the lake (Kate never leaves it, and Ramón only for brief trips), Cipriano is always in border places and has a "mobile" residence (his soldier's camp), retaining links to the nomadic life even after his marriage to Kate and his move to Villa d'Aragon, where he remains only for brief periods. Like a true Indian rooted in the spirit of place, he appreciates the sinister elements which disturb Kate,[15] and can conduct a wandering existence while remaining nonetheless faithful to his principles. Ramón and Kate, on the other hand, need to root themselves in one place, which they, however temporarily, can identify as home.[16] Cipriano is the channel that links them to the outside world.

Unlike the journeys of the heroines in the stories "The Woman Who Rode Away" and "The Princess," Kate's journey to the lake at Sayula is exhausting at the beginning — because she is still reacting to the squalid city atmosphere — but it becomes more interesting and revitalizing the closer she comes to the lake. The ferryman, with characteristic "centreless, black eyes," appears to be the messenger of mysteries concealed in the depths of the lake (perhaps the objects offered to the gods which are, according to the Quetzalcoatl legends, reemerging after generations).[17] Only when she reaches the town of Sayula does Kate feel she has found her destination:

> This is very good, thought Kate. It is not too savage, and not over civilised. It isn't broken, but it is rather out of repair. It is in contact with the world, but the world has got a very weak grip on it [*PS* 108].

Having reached such a promising place after the horrors encountered at the beginning of her trip, Kate needs a center in which to begin a new phase of life.[18] The first thing she looks for is a house different from those she knows, a self-sufficient house opening not on the outside world but on the inside, towards the heart of things: "She wanted an old Spanish house, with its inner patio of flowers and water. Turned inwards, to the few flowers walled in by shadow. To turn one's back on the cog-wheel world" (*PS* 104). She wants a place protected from the bright light and stress of the outer world, where she might live in harmony with her own soul.[19]

Although at first sight Kate has the impression that "her house was what she wanted" (*PS* 109), it does not take long to realize that to make it liveable she must exorcise the ghosts of the past inhabitants[20] and deflect the looks of the passers-by. She thus restructures the interior, verifying that for Lawrence — as demonstrated in the stories "Goose Fair," "The Christening" and "The Thorn in the Flesh" — the interior of the home is the reflection of the soul who inhabits it, especially if it is female. The steps which led Kate here had a centripetal movement, as opposed to those of the characters in *The Rainbow* and *Women in Love*; she is directed towards a place conceived of as roots and also as an extension of the self. When Ramón and Teresa visit her at the end of the novel, Teresa crosses the threshold of Kate's room, and is enchanted, but also slightly disturbed by what she sees:

> [a] room [with] different attractive things from different parts of the world...: the rather weary luxury and disorder, and the touch of barrenness, of a woman living her own life [*PS* 402].

Nevertheless, even if Kate does everything possible to make the house her own, she must always take into account the outsiders who usurp a part of it: the servant family, consisting of Juana and her three children. But if

7. Return to Origins

their indiscreet curiosity and their attitude of sustained disapproval and tacit mockery bother her, even more intolerable are those invasions from the outside that occur whenever she opens her window ("she shut her window on the street, for the invasion had begun," PS 238). Alongside the tensions created by the cohabitation of an emancipated Irishwoman and Indians, arises the rivalry between two women who, as always in Lawrence's works, are not disposed to share their domestic sovereignty ("there was a bit of a battle to be fought between the two women," PS 110). Juana's family, indifferent to the new order that Kate tries to impose on the house, does not change its habits, so that Kate's attempts to render the house more livable must always be imposed upon them with force; the conquered territory must, in typically Lawrencean fashion, be constantly defended:

> Kate felt her household a burden. In a sense, they were like parasites, they wanted to live on her life, and pull her down, pull her down [PS 151].

But the battle is lost before it is begun, because in this house she is not a sovereign but rather a guest to be treated with care (and sometimes scorn), as indicated by the nickname, Niña (Child), which Mexicans give to all foreign landladies.[21]

The other central residence in the novel is the *hacienda* of Don Ramón, truly the stronghold of the Quetzalcoatl movement, which even from the outside looks like "another world." Built in such a way that even the interiors seem open and are therefore deprived of any connotation of "closed space" ("the salon ... seemed like part of the out-of-doors, like some garden-arbor put for shade," PS 163), the house, more than a home, is a microcosm pulsating with life. The estate contains a series of outbuildings where craftsmen tirelessly work to sustain the Movement, the restitution of the old gods to Mexico.[22]

The house's isolation, emphasized by the silence and peace that reign therein, contribute to a sense of the arcane, which Kate perceives as well in the people who work for Ramón. They approach the house as though it were magical:

> Always he [the man with the basket] spoke with pleased delight, as if the place were a wonder-place to him [PS 161].

The essential element of this house is its full integration into the surrounding environment, an element reflected in the people who live there. While Don Ramón loves to expose himself, in keeping with the spirit of place, by standing nude at the window looking at the lake, his wife Doña Carlota, devoted Catholic who respects social conventions, is uneasy, stays there only briefly, and does everything she can to oppose her husband's attempts to revitalize the spirit of place, ruthlessly resisting the Quetzalcoatl movement.

Self-sufficient center though it is, Ramón's *hacienda* is not really free of contact with the outside, from which it must continually defend its identity and safety. The big gates which protect the entrance are not the only sign of the presence of danger; the inevitable attacks from the outside lead to an attempt on Ramón's life, causing the death of his most faithful servants. Ramón is gravely injured, but saved, thanks to Kate's intervention.

Notwithstanding his efforts to conduct the movement of rebirth "in another world" (*PS* 191), staying far away from politics, Ramón needs Cipriano's defense and his military help on the borders, just as, after his wife's death, he needs to endow the home with a new center, a woman who will become its caretaker.

Rebirth from the Low — The Church

In *The Plumed Serpent,* the polarity of high/low plays out as a relationship between surface and depths, especially between Christianity absorbed (along with other western cultural models) on a completely superficial level and the spirit of the ancient pagan cults buried, but not dead, in the soul of Mexico. This spirit, emerging from the "low," sparks Kate's curiosity and interest, as shown by the episode of the people's dance in the town square, which also signals her first contact with the Quetzalcoatl religious movement. At the beginning, she is struck by the expression of impenetrable indifference on the natives' faces and by the atmosphere of stagnant inertia which reigns in the square full of people, an atmosphere which resists any attempt to cheer it up by the players sent from the city, from "on high." When they leave, however, she hears the sound of drums rising from a corner of the square which upsets her deeply: a sound which "was hardly music. Rather a far-off, perfect crying in the night. But it went straight through to the soul" (*PS* 126). Kate feels life emanating from the small circle of natives playing instruments, reciting hymns and dancing bare-backed; the rest of the square "was curiously void. There was the dense clot of people round the drum, and then the outer world, seeming empty and hostile" (*PS* 121). Watching this dance, she feels a mixture of attraction, curiosity, fear and then an involuntary and irresistible involvement that ends in a true initiation ritual, a feeling rising from the depths, a new identity as Woman ("she felt a virgin again, a young virgin," *PS* 130), an identity which she does not adopt as her own because of her reluctance to let go of her old self:

7. Return to Origins

Kate wanted to hurry home with her new secret, the strange secret of her greater womanhood, that she could not get used to [*PS* 132].[23]

After this first impact with the religion practiced by the followers of Quetzalcoatl, Kate grows increasingly familiar with their ideas, founded on the principle of circularity. Even the symbol of Quetzalcoatl alludes to circularity: the serpent who bites his own tail, forming a circle with an eagle at its center. This image is quite different from the official emblem of Mexico (an eagle which presses a serpent victoriously in his claws) because it represents not the triumph of the "high" over the "low" — whatever symbolic significance one gives the two terms — but the representation of cosmic harmony existing between earthly and celestial energies, both emanations of the divine. This harmony exists in the principle of circularity which is the basis of the rebirth promised by Quetzalcoatl religion: its followers see the return of the god in Mexico as the result of his re-emergence from the depths of the earth (in which he rested at the end of his previous life cycle) in correspondence with the Christian God's return to His place of origin, since He has by now exhausted His vital energies. The cycle is contrasted to the linear conception of time typical of western civilization, which implies violent and catastrophic breaks. The western ideology of revolution is substituted by the indigenous one of continuity and alternation, in which the old order is not unseated, but leaves its place willingly to the new one: "*My name is Jesus, ... / Oh brother, Quetzalcoatl / ... Let me come home*" (*PS* 119). Aiming to return the ancient local cult to the people, Ramón is against any kind of religious war; in fact, he professes ideological tolerance: "should there not be peace between the men who strive down their different ways, to the God-Mystery?" (*PS* 266).[24] At the same time, however, he sees Christianity as profoundly extraneous to Mexico's cultural traditions: "Christianity is a religion of the spirit. The Indians cannot understand it" (*PS* 263). Because of its vision of man founded on the primacy of the spirit (therefore on will and the mind, on the mortification of the senses, on the ethic of sacrifice), the Catholic Church "does not possess the key-word to the Mexican soul" and for this reason "in Mexico ... it has no place" (*PS* 264–65).

Don Ramón's message mirrors ideas expounded by the writer in the essay "The Spirit of Place," essentially regarding the way in which every race and community reflects in its culture, its myths and traditions, the vital polarity between population and place: "There is some subtle magnetic or vital influence," says the writer, "inherent in every specific locality, and it is this influence which keeps the inhabitants stable. Thus race is ultimately as much a question of place as of heredity" (*TSM* 20). The mystery of the world is one, but the ways of approaching it are many, arising from the very essence of each place and of the community that lives there.[25]

The completion of one cycle and the beginning of a new one are possible only through the preparation of places destined for worship, which is fundamental to the self-construction of community. In *The Rainbow* and *Women in Love*, the process of disintegration of traditional values and of the sense of community is the counterpart to the centrifugal movement of the characters. In *The Plumed Serpent* the opposite occurs: a double centripetal movement which aids in the recovery of both home and community. The long journey which gradually brings Lawrence's characters from Nottinghamshire to Mexico paradoxically ends in the re-appropriation of that which was vehemently rejected in the country of origin. A place like the church, which had disappeared for some time in Lawrence's works, and in European novels symbolized a detachment from the physical world, the tendency to mysticism and the individual's aspiration to verticality (often coinciding with a flight from the quotidian and from materialism, as for Will in *The Rainbow*), reassumes a central role in *The Plumed Serpent*, but not as a refuge for the individual so much as a "place of us," expression and reference point for the entire community.

In the empty, sleepy Mexican towns, the only centers of gravity for the inhabitants are the square and the church, so these are the places in which Ramón must spread the new religion.[26] Before welcoming the risen God, however, the community must erase all signs of the past one. The church at Sayula undergoes a gradual metamorphosis, during which it is stripped of all the sacred images; these are ritualistically transported and burned on the Isle of Scorpions in the middle of the lake. The fact that the burning of the old images happens on an island, while the people observe from the shore, acquires significance insofar as it shows (as in "The Woman Who Rode Away") that the sacrifice must occur far from the place of the community, far from the center of life.[27] These images, simple wooden objects deprived of all significance, seem almost pathetic once outside the church. The church itself is "absolutely dark ... and absolutely bare" (*PS* 284), like a place without life; it reacquires a function and light once the symbol of the cross is substituted with one of Quetzalcoatl and when the throne and colors of the new God shine inside it.

Besides confirming the necessity of a place for worship inside the community, the reconsecration of the church by Don Ramón suggests that places themselves are not sacred or inviolable, but that they become so in reference to the functions they assume in the community and in their symbolic investment.

Ramón's utopian dream, the subject of many personal conversations with Cipriano and, towards the end of the novel, with Kate, is the rebirth of all the communities and peoples of the world, their liberation from the conforming principle of progress and their recovery of an identity arising from the heart of the people, from respect for the environment and for tradition.[28] If Ramón's suggestion of the necessity for aristocratic leaders to guide the community and become its spokesmen is megalomaniac and confused,[29] it is also true that he himself is without personal ambitions for power: he is ideologically tolerant and disposed to respect the diversity of religious cults.

Ramón's project gives new vitality to the Mexican community, as shown by the serene work of his faithful followers and the untiring activity of Cipriano's soldiers, but it is not without its intrinsic weakness, deriving from the fact that the living incarnations of the ancient gods are external to the environment and only partially integrated in it: Ramón, the living Quetzalcoatl, is of Spanish origin, Cipriano, the living Huitzilopochtli, is a native with an English upbringing, while Kate, the living Malintzi, is of Irish origin and newly arrived in Mexico.[30] Although Cipriano follows his role blindly and instinctively, and does not suffer from his double identity or from any negation of self in his new identity as a living divinity, Don Ramón, on the other hand, is subject to repeated crises, to moments of discomfort and imbalance which derive from the breakdown of his self in the name of Quetzalcoatl. Kate cannot help but notice this breakdown; it stops her on the threshold of conversion to the Indian cult. It is no coincidence that Ramón's ascent to the throne once occupied by the Christian God comes at the price of the death of his wife Carlota, who, in a desperate gesture that costs her life, seeks to stop her husband.

The Play of Different Viewpoints

The precariousness of the victories of Don Ramón's movement is confirmed by the fact that each victory must be defended with force. In spite of his desire to avoid politics and simply to contribute to the revival of ancient local cults, re-establishing at the same time the vital relationship between the community and the surrounding environment, Ramón must, as Cipriano intuits from the very beginning, come to terms with authority. At the end of the book, the movement inevitably acquires a political character and becomes, against its leader's wishes, a power that is imposed with force, declaring the Catholic Church illegal.[31] The continuous "manifestations" to which Don Ramón alludes are necessary to stoke the faith of the people. They consist not only of hymns and dances, but also atrocious rites, such as the execution of the traitors in front of the church in a meticulously regulated ceremony. The ruthless cruelty and cold theatricality of the ceremony deeply disturb Kate and induce her to seek refuge in the solitude of her own house.[32]

Such behavior reconfirms her ambivalent reactions to a country whose attractions hide its cruelty and horror. In reality, however, the polarity which, in her view, constitutes the very essence of the place is due not as much to the environment as to her relationship with it.

As soon as Kate, accompanied home by Cipriano, remarks, "the night is beautiful … . But the moon … isn't lovely and friendly as it is in England or Italy" (*PS* 233), her companion replies "it is the same planet" and significantly adds, "Perhaps there is in you something European, which hurts our Mexican moon" (*PS* 233). Cipriano points out the inevitable differences in viewpoint produced by the cultural codes of one's origins and by personal experiences which shape one's own sensibility. Because of this different interior constitution, Kate retreats with fear from the sensations of terror she feels in the Mexican nights, sensations which for Cipriano are an integral part of life and should be accepted as such.[33]

The contrast between Kate's and Cipriano's viewpoints becomes more extreme in regard to Ramón. Both gravitate towards him and consider him their central reference point, but Kate emphasizes his European origins to justify her attraction: "Don Ramón isn't really Mexican … . He feels European" (*PS* 237), while for Cipriano, Ramón is the very incarnation of the country ("To me he is—Mexico," *PS* 237).

Kate's difficulty in integrating herself into Mexican life is linked, in the final analysis, to the instability of the cultural structures which formed her personality, yet if she were to obliterate them (if that were even possible), her own personality would cease to exist. For precisely this reason, the exotic adventures which Lawrence narrates in his novels of these years never end well. For this same reason, the flight to an Other place, no matter how stimulating, can never lead to the desired freedom, as the Australian novels also prove: in adapting himself to new, virgin places, in fact, the character always ends up clinging to known parameters which, even though rejected because they are sterile and obsolete, remain always a part of the self. Although at the beginning of the novel, Kate was perfectly convinced that she did not want to return to Europe or America, the memory of her origins and her clinging to a vague nostalgia of the past increasingly become a means of protecting herself from changes that the unknown imposes, but that the self or part of the self refuses to accept. Thus, Kate's inner conflict escalates when she proceeds from observing the new religious movement to being an integral part of it. Whereas Ramón and Cipriano live *inside* the rituals of rebirth of the Indian God, identifying themselves completely with their new roles, Kate remains always a

7. Return to Origins

spectator who observes from *outside*. This particular position, which permits her to observe from a distance the life going on around her, emerges as early as her first contact with the Quetzalcoatl movement, when, attracted but also frightened by the dance, she defends her own integrity by staying "on the fringe" (*PS* 122). She observes from the threshold without ever completely crossing it. She abandons herself to the dance for only a moment but always retains the privileged position of observer, capable of holding every reaction under control. When this capacity for control weakens, and the observing self is about to become one with the acting self, Kate quickly steps back. This tendency to be always the observer is also confirmed by the fact that in moments of solitude, she likes to sit on the veranda of her house or on the lake shore and observe from a distance the life that is going on around her, without taking part.[34] It is not always she who chooses this role, for at times it is imposed on her because she is female, as in the episode in which she attends from the balcony, with Doña Carlota, one of the first celebrations of the Indian God, and in the episode of Carlota's death (which is also a turning point in the novel) and Don Ramón's ascent of the throne as the living Quetzalcoatl. Even during this ceremony, Kate, who comes from Catholic Ireland, is next to the devout Catholic Carlota, and the proximity is not coincidental: in effect, the physical death of Ramón's wife prefigures the inner death of the protagonist, which will occur when she finds herself incapable of returning to her old life, without yet being ready for the new one proffered by the Movement and Cipriano:

> Ramón and Cipriano no doubt were right for themselves, for their people and country. But for herself, ultimately, ultimately she belonged elsewhere [*PS* 387].

The fight between her old and new selves elicits, especially in the second half of the novel, a doubling of Kate's personality, so that in certain moments she seems invested in her new identity, observing herself while she acts her new role, both actress and spectator of herself,[35] a situation which, paradoxically, she does not terminate even when she enters ritualistically into the new community and begins a new life after her marriage to Cipriano. Kate refuses to live in the same house with him, or to give civil sanction to their religious wedding, and avidly defends her own individuality and independence, continually considering the possibility of flight, and even preparing it down to the last detail, only to abandon it later. This indecisive behavior characterizes the entire ending portion of the novel, in which Kate oscillates continually between opposite propositions and takes a step backward for every step forward. Even though she accepts the throne as Malintzi and becomes Cipriano's bride, moving with him to Villa d'Aragon, she does it with the conviction that she will leave immediately for Europe. In reality, it is from herself that she tries to escape, so that the possibility of retreat, every time she contemplates it, does not seem feasible. Her desire to shed the old self and open herself to a new identity is never fulfilled; she ends up refusing the responsibility of making a definite decision, attributing her staying to the desire of others that she should not part. The final sentence of the novel—"You won't let me go!" (*PS* 444)—clearly reveals the intention to lean on someone else in order to avoid a departure, something which she had always resisted, especially in this country—a guide *outside* her own will.

Thus, even her quest does not reach fulfillment; she only partially crosses the threshold on which the characters of *The Rainbow* and *Women in Love* stopped. Even so, the open ending of the novel seems to suggest the possibility that finally, whether dragged along or *sua sponte*, she will take the final decisive steps towards a new life.

Conclusion

The eternal silence of these spaces frightens me.
— Blaise Pascal

The tragic ending of the American stories and the uncertain one of *The Plumed Serpent* point out the irremediable contradiction inherent in the attempt to seek personal regeneration through relationship with a radically Other reality. Because of its "otherness," such a reality is incomprehensible and unapproachable, thus signifying for individuals a total (and therefore impossible) erasure of the cultural codes which *are* their own identity.

America is an unfeasible destination for Lawrence who, after his Mexican novel, tried to find new avenues, and who previously had tried an alternative route in Australia (reflected in the two Australian novels), but in that case as well, without positive results. That visit finished with the void in *The Boy in the Bush* and ended circularly with the protagonist's return to England after the death of Kangaroo in the eponymous novel.[1] It was inevitable that after exploring the extreme poles of the known world and experiencing their particularities—always problematic for western man—the writer turned back to his point of origin, England. This is where he sets *Lady Chatterley's Lover*, the last novel which, although artistically not one of Lawrence's greatest achievements, is more ideologically positive than any of the other works discussed here, perhaps because in it the writer returns to less ambitious objectives, abandoning every hope of rebirth for the entire community and limiting the range of the quest to individual existence.

In light of this goal, and from a spatial viewpoint, Lawrence's later work hinges on the opposition between the line and the circle, or between the open and the closed, that is between *movement* onward towards new, always more distant places versus *staying* within the circularity of a world with fixed, but controllable limits, which is in the end the only effectively habitable space. Whereas the "line" is oriented in the direction of large open spaces (which are never actually fully reached), the solemn, disturbing silence of the Australian bush, or the mysterious but harsh and hostile landscapes of the Rocky Mountains (*St. Mawr*), in *The Plumed Serpent* the "circle" is formed by the circumscribed horizons of places culturally marked by human beings (albeit foreign) within which Kate manages, in some degree, to find an orientation; and in *Lady Chatterley's Lover*, the circle is a familiar, circumscribed environment, the woods near her husband's ancestral home, which makes it possible for the protagonist Connie to find a haven for her existential quest through the rediscovery of her own instincts.

In both novels we find a movement from social and cultural centers (Dresden, London, Mexico City) towards isolated, marginal places which coincide circularly with the historical and mythical heredity of the country, a heredity which, however, is Other for Irish Kate, but is her "own" for British Connie.[2] The solution, albeit partial, of the central problem around which all of Lawrence's works revolve is found, finally, in a place somehow protected from the alienating forms of industrialized society, a place where it is possible to recover, starting from the world of below, the true values of rural Old England. This represents a return to the point of departure of Lawrence's literary career: the woods of his last novel, insofar as they are a refuge, are not functionally very different from the garden in *The White Peacock*.

In almost all of the works written after the twenties, it is possible to find the motif of flight from an alienating environment, whether it is the lordly manor which becomes a prison (*Lady Chatterley's Lover*) or the bright lights of cities regulated by frenetic, inhuman rhythms, like Mexico City, London, and also Sydney in *Kangaroo* and isolated Perth in *The Boy in the Bush*. The flight occurs alternately in two directions—towards the open and the primitive or towards the closed and the safe—presenting greater problems the greater the Otherness of the destination, as seen especially in the Australian novels. These constitute, in more than a literal sense, the most distant point to which the Lawrencean quest extends, and therefore also the place which initially appears to the writer the most apt for the utopian project which he tenaciously planned for several years, after the collapse of Europe at the end of World War I. He wished to establish a community, Rananim, in a faraway space which was historically and culturally untouched. In both *Kangaroo* and *The Boy in the Bush*, the protagonists, after having repudiated the Old Continent, are involved in local attempts to rejuvenate the community under the guidance of leaders who, notwithstanding their personal charisma, cannot actualize their own utopian projects. Kangaroo, who would seem to carry in his body the spirit of place (he resembles a kangaroo), fails because his abstract ideals of universal love are completely out of place in the locale where he wishes to apply them — so out of place that he is killed. In *The Boy in the Bush*, Jack Grant, of mixed Anglo-Australian blood, is driven from the Old Continent, whose cultural and social heredity he scorns. Wishing to begin a new life in the uncontaminated wilderness of Australia's interior, he is incapable of convincing a small group of people to follow him. He wishes to establish a utopia in a place which is as far as possible from any human presence, where, like the old biblical patriarchs, he plans to live in harmony with nature, surrounded by the affection of several wives.

The failures in both novels are caused not so much by the radical Otherness of the "margins" in which they take place, as by the persistence in the margins of the cultural codes of the "center," codes which, in young Australia, are a deformity and a degeneration of those received from England's heritage. However, as the relationship with society fails, so too does the relationship with nature in Australia, where the peculiarities of the bush, that environment so attractively different, where man cannot understand its system of communication and thus loses himself,[3] extends a powerful challenge to both protagonists, but one that they, especially Somers in *Kangaroo*, are not ready to meet:

> I don't love people. But this place — it goes into my marrow, and makes me feel drunk. I love Australia … . I never was so tempted in my life. Australia tempts me. *Retro me*— … . I don't want to give in to the place. It's too strong. It would lure me quite away from myself [*K* 347–48].

Whereas Jack Grant gets lost in the bush in what appears a true descent into Hell ("the bush has got me … and now it will take life from me … . I shall wander in the bush throughout eternity" *BB* 287), which condemns him, in the end, to a sterile isolation from humanity, the adult Somers realizes that abandoning himself to the magic silence of the bush, no matter how stimulating, would deprive him of his identity (like the woman in "The Woman Who Rode Away"), which is ineradicably linked to his cultural heredity.

The longing to free oneself from codes and the incapacity to completely renounce them, in interaction with the virgin space, characterizes *St. Mawr* as well. Tired of social conventions and awakened to new life through the vitality of the horse St. Mawr, the protagonist Lou Witt leaves England, her husband, and her familiar existence to go to America. Disappointed by the empty social life in the New Continent, she seeks refuge in the uncontaminated nature of Old America, the heart of the Rocky Mountains. But as attractive as the natural beauty is and as much as she desires to insert herself into it, she is unable to reach harmony with the spirit of place, which is hostile, regulated by incomprehensible laws which have already defeated those who tried before her to form a connection with it:

> ... most mysterious but worst of all, the animosity of the spirit of place: the crude, half-created spirit of place, like some serpent-bird forever attacking man, in a hatred of man's onward-struggle towards further creation [*SM* 150].

In *St. Mawr*, as in many of Lawrence's later works, the "spirit of place," being the result of the encounter between the nature of a certain place and of the community of people who inhabit it or have inhabited it in the past, tends to be stripped of its human components and to become simply the emanation of a "spirit" present in things and in landscape, an elusive, yet nonetheless imposing will which the individual cannot oppose and by which he feels threatened and almost crushed. As such, Lawrence's "spirit of place" is similar to the "fate" of Thomas Hardy, a writer who profoundly influenced Lawrence's early works and to whose influence there would seem to be a "return" in the later ones. This influence is seen particularly in the fear of violent, implacable nature, which makes the adolescents in *The White Peacock*, the lovers in *The Trespasser*, and Miriam in *Sons and Lovers* take precarious refuge in various "gardens." But in the later works this fear mutates, acquiring almost religious connotations, into the desire for contact with a living, uncontaminated presence, a numinous being which has not yet vanished from mechanized civilization. This desire is the object of the writer's and characters' quests in the spatially and temporally remote places in which the later works are set. In the end, however, this "presence" eludes them and refuses access to the intruder, compelling them to flee again, this time back to their point of departure. This happens in *St. Mawr*, the novella whose interest, apart from its artistic merits, lies largely in the theme of the double journey: that which first brings the protagonist from the New World to England and then back to her place of origin, where she feels disappointed and disgusted by the empty, frenetic life of American society. Then, venturing into the Rocky Mountains, she stops short on the threshold of the wilderness, disoriented by a foreign spirit of place which is hostile in its primitiveness. Her stopping suggests that she will turn towards another, more friendly, comprehensible, and human place.

St. Mawr represents a kind of bridge between the exotic or primitive phase of Lawrence's work and the last phase, represented by *Lady Chatterley's Lover*, a work in which the writer returns to his own country, abandoning the "line" in favor of the "circle," the open in favor of the closed.[4] Spatially, *Lady Chatterley's Lover* presents a schematic structure based on allegoric intentions and the idea of circularity: the external circle is formed by the mining village, in which is found Clifford Chatterley's estate, a microcosm upon which the whole novel centers. The novel is divided between the manor (place of the mind, of sterility and in the end, of death) and the gamekeeper's woods, in which is located his hut, place of Eros and personal regeneration.[5] In the very middle of the woods, the protagonist — significantly, a lady — experiences a true return to life, emphasizing in an almost too obvious way the regenerative effects of the spirit of place (though assisted by the ardour and amorous approaches of a passionate gamekeeper) and suggesting that regeneration can more readily occur in a known, familiar place than in disorienting, exotic locations.

Again by virtue of the gamekeeper, who willingly assumes the role of mentor, Connie rediscovers the familiar place, seeing it with new eyes, and getting in touch with the spirit of place, which has been asleep but not dead. She rediscovers the lost dimension of the primordial, renewing her relationship with her own deep roots. Although the primitive in Other places such as Mexico and Australia has a deleterious effect on the outsider, jeopardizing not only his identity but also his physical constitution ("it takes about four or five years for your blood properly to thin down .... The blood is thinner out here than in the Old Country," *K* 145), in familiar places (like the woods in *Lady Chatterley's Lover* which is a "place of us"), it turns out to be a source of therapeutic potential.

That Connie's experience is a return to nature and, more specifically, to her own roots, is perhaps too obvious. But it would be unfair to Lawrence to dismiss this solution out of hand. In reference to the binary of culture/nature on which he bases his axiological system, nature becomes, in his last works, the foundation of a radically new culture, which then reveals itself as, in essence, radically old, inasmuch as it is the recovery of forgotten ways in which man was in touch with the profound and the arcane before mechanized civilization.

In this sense, the solution he proposes in *Lady Chatterley's Lover* is not so far from the solution proposed in *The Plumed Serpent*, even though in *Lady Chatterley's Lover* he removes the political dimension of the Mexican novel and stays within the limits of a strictly personal dimension which finds definition in discussions between Connie and the gamekeeper.

This new private mode — the most private possible, if we think of the circumstances in which they usually hold these discussions — in which Lawrence's message is conveyed, necessarily reduces the messianic tensions of the writer's work, and thus contributes to the applicability of the message itself. Kate's awareness, at the end of *The Plumed Serpent*, that the rebirth attempted by Ramón would work only in Mexico, is reflected in Somers' thoughts in *Kangaroo* ("Every continent has its own way, and its own needs," *K* 112), and also in the travel book written in this period, *Sketches of Etruscan Places*, in which Lawrence, opposing the vitality of Etruscan culture to the destructive conformity of Roman imperialism, proclaims the inevitable failure of every ideological and cultural model which proposes itself *a priori* as universally valid and adaptable to every environment. While the intervention of the "high" (such as the authoritarian interventions of the Roman and British empires) kills man, the only possibility is that of a rebirth from the "low," inside a protected place, a temple in which it is possible to renew, in an attitude of religious respect, the relationship with spirit of place:

> From the old wood came an ancient melancholy, somehow soothing to her, better than the harsh insentience of the outer world. She liked the *inwardness* of the remnant of forest, the unspeaking reticence of the old trees. They seemed a very power of silence, and yet, a vital presence [*LCL* 65].

By means of this relationship with the spirit of place, one re-establishes dialog with the world and creates a new type of communication. At the end of *Women in Love* we find a fragmentation of language in the empty, incomprehensible, polyglot stuttering of Loerke (perhaps an involuntary parody of Eliot's *Waste Land*); in the Australian novels the progressive rejection of the code (linguistic and cultural) imported from England, inadequate to the reality of the bush, proceeds apace with the discovery of a new language made of silence and sounds which are the true expression of the numinous in the immensity of the Australian outback: "Coo-ee! Coo-ee! A marvelous sound .... It seemed to Jack, this sound in the bush was like God" (*BB* 98); "The thud, the pulse of the waves: that was his nearest throb of emotion" (*K* 329). Also in *St. Mawr* we find silence and a deep relationship established by the exchange of looks as an alternate means of communication to empty, polite conversation, while in *The Plumed Serpent*, rebirth coincides with the attempt to substitute a mythical language of hymns for rational communication, a language which in *Lady Chatterley's Lover* becomes the corporal conversation of senses, silence and gestures.[6]

Lawrence's undeniable vagueness (which becomes greater the more he tries to explain his convictions) makes this idea of necessary correlation between personal regeneration and the creation of a new language seem rather nebulous. Nevertheless his way of putting language in vital relationship to the specificity of place is of contemporary scholarly interest (suffice it to think of the lively critical/theoretical debate in the field of postcolonial literature). Such a relationship involves not only a cultural aspect, a relativistic attitude implying, in modern terms, the rejection of every kind of centricity, but also an ethical aspect, an insistence on the value of mutual *respect*, not only between community and community, between individual and individual, but also respect of the individual for the self.

Notes

Introduction

1. See Jo A. Isaak, *The Ruin of Representation in Modernist Art and Texts*, UMI Research Press, Ann Arbor 1986, in particular the chapter on Joyce and the Cubist aesthetic, and the essay by Joseph Frank entitled "Spatial Form in Modern Literature" (1945), republished in *The Widening Gyre: Crisis and Mastery in Modern Literature*, Rutgers UP, New Brunswick 1963, pp. 3–62, later expanded and furnished with responses to his critics in *The Idea of Spatial Form*, Rutgers UP, New Brunswick 1991.

2. On Lawrence's relationship with avant-garde visual art, see the pioneering essay by Jack Lindsay, "The Impact of Modernism on Lawrence" in Mervyn Levy (ed.), *Paintings of D.H. Lawrence*, Cory, Adams and MacKay, London 1964, pp. 35–53; Paul Eggert, "Lawrence and the Futurists: The Breakthrough in His Art," *Meridian* 1 (1982), pp. 21–32; Kim A. Herzinger, "'Another Language Almost': The Impact of Futurism, Imagism and Vorticism," in *D. H. Lawrence in His Time: 1908–1915*, Associated University Presses, London and Toronto 1982, pp. 120–40; Giovanni Cianci, "D.H. Lawrence and Futurism/Vorticism," *Arbeiten zur Anglistik und Amerikanistik* 8 (1983), pp. 41–53; Vita Fortunati, "The Visual Arts and the Novel: The Contrasting Cases of Ford Madox Ford and D. H. Lawrence," *Etudes Lawrenciennes* 10 (1994), pp. 129–43, and Jack Stewart, *The Vital Art of D.H. Lawrence: Vision and Expression*, Southern Illinois UP, Carbondale and Edwardsville 1999. Interesting considerations of the subject also occur in Christopher Butler, *Early Modernism*, Clarendon Press, Oxford 1994; Marianna Torgovnick, *The Visual Arts, Pictorialism and the Novel: James, Lawrence and Woolf*, Princeton UP, Princeton 1985; in Gregory L. Ulmer, "D. H. Lawrence, Wilhelm Worringer, and the Aesthetics of Modernism," *D. H. Lawrence Review* 10 (1977), pp. 165–81; and in Emile Delavenay, "Lawrence and the Futurists," in Lawrence B. Gamache and

Ian S. MacNiven (eds), *The Modernists: Studies in a Literary Phenomenon*, Associated University Presses, London and Toronto 1987, pp. 140–62. On the relationship between Lawrence and Modernism, see also Ornella De Zordo, *The Parable of Transition: A Study of D. H. Lawrence and Modernism*, ETS, Pisa 1987; Tony Pinkney, *D. H. Lawrence*, Harvester Wheatsheaf, Hemel Hempstead 1990; Nancy Kushigan, *Pictures and Fictions: Visual Modernism and the Pre-War Novels of D.H. Lawrence*, Peter Lang, New York 1990; Akos Doman, *Die andere Moderne: Knut Hamsun, D.H. Lawrence und die lebensphilosophische Stromung des literarischen Modernismus*, Bouvier, Bonn 1995; and Terri A. Mester, *Movement and Modernism: Yeats, Eliot, Lawrence, Williams, and Early Twentieth-Century Dance*, University of Arkansas Press, Fayetteville 1997.

3. According to Francesco Remotti, *Luoghi e corpi. Antropologia dello spazio, del tempo e del potere*, Bollati Boringhieri, Torino 1993, p. 31, "every society is made of places and bodies, that is, it consists of bodies which live, work, interact, and dwell in certain places ... every society spreads out into a space, articulates and organizes itself in it, designating certain specific places in its territory which are destined to certain specific activities." (translation mine).

4. See, in this regard, Remotti, *Luoghi e corpi*, cit, pp. 36–46, on the importance of "marking" and of "writing" in the process of affirmation and differentiation of a culture.

5. Martin Heidegger, "Art and Space" (1969), trans. by Charles H. Seibert, *Man and World* 6 (1973), pp. 3–8, states: "Whereof does it speak in the word 'space'? Clearing-away (*Räumen*) is uttered therein. This means: to clear out (*roden*), to free from wilderness. Clearing-away brings forth the free, the openness for man's settling and dwelling ... clearing-away is the release of places toward which the fate of dwelling man turns in the preserve of the home or in the brokenness of homelessness or in complete indifference of the two" (p. 5).

6. In his research on forms of human settlement, Christian Norberg-Schulz, *The concept of dwelling: On the way to figurative architecture* (1984), Rizzoli, New York 1985, p. 9, observes that "place ... unites a group of human beings, it is something which gives them a common identity and hence a basis for a fellowship or society."

7. Jean Piaget, in his studies on space, insists on the fact that spatial representations are formed by the organization of *actions* done upon objects in space. The adult representation of space, moreover, is not an immediate "reproduction" of the environment on the part of the perceptive apparatus, but the result of intellectual manipulations of the spatial environment. Cf. John H. Flavell, "Space, Geometry, Chance, Adolescent Reasoning, and Perception," in *The Developmental Psychology of Jean Piaget*, With a foreword by Jean Piaget, D. Van Nostrand, Princeton (N.J.) 1963, pp. 327–56.

8. Franco La Cecla, *Perdersi. L'uomo senza ambiente*, Laterza, Bari 1988, pp. 92–100, emphasizes the importance assumed by the dialectical relationship with the unknown in reinforcing the individual obligation to the collective, noting that, in cultures which "live a location," the forest, the unknown beyond the place of community, are essential to that end, inasmuch as they permit us to consider our own place from another viewpoint, to evaluate it in relation to all of the cosmos, to discern its weaknesses and possible threats from the outside. Jurij M. Lotman

Notes: Introduction

and Boris A. Uspenskij, *Tipologia della cultura*, ed. Remo Faccani and Marzio Marzaduri, Bompiani, Milano 1987, pp. 145–81, show that the frontier, the threshold between inside and outside, the known and the unknown, is an essential element in the spatial metalanguage used for the description of culture. By these means, in every society and cultural system, are determined the world of organization and good, and the world of disorganization, chaos, and evil.

9. In this regard, Michel Foucault, "Of Other Spaces" (1984), trans. by Jay Miscowiec, *Diacritics* 16 (1986), pp. 22–27, observes that "our life is still governed by a certain number of oppositions that remain inviolable ... that we regard as simple givens: for example between private space and public space, between family space and social space, between cultural space and useful space, between the space of leisure and that of work. All these are still nurtured by the hidden presence of the sacred" (p. 23).

10. The opposition between "places of us," that is, of the social community, and "places of others" identified with institutions, with order imposed by the outside, in other words, with power, is suggested by Remotti, *Luoghi e corpi*, cit., pp. 11–75.

11. Cf. La Cecla, *Perdersi*, cit. pp. 100–5.

12. Stephen Kern, *The Culture of Time and Space 1880–1918*, CUP, Cambridge (Mass.) 1983, offers a overall view of changing concepts of time and space found in various fields of knowledge and of their effect on the arts. Frank's essays, collected in the monograph *The Idea of Spatial Form*, cit., insist on the prevalence of the synchronic aspect over the diachronic in the avant-garde literary texts of the early 1900s. Interesting points on the subject are offered by Eric S. Rabkin, "Spatial Form and Plot," *Critical Inquiry* 4 (1977), pp. 253–70; William Holtz, "Spatial Form in Modern Literature: A Reconsideration," *Critical Inquiry* 4 (1977), pp. 271–83, Garbiel Zoran, "Towards a Theory of Space in Narrative," *Poetics Today* 5 (1984), pp. 309–35; and Isaak, *The Ruin of Representation in Modernist Art and Texts*, cit. Particular attention to spatial form in the novel is given by Joseph Kestner in *The Spatiality of the Novel*, Wayne State UP, Detroit 1978; in Jeffrey R. Smitten and Ann Daghistany (eds), *Spatial Form in Narrative*, Cornell UP, Ithaca and London 1981, furnished with an extensive bibliography; and in Ruth Ronen, "Space in Fiction," *Poetics Today* 7 (1986), pp. 421–38. Regarding the crisis of traditional diachronic succession and the prevalence of synchronicity and simultaneity in relation to the modern metropolis, see also Carlo Pagetti and Marialuisa Bignami, "La coscienza narrativa tra vecchio e nuovo secolo," and Carlo Pagetti, Luisa Villa, Ruggero Bianchi, Giovanni Cianci, Massimo Bacigalupo, Renzo S. Crivelli, "La metropoli modernista," in Giovanni Cianci (ed.), *Modernismo/Modernismi*, Principato, Milano 1991, pp. 63–82 and 476–508.

13. Lotman, *Tipologia della cultura*, cit., emphasizes the distinction between fixed and mobile spaces, between passable places and closed boundaries, showing how the fixed elements in a literary text form the cosmogonic, geographic and social structure, the so-called "field" of the hero.

14. Lotman, *Tipologia della cultura*, cit., p. 154, "the space of a cultural text represents the universal totality of the elements of a given culture, since it is the model of the *whole*" (translation mine).

15. The epochal episteme and the system of anthropological archetypes respectively reflect a diachronic and a synchronic perspective. "System of anthropological

archetypes" refers to a model of reading space, an interpretation of reality belonging to a culture not "fitting" into history. See in this regard the chapter "Cultura" in Remotti, *Luoghi e corpi*, cit. pp. 11–46, in particular the section dedicated to the nature of anthropological concepts, where the author insists on the necessity of abandoning the pretense of "elaborating models and applying their conceptual grid to various ethnographic contexts," showing that "when encountering diverse societies, anthropologists find not only strange and bizarre customs, not only thoughts that are at least as deep as their own, but also other anthropologies: customs which represent human beings differently, thoughts which conceive differently, yet always interestingly, human reality" (pp. 19–21). (translation mine).

16. The idea of the presence of poetry in nature, which feeds individuals' dreams of beauty and happiness, and of the deterministic laws of cause and effect decisively indifferent to their aspirations and needs, so that they become tragic victims of a system of which they are a part, but whose laws they do not understand, is drawn by Lawrence from Thomas Hardy. In "Study of Thomas Hardy," Lawrence states in fact that he has found "a constant revelation in Hardy's novels: that there exists a great background, vital and vivid, which matters more than the people who move upon it ... . Upon the vast, incomprehensible pattern of some primal morality ... is drawn the little, pathetic pattern of man's moral life and struggle" (*Hardy*, 28–29). On the influence of evolutionary theory upon the works of Hardy and Lawrence, see Roger Ebbatson, *Lawrence and the Nature Tradition: A Theme in English Fiction, 1859–1914*, Harvester Press, Brighton 1980; also by Ebbatson, *The Evolutionary Self: Hardy, Forster, Lawrence*, Harvester Press, Brighton 1982, and Lawrence Jones, "Imagery and the 'Idiosyncratic Mode of Regard': Eliot, Hardy, and Lawrence," *Ariel* 12 (1981), pp. 29–49. After recognizing the presence of an evolutionary perspective in all three of the writers, the critic analyzes the way in which common images relative to the man/nature relationship are developed in completely different ways in each of them, such that they lead to opposite solutions. In reference to Hardy as master of the "naturist novel," see John Alcorn, *The Nature Novel from Hardy to Lawrence*, Columbia UP, New York 1977. See also Raney Stanford, "Thomas Hardy and Lawrence's *The White Peacock*," *Modern Fiction Studies* 5 (1959), pp. 19–28; Richard Swigg, *Lawrence, Hardy and American Literature*, OUP, New York 1972; Robert Langbaum, "Lawrence and Hardy," in Jeffrey Meyers (ed.), *D. H. Lawrence and Tradition*, Athlone, London 1985, pp. 69–90; and Perry Meisel, "Hardy, Lawrence, and the Disruptions of Nature," in *The Myth of the Modern: A Study in British Literature and Criticism after 1850*, Yale UP, New Haven 1987, pp. 11–36.

Chapter 1

1. Marco Modenesi, "Verso una definizione del romanzo decadente," in Paolo Amalfitano (ed.), *Il romanzo tra i due secoli (1880–1918)*, Bulzoni, Roma 1993, pp. 3–19, argues that the decadent novel aims at a breakdown of diegesis and a reduction of the narrative nucleus to its essentials, which, on the one hand, accentuates the static quality of the narrative and on the other hand, the tendency of various

episodes to gravitate towards it. From a spatial point of view and in relation to the function of places, *The White Peacock* fits perfectly into this classification. The fundamental narrative nucleus, which binds the three parts of the novel (even if predominantly in the first part), is made up of characters' movements to and from the mill, which is their center of gravity.

2. To the couples Lettie/Leslie, George/Meg, Cyril/Emily must be added those belonging to the preceding generation, which Lawrence uses to verify the inevitability of the fading of every love relationship. In some cases, this is motivated by the woman's "tyranny" in the erotic sphere (as in the case of Lady Crystabel and the gamekeeper) or inside the domestic walls (as in the case of Cyril's mother, who has completely crushed her husband, denying him access to the house after his betrayal). Relationships with the outcasts generally occur in isolated or transient places: for example, Cyril speaks with his father while accompanying him on the main road, and with Annable, in the woods.

3. Notice, in this regard, the importance of the positioning of the three residences and of their reciprocal distance (Strelley Mill, Woodside, Highclose): "Her path lay through the wood in the opposite direction from Strelley Mill [Lettie is going to Highclose], down the red drive across the tree-scattered space to the highroad. This road ran along the end of our lakelet, Nethermere, for about a quarter of a mile. Nethermere is the lowest in a chain of three ponds. The other two are the upper and lower mill-ponds at Strelley: this is the largest and most charming piece of water, a mile long and about a quarter of a mile in width. Our wood runs down to the water's edge. On the opposite side, on a hill beyond the farthest corner of the lake, stands Highclose. It looks across the water at us in Woodside with one eye as it were, while our cottage casts a sidelong glance back again at the proud house, and peeps coyly through the trees" (*WP* 9).

4. The tendency to idealize the environment, to transfigure reality into poetic and idyllic terms is recognized by Lawrence himself: "to me, as a child and a young man, it [the country around Eastwood] was still the old England of the forest and agricultural past; there were no motor-cars, the mines were, in a sense, an accident in the landscape, and Robin Hood and his merry men were not very far away" (*NMC* 133).

5. The minute attention to detail in the description of nature, where nothing is left to chance, nothing escapes notice, and the landscape imagery acquires traces of Pre-Raphaelite painting, is emphasized by Claude M. Sinzelle, "Naturalism in the Treatment of the Natural and Human Background in *The White Peacock*," in *The Geographical Background of the Early Works of D. H. Lawrence*, Didier, Paris 1964, pp. 30–46. The importance of pictorial images as a fundamental element in the development of Lawrence's visual perception is discussed in detail by Keith Alldritt in *The Visual Imagination of D. H. Lawrence*, Edward Arnold, London 1971, pp. 3–15; and by Jack Stewart, *The Vital Art of D.H. Lawrence*, cit. On the Pre-Raphaelite influence in D. H. Lawrence's works and in particular on the close relationship between Maurice Greiffenhagen's *Idyll* and *The White Peacock*, see Jeffrey Meyers, "Maurice Greiffenhagen and *The White Peacock*," in *Painting and the Novel*, Manchester UP, Manchester 1975, pp. 46–52. See also Jack F. Stewart, "Landscape Painting and Pre-Raphaelitism in *The White Peacock*," *D.H. Lawrence* [*Review* 27 (1997–98), pp. 3–25].

6. To the sober, orderly interior of Strelley Mill is contrasted Annable's house at the Kennels. It too is an "island," for its position at the borders of the woods and its distance from other habitations. The gamekeeper's residence is the mirror of the "jungle" in which he has chosen to live. In its untidy squalor, it resembles a den more than a home: "The barred windows of the cottages were grey with dust; there was no need now to protect the windows from cattle, dog or man. One of the three houses was inhabited ... . The kitchen was large, but scantily furnished; save, indeed, for children" (*WP* 70). On the image of Annable's kitchen as a territory of aggression and violence towards those weaker than him, "where nothing is idealized and violence lies close to the surface," cf. Margaret Storch, "The Lacerated Male: Ambivalent Images of Women in *The White Peacock*," *D. H. Lawrence Review* 21 (1989) pp. 117–36.

7. Christopher Brown, "As Cyril Likes It: Pastoral Reality and Illusion in *The White Peacock*," *Essays in Literature* 6 (1979) pp. 187–93, discerns in the particular nature of the Arcadia, temporarily shared by the characters, the cause of its inevitable decline. Whereas in the novels *Women in Love* and *Lady Chatterley's Lover*, "the Arcadian experience ... is viewed as a healthy and health-inducing alternative to the dominant culture," in *The White Peacock* "Lawrence emphasized the darker, equivocal side of the pastoral tradition: Arcadia tends toward microcosm rather than idyllic alternative" (pp. 187–88). According to the critic, the dissolution of the idyll is determined by internal conflicts and not from outside threats, so that "Lawrence's Arcadia manifests in miniature the very elements which are found deplorable in the outer world and which bring about the novel's sad conclusion" (p. 189).

8. Appropriation, in one form or another, is common to all of the characters, for whom it is an instrument of security and guarantee of identity. The mill is materially necessary for the Saxton family who experiences the anxiety of the dispossession/uprooting, of the loss of their home at the moment of expulsion, and it is psychologically essential to Cyril, who feels nostalgia for his home "center" in disorienting London. It is fundamental for Lettie, who is always conscious of the influence and attraction that her presence exerts at the mill, although the mill's inhabitants sometimes perceive Lettie's appropriation of the place as a violation of their intimacy.

9. For example, after the upsetting encounter with reality provoked by Emily's killing of the dog, the two characters exorcize the brutality of the episode by a ritualistic immersion in nature, by covering and crowning themselves with berries: "'I [Emily] daren't think of it. Get me some of those berries ... . I have always wanted to put red berries in my hair' ... 'There!' said I [Cyril] 'You're crowned'" (*WP* 68–69).

10. Remo Ceserani, "Su alcuni simboli della tradizione e della modernità in Thomas Hardy: la cattedrale e la stazione ferroviaria," in Amalfitano (ed.), *Il romanzo tra i due secoli (1880–1918)*, cit., pp. 21–38, emphasizes the importance of "walking together" as a common occasion of encounter, communication and intimacy, showing that the act of walking is linked to the ancient social practice of courtship and young love, to which refers the expression "to walk out with" in the language of rural society.

11. To arrive at the mill, in fact, one must descend, whereas Woodside is on

the shore of a lake (and therefore on a flat surface) and Highclose is on top of a hill.

12. A function that he enacts, in actuality, in a merely narrative sense, by virtue of his role as omnipresent observer.

13. A principle symbolized, as in *The Mill on the Floss* (a work which Lawrence surely knew), by the wheel of the mill. On the influence of George Eliot's works in *The White Peacock*, see Michael Black, "A Bit of Both: George Eliot and D. H. Lawrence," *Critical Review* (Canberra) 29 (1989), pp. 89–109; H. M. Daleski, "Lawrence and George Eliot: The Genesis of *The White Peacock*," in Meyers (ed.), *D. H. Lawrence and Tradition*, cit., pp. 51–68; and Pinkney, *D. H. Lawrence*, cit., pp. 5–27.

14. Concerning this scene, Vita Fortunati, "'The word unsaid': il tema dell'omosessualità nella narrativa di D. H. Lawrence," in Carla Comellini and Vita Fortunati (eds), *D. H. Lawrence cent'anni dopo. Nuove prospettive della critica lawrenciana*, Pàtron, Bologna 1991, pp. 117–28, emphasizes Lawrence's recourse to great archetypes of the past, in this case, that of David and Jonathan, "to accentuate the ideal and sacred aspect of 'male friendship'" (p. 122) translation mine. According to Pinkney, *D. H. Lawrence*, cit., p. 16, "homosexuality is not here as a theme in its own right ... . It is as yet, rather, the novel's narrative means of rendering a general creative pleasurableness of the labour process—a sexuality which embraces the landscape as well as the lover."

15. Ebbatson, *Lawrence and the Nature Tradition*, cit., pp. 44–60, interprets the inevitable end of the "poetic" valley of Nethermere in an evolutionary way. Insofar as it is a closed, isolated community, the valley is destined to destruction from the outside, more "fit" to accomplish the process of transformation and evolution of nature. A correlation between the characters' downward spiral and their inability to adapt is posited by Alastair Niven, *D. H. Lawrence: The Novels*, CUP, Cambridge 1978, p. 22, for whom "*The White Peacock* stopped too soon ... because he [Lawrence] had not shown in Lettie and George any capacity to develop *after* their fatefully wrong choices have been made; they just seem to wither or stagnate."

16. The mill is always represented as an open place where the characters enter without knocking or ringing, unlike Woodside, where the entrance is guarded by Rebecca, and Highclose, where a hedge borders the garden; this situation will last, however, only until the mill itself is opened to day-laborers, strangers to the "idyll" of which it was the center.

17. Cf. Lotman, *Tipologia della cultura*, cit., pp. 145–81.

18. Abrupt, upsetting encounters with reality occur constantly in the second part of the novel: the most important two episodes are when Annable suddenly appears during the meditation on the mystery of the snowdrops, and the shout of the man defending his private property when George and Lettie, sitting near the fountain, dream of a life as free as that of the fish.

19. In the episode of the gamekeeper, the threat of violence which will also affect the mill, for the moment still "peaceful, with the blue smoke rising as winsomely and carelessly as ever" (*WP* 157), is announced by the restriction of usable space caused by the chaotic excess of nature. Not only is the church's threshold covered by grass and the ruins of an ancient religion disfigured by mice and birds, but also the stairway, full of wild roses, has become *impassable*.

20. The dispersal, shown spatially by the characters' physical as well as psychological moving away, highlights the paradigm of circularity inasmuch as the characters' moves towards various cardinal points are followed by a return to their places of origin, by resettling themselves in a circumscribed area, even if communication is no longer possible.

21. In this regard, note, during the trip to Nottingham, the episode of taking tea at the fair in Colwick Park, where George, with a clumsy ostentation of social *savoir faire*, orders oysters, and the disturbing effect that the performance of *Carmen* has on him and Meg, because it is an encounter with an exotic, attractive and unknown world.

22. La Cecla, *Perdersi*, cit., p. 28, emphasizes how "to bring oneself along means to colonize with one's presence every step of the journey ... . One can no longer get lost because the places are consumed by the order which one brings to them; they are not given any chance to become places with which it is possible to interact." (translation mine).

23. W. M. Verhoeven, "D. H. Lawrence's Duality Concept in *The White Peacock*," *Neophilologus* 69 (1985), pp. 294–317, points out in Emily's house "a revival of Strelley Mill, the symbol of robust and vital life of the senses that Lawrence has caused to fall victim to the materialism of the age" (p. 316).

Chapter 2

1. On the difficulty of arranging the short stories and the early novels chronologically, see John Worthen, "Short Story and Autobiography: Kinds of Detachment in D. H. Lawrence's Early Fiction," *Renaissance and Modern Studies* 29 (1985), pp. 1–15. For an analysis of the genesis of the collection see Brian H. Finney, "D.H. Lawrence's Progress to Maturity: From Holograph Manuscript to Final Publication of *The Prussian Officer and Other Stories*," *Studies in Bibliography* 28 (1975), pp. 321–32, and John Worthen's introduction to *The Prussian Officer and Other Stories*, CUP, Cambridge 1983, pp. xix-li. See also Keith Cushman, *D. H. Lawrence at Work: The Emergence of the 'Prussian Officer' Stories*, Harvester, Sussex 1978; Janice H. Harris, *The Short Fiction of D. H. Lawrence*, Rutgers UP, New Brunswick 1984; and Michael Black, *D. H. Lawrence: The Early Fiction*, Macmillan, London 1986, pp. 111–49 and 188–256.

2. A mythical-ritualistic reading of *The Prussian Officer*, focused mostly on the material that Lawrence took from recent studies in anthropology and in particular from his reading of *The Golden Bough* by James G. Frazer, is undertaken by John B. Vickery, "Myth and Ritual in the Shorter Fiction of D H. Lawrence," *Modern Fiction Studies* 5 (1959), pp. 65–82, republished with updates and revisions in *The Literary Impact of The Golden Bough*, Princeton UP, Princeton 1973, pp. 294–325.

3. On the paradoxical relationship between the officer and his attendant see Gary Adelman, "Beyond the Pleasure Principle: An Analysis of D. H. Lawrence's 'The Prussian Officer,'" *Studies in Short Fiction* 1 (1963), pp. 8–15; Ann Englander, "'The Prussian Officer': The Self Divided," *Sewanee Review* 71 (1963),

pp. 605–19; and Serena Cenni, "Psico-narrazione e monologo interiore in 'The Prussian Officer' e 'The Fox'," in Comellini and Fortunati (eds), *D. H. Lawrence cent'anni dopo*, cit., pp. 29–46.

4. "And then he saw the thin, strong throat of the elder man moving up and down as he drank, the strong jaw working. And the instinct which had been jerking at the young man's wrists suddenly jerked free" (*PO* 14).

5. Her father continued to eat for a few moments, then he said: 'Have a chop — here's one!' ... Lois was insulted, but she gave no sign. She sat down and took a cup of coffee, making no pretence to eat" (*PO* 139).

6. The story presents the same triangle (the noble savage, the well-mannered citizen, and the *femme fatale*) upon which many Lawrencean works focus, beginning with *The White Peacock*. However, it should be emphasized that here the protagonist Hilda makes a life choice opposite to Lettie's, and from that choice she draws a greater "sovereignty" than Lettie's, which extends to all spaces, both inside and outside. On the affinities between "The Shades of Spring" and *The White Peacock*, see Black, *D. H. Lawrence: The Early Fiction*, cit., pp. 122–29.

7. "Mr. Lindley kept a special tone for him, kind, indulgent, but patronising. Durant took it all without criticism or offence, just submitting. But he did not want to eat — that troubled him, to have to eat in their presence. *He knew he was out of place*. But it was his duty to stay yet awhile" (*PO* 79, emphasis mine).

8. The celebration of the two rites (the bourgeois tea and the Christian baptism) reunite members of the family and the priest around the domestic hearth, which becomes a place, not of union between family members, but of a series of conflicts, from which the story draws its dramatic structure. These conflicts reveal two oppositions: between *convention* and *the sacred*, and between *convention* and *nature*. The first is shown in the image of the water for the baptism, paradoxically "placed ... there among the tea-things" (*PO* 177), and in the contrast between the father's prayers, as he blesses the baby's entry into the world, and the empty formulae of the ritual baptism celebrated by the clergyman; the second is shown in the antagonism which separates Hilda, the intellectual of the family, fierce guardian of social dignity, from the girl-mother and her brother, the latter is a completely instinctive miner who scornfully refuses the falsity of the rite and the hypocritical purchase of sweets from a bakery, whose boy is the very father of the child.

9. "There *was* a difference between the Rowbothams and the common collier-folk: Woodbine Cottage was a superior house to most, and was built in pride by the old man" (*PO* 176).

10. In "Odour of Chrysanthemums" the domestic interior seems to be the only "humanly" inhabitable space, since the external environment is a dark "mechanical forest" full of deafening noises where one can easily get lost or imprisoned, like the woman at the beginning of the story, "insignificantly trapped between the jolting black waggons and the hedge" (*PO* 181). On the image of man and nature, victims of a mechanized universe, immersed in an atmosphere of death, see Keith Sagar's comments in *The Art of D. H. Lawrence*, CUP, Cambridge 1966, pp. 14–15, and Claudio Gorlier's essay, "Uccidere il porcospino. Ipotesi sui racconti di Lawrence," *Il Verri* 17 (1980), pp. 37–49.

11. In "Odour of Chrysanthemums," the flower which attracts the daughter by its beauty and the intensity of its perfume, is violently refused and pushed away

by the mother because it is an incarnation of a spent life, wasted next to her husband: "No .... Not to me [do they smell beautiful]. It was chrysanthemums when I married him, and chrysanthemums when you were born, and the first time they ever brought him home drunk he'd got brown chrysanthemums in his buttonhole" (*PO* 186).

12. Worthen, "Short Story and Autobiography: Kinds of Detachment in D. H. Lawrence's Early Fiction," cit., pp. 9–11, points out the origins of Syson's failure in his idealization and sentimentalizing of the surrounding environment, which renders him unable to participate in real life, which he perceives only through a kind of "stained glass."

13. "'Why, would you *like* me to kill the moles then?' she asked, tentatively, after a while. 'They do us a lot of damage,' he said, standing firm on his ground, angered .... And the next day, after a secret, persistent hunt, she found another mole playing in the heat. She killed it, and ... took him the dead creature" (*PO* 119–20).

14. On the liberating effect which their sexual relationship has on both partners, see John Worthen, "The Roles of Women: 'The Thorn in the Flesh' and 'Odour of Chrysanthemums,'" in *D. H. Lawrence*, Edward Arnold, London 1991, pp. 32–41.

15. Jack F. Stewart, "Expressionism in 'The Prussian Officer,'" *D. H. Lawrence Review* 18 (1985–86), pp. 275–89, proposes an interesting reading of the story, pointing out close links between the man-universe relationship and expressionist painting and emphasizing that "Lawrence's imagery presents a distorted, hallucinatory world, seen through a consciousness stripped of volition and reeling from sunstroke, thirst, and emotional trauma. Themes of regression and disintegration are intrinsic to expressionism: they may be linked either with regeneration ... or with annihilation" (p. 276).

16. In "A Fragment of Stained Glass" the decision to cut ties with the world is possible only by an escape to the woods, where the lovers can "join the outlaws" (*PO* 94). The woods, however, even though they are a necessary passage for achieving liberty, are inhabited by dark and uncontrollable forces which make them intolerable for man: "I will not sleep in the wood, ... for I am afraid. I had better be afraid of the voice of man and dogs, than the sounds in the woods" (*PO* 93). And the dark terrors are justified and explained by the end of the story, which presents the two lovers awakened by the approach of wolves. The epilogue supplied by the external narrator, "they lived happily ever after" (*PO* 97) rings clearly as an ironic homage to the conventions of fable.

Chapter 3

1. Already upon its first appearance in print, *The Trespasser* did not enjoy a favorable reception. It is enough to recall that Ford Madox Ford, who had warmly supported the publication of *The White Peacock* by Heinemann, condemned the second novel outright, describing it as "a rotten work of genius" (*Letters* i. 339), brimming with eroticism. His condemnation, along with Lawrence's own words

in a letter to his editor, "execrable bad art [with] no idea of progressive action ... finally, pornographic" (*Letters* i. 229), found an echo in later criticism which, although indulgent with regard to *The White Peacock*, was very severe with *The Trespasser*. Later critical studies like that of Jacqueline Gouirand, "*The Trespasser*: aspects génétiques," *Etudes Lawrenciennes* 1 (1986), pp. 41–57, and two essays by A. R. Atkins, "Recognizing the 'Stranger' in D. H. Lawrence's *The Trespasser*," *Cambridge Quarterly* 20 (1991), pp. 1–20, and "Textual Influences on D. H. Lawrence's 'The Saga of Siegmund'," *D. H. Lawrence Review* 24 (1992), pp. 27–26, are principally concerned with reconstructing the genesis of the novel by comparing the two versions. See also Elizabeth Mansfield's introduction to *The Trespasser*, CUP, Cambridge 1981, pp. 3–37. In reference to German culture's impact on Lawrence, see John L. Digaetani, "Situational Myths: Richard Wagner and D. H. Lawrence," in *Richard Wagner and the Modern British Novel*, Associated University Presses, London 1978, pp. 58–89; Raymond Furness, "Wagner and Myth," in *Wagner and Literature*, Manchester UP, Manchester 1982, pp. 79–107; and Pinkney, "Northerness and Modernism: *The Trespasser, The Rainbow, Women in Love*," in *D. H. Lawrence*, cit., pp. 54–99. In the field of gender studies, some attention has been given to the novel by Jane Heath, "Helen Corke and D. H. Lawrence: Sexual Identity and Literary Relations," *Feminist Studies* 11 (1985), pp. 317–42, in which she examines the relationship between *The Trespasser* and "The Freshwater Diary" of Helen Corke in light of the interpersonal relationship between the two authors. A notable recent study is the monograph by Cecilia Björkén, *Into the Isle of Self: Nietzschean Patterns and Contrasts in D. H. Lawrence's* The Trespasser, Lund UP, Lund 1996.

2. His difficulties are evidenced in a 1910 letter, written when Lawrence was still working on the first version of *The Trespasser*: "I shall never do anything decent till I can grow up and cut my beastly long curls of poetry" (*Letters* i. 167). Concerning this, John Worthen, "The Saga of Siegmund," in *D. H. Lawrence: The Early Years 1885–1912*, CUP, Cambridge 1991, pp. 260–62, investigates the writer's personal struggle to free himself from the "literary world for which, in one sense, the novel was precisely designed." The explicit "distaste for the literary world" demonstrates, for the biographer, that "[Lawrence] knew that the 'literary element' was sticking to the roots of the 'growing things' which he himself was trying to create."

3. Concerning the Isle of Wight setting, Anthony Beal, *D. H. Lawrence*, Oliver and Boyd, Edinburgh 1961, p. 13, states that the island "is made to play an integral part in the emotions of the lovers ... their time together is an escape from everyday reality into an almost mythological world." Niven, *D. H. Lawrence: The Novels*, cit., pp. 27–29, emphasizes instead how the choice of a setting rather unfamiliar to Lawrence arises from the fact that, in his opinion, "in his second novel Lawrence seems to have experimented with forms and methods quite different from those of *The White Peacock*"; the critic assigns to the island the function of catalyst for Siegmund's failure. Inasmuch as he is a city man, "a victim ... of the suburban responsibilities forced upon the city-dweller," Siegmund is unable, even though a musician, to hear the music "thrilling the atmosphere on the Isle of Wight as though it were Prospero's enchanted isle." For Black, *D. H. Lawrence: The Early Fiction*, cit., p. 79, the theme of the island vacation as escape from daily responsi-

bility intensifies that sense of suffocating claustrophobia which permeates the whole novel: "*The Trespasser* feels claustrophobic because it adheres so closely to the working out of the relationship between two people, for a moment isolated in a holiday-realm which is not where their ordinary living takes place, where they can concentrate on what is happening within them, and relate it to the magic of their stolen days in high summer."

4. According to Niven, *D. H. Lawrence: The Novels*, cit., p. 33, the harmony of the two lovers, their "interfusion of two beings in their passion," is feverishly reached only "in single moments" and leads Siegmund to suicide because of the nature of romantic ecstasy: frenetic and unrepeatable. The critic points out that Lawrence is still far from that idea of a relationship between the sexes which will inform *Women in Love*, in which the perfect union between two lovers will be possible as long as they show themselves capable of "remain[ing] separate and themselves even in the intensity of their passion." The overheating of Siegmund's and Helena's passion and the brevity of their union are caused by their will to fuse, completely annihilating the distance between them and the acceptance of the otherness of their partner.

5. Ebbatson, *Lawrence and the Nature Tradition*, cit., pp. 61–63, attributes Siegmund's failure to his inability to adequately "read" Nature's message, to shake off the cultural and aesthetic patrimony which he carries and which makes him a slave of his mystifications, unable to "take part in the great battle of action ... . From this struggle for survival, even in the ecstatic idyll of love, Siegmund turns away ... . This aestheticism makes Siegmund's relation to Nature ultimately too frenzied." The ending of the novel "in domestic tragedy," emphasizes the critic, "reflects upon the inadequacy of the human response to the redemptive potentialities revealed on the island."

6. In the utopian tradition the island is always viewed as virgin ground in which the construction of an ideal world is made possible by the absence of conventions, laws and institutions which restrict human beings in the real world.

7. The fundamentally renunciative *animus* of the protagonist, unable even to think of cutting off from his petit-bourgeois existence, is evidenced by the way in which he thinks of the "flight" itself: "he was going to break free altogether, to have *at least a few days* purely for his own joy" (*T* 49, emphasis mine).

8. This method of connecting a character's existential dilemmas to a choice between two places recalls certain stories of *The Prussian Officer* in which the heroine (Louisa in "Daughters of the Vicar," Frances in "Second Best" and Hilda in "The Shades of Spring") leaves behind her old existence by moving to another place. In *The Trespasser* it is instead a man who finds himself in such a dilemma and in his case there is no real choice, something that determines (in contrast to the female characters mentioned above) his existential failure.

9. Concerning this, Inge P. Nielsen and Karsten H. Nielsen, "The Modernism of D. H. Lawrence and the Discourses of Decadence: Sexuality and Tradition in *The Trespasser, Fantasia of the Unconscious*, and *Aaron's Rod*," *Arcadia* 25 (1990), pp. 270–86, observe that the language Lawrence uses to render the island experience entirely reflects his choice of "decadent discourse," that is, a "language of ornament [which] offers no material from which knowledge can be extracted; it stages isolated situations with no other purpose than that of presenting to the

moment of perception a maximum concentration of sensual impressions" (p. 277).

10. This lack is symbolized by an element, the fog — present at both Siegmund's arrival on the island and his departure — which points out the absence of a real grip on reality on the part of the two lovers and which becomes the occasion for one of several moments of separation between them: both, under the circumstances, believe they hear a magical siren song (probably the sound of a ship's horn), but they differ in discerning which tone it is: an "E" for Helena and a "F" for Siegmund.

11. In the chapter "Convenzione," Remotti, *Luoghi e corpi*, cit., pp. 108–48, dedicates ample space to the dramaturgic metaphor in substitution for the organic and architectonic one in relation to society. From this viewpoint (argued in works by Erving Goffman, Victor W. Turner and Clifford Geertz) the individual is both actor (he "acts" in front of others) and character (his ego is formed in the context of acting, through its rules and conventions). It is impossible to take off the mask because no "real" individual exists behind it, insofar as the man's interior is also constituted by "fictions," constructs and cultural costumes, by a totality of "what ifs." Culture is presented therefore as a complex of costumes in which man dresses to "act" his own life. In *The Trespasser* there are many instances of the dramaturgic metaphor to describe the island experience. For example we see it in the following passages: "Siegmund, with his face expressionless as a mask, sat staring out at the mist" (*T* 58); "'The mist is Lethe. It is enough for us if its spell lasts five days.' ... They walked on joyfully, locking behind them the doors of forgetfulness ... . It was a splendid, flaming bridal chamber where he had come to Helena" (*T* 61); "The days used to walk in procession like seven marionettes, each in order and costume, going endlessly round" (*T* 98); "'And there shall be no more sea,' she quoted to herself" (*T* 119). Even Siegmund's suicide is like a "performance": "He was hardly conscious of anything he did ... . Yet he *performed* his purpose methodically and exactly ... . It was a mesmeric *performance* in which the agent trembled with convulsive sickness" (*T* 204, emphasis mine). The way in which the corpse is discovered and removed from the stage also conforms to the dramaturgic metaphor: the window-cleaner, stranger to the tragedy, functions to remove "the past" from the stage and prepare the set for the new act, that of the novel's frame.

12. These are, for example, the interiors, the single rooms, the stations and most of all, the train compartments, focused on according to the plot's development.

13. For this reason it favors the identification of the Absolute and the infinite with Nothing and therefore with death, which becomes, à la Wagner, "temptation" and object of longing for the two lovers, especially Siegmund: "Helena drew him to the edge of the cliff ... . 'Shall we walk over, then?' said Siegmund, glancing downwards ... . How could he play with the idea of death, and the five great days in front! She was afraid of him just then" (*T* 60–61).

14. But the island itself turns out to be a disorienting, labyrinthine place for the two protagonists, as we see in the episode where they get lost, Helena's persistent recourse to the map, and their continual search for landmarks (such as the white cross on the hill).

15. The devastating effect of the sunstroke links this episode with the tragic end of Schoner in "The Prussian Officer," who dies of sunstroke in the wood follow-

ing his struggle with the officer. Ebbatson, *Lawrence and the Nature Tradition*, cit., p. 71, interprets the strong presence of the sun in the novel as a symbol of fertility, a means of rebirth and resurrection, element which in his opinion demonstrates that *The Trespasser* "reflects Haeckel's conviction that the 'whole marvellous panorama of life that spreads over the surface of our globe is, in the last analysis, transformed sunlight.'" In actuality, the sun has destructive effects on both of the protagonists.

16. "[Siegmund] found the cold mystery of the deep sand also thrilling. He pushed in his hands again and deeper, enjoying the almost hurt of the dark, heavy coldness ... . under all, was this deep mass of cold, that the softness and warmth merely floated upon" (*T* 88–89).

17. While his own house in London appears strange and melancholy to Helena, the island cottage is decisively an idyllic place for her: "This is one of the few places that has ever felt like home to me" (*T* 142), a detail which confirms her propensity to mystify reality.

18. The landlady is always a somewhat awkward presence: consider, for example, the effect produced by her voice, coming from the upper floor, the first night, when Siegmund and Helena are experiencing an intimate moment, and especially, her harsh disapproval in the episode where the two protagonists come in late at night after being lost in the dark.

19. In a less clear, but probably deliberate way, the cross creates an ideological opposition between the symbol of Christianity (seen by Lawrence as the exaltation of an asceticism which denies life and joy) and the values of a pagan religion of Nature with which the protagonists' names — Siegmund and Helena refer respectively to the German and Greek mythology — are associated.

20. While in the "world of above" the two lovers restrain their effusions, because they are always fearful of being seen, in the "world of below," in the niches that mark the border with the infinite, occur the most intense moments of union and of conflict between them.

21. Notice Siegmund's comments at the scene of sheep washing: "'Don't they seem a long way off?' he said, staring at the bucolic scene. 'They are farther than Theocritus — down there is farther than Sicily, and more than twenty centuries from us. — I wish it weren't" (*T* 117). The pastoral world, where life is connected to earth and its natural cycles, repeatedly attracts Siegmund, even though it is always distant and unreachable. Whereas on the island he observes the sheep washing scene from above, during his return journey he fantasizes such a remote, archaic life, transfiguring the images from the train window, modified by the speed of the train: "Siegmund looked at the farm, folded in a hollow, and he wondered what fortunate folk were there, nourished and quiet, hearing the vague roar of the train that was carrying him home" (*T* 164). Regarding the distance — not only physical — that the train ride determines with respect to a rural society by now in its final phase, see the comment by Remo Ceserani, *Treni di carta*, Marietti, Genova 1993, p. 171, in reference to the imagery of the railway in Lawrence's work, where "the railway motif [accompanies] the contrasting theme of the ancient life of rural England and the confused, corrupt life of industrial England which has invaded the old places ... opened tunnels in the mountains ... and brought mechanization everywhere." (translation mine).

Chapter 4

1. "I hated the Psychoanalysis Review of *Sons and Lovers* ... . I think 'complexes' are vicious half-statements of the Freudians: sort of can't see wood for trees. When you've said Mutter-complex, you've said nothing — no more than if you called hysteria a nervous disease. Hysteria isn't nerves, a complex is not simply a sex relation: far from it. — My poor book: it was, as art, a fairly complete truth: so they carve a half lie out of it, and say 'Voilà'" (*Letters* ii. 655). Lawrence's reaction was to Alfred B. Kuttner's essay, "*Sons and Lovers*: A Freudian Appreciation," *Psychoanalytic Review* 3 (1916), pp. 295–317. Other than Kuttner, see, in this regard, Daniel Weiss, "Oedipus in Nottinghamshire," *Literature and Psychology* 7 (1957), pp. 33–42; Alfred Kazin, "Sons, Lovers and Mothers," *Partisan Review* 29 (1962), pp. 373–85; Evelyn J. Hinz, "*Sons and Lovers*: The Archetypal Dimensions of Lawrence's Oedipal Tragedy," *D. H. Lawrence Review* 5 (1972), pp. 26–53; Shirley Panken, "Some Psychodynamics in *Sons and Lovers*: A New Look at the Oedipal Theme," *Psychoanalytic Review* 16 (1974–75), pp. 571–89; Giles R. Mitchell, "*Sons and Lovers* and the Oedipal Project," *D. H. Lawrence Review* 13 (1980), pp. 209–19; T. H. Adamowski, "The Father of All Things: The Oral and the Oedipal in *Sons and Lovers*," *Mosaic* 14 (1981), pp. 69–88; and, among more recent studies, Robert Burden, "Libidinal Structure and the Representation of Desire in *Sons and Lovers*," *The Journal of the D. H. Lawrence Society* (1994–95), pp. 21–38.

2. For the links between *Sons and Lovers* and the author's biography, see Worthen, *D. H. Lawrence: The Early Years 1885–1912*, cit. Tracing Lawrence's life and artistic development step by step, Worthen highlights the convergences, but even more so, the divergences between young Lawrence's life at Eastwood and Paul's, emphasizing repeatedly that "*Sons and Lovers* is a misleading guide to the events of real life" (p. 160).

3. Recognized by the author himself in a letter of 30 December 1913 to Edward Garnett: "I shan't write in the same manner as *Sons and Lovers* again, I think: in that hard, violent style full of sensation and presentation" (*Letters* ii. 132).

4. Cianci, "D. H. Lawrence and Futurism/Vorticism," cit., points out in this phase the manifestation of Lawrence's interest in avant-garde art and its reflection in a new type of writing. On the relationship between Lawrence and Modernism, please see Note 2 to the Introduction.

5. In *Sons and Lovers* there reappear all the important locations present both in *The White Peacock* (the garden, the woods, the pond, Strelley Mill), and in *The Trespasser* (the sea, city life) together with a realistic and minute attention for the noises and greyness of the mining world that also characterizes some of the stories in *The Prussian Officer*. There is even reference to military discipline and the fight against it.

6. The way in which the writer emphasizes the environment's influence on characters' formation seems close to a Marxist type of determinism in which the individual and his development are closely connected to systems of production and the economic structure of the environment. The sociological implications of the novel's characters, in particular Mrs. Morel, are analyzed by Terry Eagleton in *Exiles and Emigrés: Studies in Modern Literature*, Chatto and Windus, London 1970, pp. 192–200. A socio-cultural reading of the text (though not Marxist) seems

to be encouraged by Paul in a central point in the novel, when his inability to openly declare his love for a girl, to get close to her physically, is explained and justified, if only in part, as a common situation for many young men of his age who come from mining families. Cf. *Sons and Lovers* 322–23.

7. Such a partition corresponds to another in the second part, where four chapters are dedicated to Willey Farm and the relationship with Miriam, and four to Clara and the city. The passage occurs with the interposition of a chapter, "Clara," which, other than introducing the character and anticipating the relationship with the city, functions as a preparation for the next, entitled, "The Test on Miriam"; here, the character's defeat is accompanied by an abandonment of the "Farm" and of all the world which it, up until now, represented.

8. Lotman, *Tipologia della cultura*, cit., pp. 193–248, emphasizes the importance of the relationship between specific places and actions (more or less possible inside them) "inasmuch as a simple listing of places in which certain episodes *cannot* happen enables us to trace the frontiers of the world which finds expression in the text, while the totality of the places in which they *can* be transferred gives us the variations of an invariable model" (p. 202). (translation mine).

9. William's destruction, as he is caught between the city and his domestic universe, is foreshadowed in the first chapter by his oscillation between the fair ("the wakes"), which attracts him by its exotic, unknown, marvellous aspect (a foreshadowing of the city's multiple faces), and his mother, an oscillation which renders him: "cut to the heart to let her go, and yet unable to leave the wakes ... . Since she had gone, he had not enjoyed his wakes" (*SL* 12–13).

10. In this way, a relationship of analogy and also of opposition is established between Paul Morel and the protagonists of the two short stories written in the same years, "Second Best," and "Daughters of the Vicar," who left behind the urban world of bourgeois sophistication and opted for a natural and instinctive life instead. Paul makes the opposite choice, but it coincides, paradoxically, with theirs, since it is that of "real life."

11. Lawrence's place naming, Bestwood for Eastwood, suggests a hierarchy of places in which *Best*wood, place of bourgeois houses, is on top (its superiority suggested not only by the first part of the name, "Best," but also by the word *wood*, which is connected to nature and to an environment opposed to industrialization and is therefore more liveable). At the base of the hierarchy is "the Bottoms," where the miners live: "Mrs. Morel was not anxious to move into the Bottoms ... when she descended to it from Bestwood" (*SL* 10).

12. J. R. Watson, "'The country of my heart': D. H. Lawrence and the East Midlands Landscape," in Gāmini Salgādo and G. K. Das (eds), *The Spirit of D. H. Lawrence*, Macmillan, London 1988, pp. 16–31, proposes a comparison between the landscape described by Lawrence, "known and familiar ... and, above all, understood," and today's: "Even today, the landscape of the Nottinghamshire-Derbyshire border is the same kind of broken semi-industrial scene, with buildings interspersed with field and farmland. It contains within itself, as Lawrence saw so clearly, the central change of modern England, the movement from agrarian openness and small-scale cottage industry to a fully industrialised environment" (p. 26).

13. Gerald Doherty, "The Dialectic of Space in D. H. Lawrence's *Sons and*

Lovers," *Modern Fiction Studies* 39 (1993), pp. 327–43, points out that the novel "insistently oscillates between claustrophobic, protective enclosures and unlimited vistas," and describes the miners' houses as "hermetic space, each dwelling with its own small rectangular rooms is a micro-image of the larger configuration of which it forms a part," inside of which the inhabitants "are compacted, crowded together, engaged in the kind of repetitive routines that extreme contiguity imposes upon them" (pp. 229–30).

14. In the chapter "House and Universe," Gaston Bachelard, *The Poetics of Space* (1958), trans. by Maria Jolas, Beacon Press, Boston 1969, pp. 38–73, shows how the archetypical home, is closely connected to its universality, to its being for its inhabitants, the center of the world. In this regard, it is necessary to have contact with the space outside the house, with the unknown, with the force of the elements, for the house to constitute a protection and fixed point in the life of its inhabitants. In planned housing, particularly in the city, but also in row houses like the miners', outside space is lacking and the inhabitants must continually seek it elsewhere.

15. Rural life, connected with fields and farm, brings a different type of socialization related mostly to festivals that involve the whole community. The pub, other than being a prevalently masculine place, is an extension of the camaraderie that the miners enjoy in the mine.

16. To be precise, the husband's admission is limited to the threshold. He may visit his wife, but only for a short period and by maintaining a certain distance from her person. By now totally deprived of power in the domestic universe, he does not dare come closer, as if only distance renders still possible a *modus vivendi* in the same environment.

17. The antagonism in this family seems to characterize all the miners' families and Lawrence suggests it is closely connected to the process of alienation occurring in the working class.

18. Nigel Kelsey, *D. H. Lawrence: Sexual Crisis*, Macmillan, London 1991, notices in Morel's distancing, Mrs. Morel's conquering of the space in the domestic universe: "in Morel's absence Mrs. Morel, the real driving force of the household, gradually inculcates an array of bourgeois values from which the uneducated Morel is acutely alienated" (p. 82). Imposing her own code on the house and the children, Mrs. Morel causes Morel to be "ideologically stripped of his humanity, reduced to a husk, a functional machine, both by the industry that employs him and the household members who need him financially. Morel's presence is wanted only as a reminder that he is safe and economically viable" (p. 83). According to Terry Eagleton, "Psychoanalysis (*Sons and Lovers*)" (1983), in Peter Widdowson (ed.), *D. H. Lawrence*, Longman, London 1992, pp. 62–66, Mrs. Morel's wielding of power in the domestic universe and the consequent unseating of Mr. Morel reflect "the 'sexual division of labour,' which in capitalist society takes the form of the male parent being used as labour-power in the productive process while the female parent is left to provide the material and emotional 'maintenance' of him and the labour-force of the future (the children)" (p. 63). See also Paul Delany, "*Sons and Lovers*: The Morel Marriage as a War of Position," *D. H. Lawrence Review* 21 (1989), pp. 153–65.

19. Notice, for example, Morel's serenity, when at dawn he can sit near the fire,

eat his meal with a knife, without the ceremony of family meals at table: "with his family about, meals were never so pleasant ... . Then, in solitude, he ate, and drank, often sitting, in cold weather, on a little stool with his back to the warm chimney piece, his food on the fender, his cup on the hearth" (*SL* 37–38).

20. Time is spent at home with the firstborn during recurring rituals such as sharing breakfast before he goes to work, helping him dress, etc.

21. Garnett cut certain passages dedicated to William, decisively reducing this character's importance in the novel. In this regard, Michael Black, "A Kind of Bristling in the Darkness: Memory and Metaphor in Lawrence," *Critical Review* (Melbourne) 32 (1992), pp. 29–44, observes that "now that the complete text of the novel is at last available in the Cambridge edition, we can see the care with which William's case is established as a precedent for Paul's, so justifying the plural nouns in the title. This in turn alerts us to the formal parallels between the climaxes at the end of each Part" (p. 32). The Cambridge edition of *Sons and Lovers* (1992) integrates for the first time the parts cut by Edward Garnett in the 1913 edition (10% of the length of the novel). See, in this regard, Helen Baron and Carl Baron's introduction to the CUP edition, pp. xxi–lxxi; and, also by Helen Baron, the essay "Editing *Sons and Lovers*," *The Journal of the D. H. Lawrence Society* (1994–95), pp. 8–20. Opinions favorable to Garnett's cuts, "frequently aimed at tightening scenes of situational drama, eliminating repetitive elements in them, helping them to become more richly suggestive or more sharply visualized" (p. 47) as well as a detailed analysis of the passages about William are found in Paul Eggert, "Opening Up the Text: The Case of *Sons and Lovers*," in Keith Brown (ed.), *Rethinking Lawrence*, Open UP, Milton Keynes and Philadelphia 1990, pp. 38–52.

22. The element of distinction in the Morel's house, other than foreshadowing the future family houses, positioned higher in the town and therefore higher socially, constitutes a connection with the story "The Christening," where the respectable house built by the protagonist, an old miner, is figured as the fruit of a fierce struggle for a higher position, a struggle frustrated by the scandal of an illegitimate son.

23. Regarding Mrs. Morel's position in the inside/outside, public/private opposition, Kelsey, *D. H. Lawrence: Sexual Crisis*, cit., pp. 94–96, observes that "it is from the private stability of the household, moreover, that Mrs. Morel employs the tactics of a political-social exclusion of a section of the public ... hegemonically enshrining her own specific *public* identification within the private sphere ... . Mrs. Morel's major victories, however, occur as a result of her battling hard both *for* and *within* the private sphere. To effect a political identification with the household, to fight so intensely for its internal ideological dynamics, the place as for so many women of her work and leisure, is to fight for a realm of influence and power however limited, for her own self-determination and relative independence."

24. Each spouse adheres to his/her own code and the inevitable conflicts which consequently arise between them are interpreted by Graham Holderness, *D. H. Lawrence: History, Ideology and Fiction*, Gill and Macmillan, Dublin 1982, as Morel's attempt to impose the rigid system of values belonging to his own community and Mrs. Morel's struggle to overcome the social conventions of the working class community where she now belongs. The domestic conflict is therefore substantially a conflict of values which "shows Mr. Morel trying to establish the norms

and conventions of the community, and Mrs. Morel trying to transcend them by individual appropriation of the child, making him different, isolated from the collective life of the community" (p. 144).

25. The longest journey undergone spontaneously by Morel is the walking trip to Nottingham with his miner friend: a traditional trip for the Bestwood community, which entails stopping at a number of pubs along the way, in a growing euphoria that climaxes in the arrival at the city. His other trip is the obligatory one to London to meet his wife after William's death.

26. "Don't think I didn't like your *house* Annie … . But it's nice to be in my own *home* again" (*SL* 422, emphasis mine). On the concept of appropriation of a living space as an essential part of one's identity, see Emma Corigliano, *Tempo spazio identità. No place like home*, Angeli, Milano 1991, pp. 26–30, and Norberg-Schulz, *The concept of dwelling*, cit., pp. 13–30.

27. Black, "A Kind of Bristling in the Darkness: Memory and Metaphor in Lawrence," cit., pp. 29–30, notes in the opposition between the security provided by the light inside the house, made precarious by the parents' discord, and the threat from the outside, symbolized by the rustling of the wind, by the darkness and immensity of the void, a structural element of the novel, in other words the opposition between the necessity for protection inside the domestic walls (the center) and the threatening unknown of the outside world: "The good feeling corresponds with being in a circle of warm friendly light, especially in the home … . Yet the safety of the house is precarious if the parents are at odds … the position of the house on the hillside, facing the shell-shape of hollowed-out land in front, is a central part of the feeling of being threatened … . The house is precariously perched above a void…; and hostile forces, typified by the wind, are threatening to dislodge it into that void."

28. According to Holderness, *D. H. Lawrence: History, Ideology and Fiction*, cit., p. 147, William's death and Paul's inability to detach himself from the domestic environment are the immediate consequences of Mrs. Morel's fierce efforts to project her sons towards the middle class, distancing them from their own class and community by a process which, instead of freeing them, relegates them to isolation and separation: "this process destroys William and leads Paul into a position of isolated singleness where he is wholly dependent on his mother, so that her death leaves him alone and abandoned, himself drifting towards death."

29. Michael Black, *D. H. Lawrence: Sons and Lovers*, CUP, Cambridge 1992, p. 77, notices in Paul's fear of losing his mother and the stability which she represents the true essence of the threat from the outside world and the unknown which it symbolizes: "the positive forces—stability, solidity, support, warmth, love—are located in the mother through the analogues (lamplight in the home, and the lamppost outside). The universal light, the darkness, the space, which 'scoop' at the land … and into which he fears to be sucked, are actually … the obverse of the same force: dependency, the fear of being bereft."

30. Doherty, "The Dialectic of Space in D. H. Lawrence's *Sons and Lovers*," cit., p. 334, describes the second part of the novel as "a general release from the claustrophobic oppression that dominated Part One." Such "release" entails, on the one hand, "descriptions of group-walks in the countryside, visits to the seaside and to cities, a break-out from domestic entrapment," while on the other hand,

the widening of horizons renders the protagonist "a subject in process, open to all the ontological *Angst* that the unlimiting of spatial horizons brings in its wake."

31. The idea of a female presiding at the domestic hearth, the center to which the man returns, is discussed by Lawrence in *Fantasia of the Unconscious*, in which it is viewed as an essential element in the balance and harmony between the sexes: "there should be a great balance between the sexes. Man, in the daytime, must follow his own soul's greatest impulse, and give himself to life-work and risk himself to death…, the woman has her world, her positivity: the world of love, of emotion, of sympathy. And it behoves every man in his hour to take off his shoes and relax and give himself to his woman and her world … . Primarily and supremely man is *always* the pioneer of life, adventuring onward into the unknown, alone with his own temerarious, dauntless soul. Woman for him exists only in the twilight, by the camp fire, when day has departed" (*FU* 100–1, 109).

32. An example is the episode in which Mrs. Morel, discovering an unfamiliar flower in her garden, of exotic provenance ("I guess they come from Switzerland where they say they have such lovely things," *SL* 199), immediately calls Paul to share with him the marvel and excitement of the discovery.

33. The isolation is emphasized by the inhabitants themselves, especially by the lady of the house, who welcomes Mrs. Morel and Paul by referring to the rarity of the event: "I *am* glad to see you … . We're only too thankful to see a new face, it's so lost up here" (*SL* 154). In the chapter "Identity," Remotti, *Luoghi e corpi*, cit., pp. 76–107, shows the constant need to compare one's place with the outside world, with the diversity of other places, a comparison which on the one hand jeopardizes one's identity, but also saves one from isolation, paralysis and death.

34. The quotation is not identified. In the notes to *Sons and Lovers* (CUP, 1992), the translation is given without reference to the source, pointing out, however, that it is part of the fin de siècle cultural climate (highlighting a literary *topos* connected to the decline of aristocratic property-holding) and indicating the recurrence of the same concept in other works by D. H. Lawrence such as *The White Peacock*, *Twilight in Italy*, "Study of Thomas Hardy" and *Women in Love* (cf. *SL*, "Explanatory Notes," p. 535).

35. "This atmosphere, where everything took a religious value, came with a subtle fascination to him … . His own mother was logical. Here there was something different, something he loved, something that at times he hated" (*SL* 177–78).

36. Regarding this character, usually attacked by critics as the quintessence of sterile spiritualization, Adrienne E. Gavin, "Miriam's Mirror: Reflections on the Labelling of Miriam Leivers," *D. H. Lawrence Review* 24 (1992), pp. 27–41, observes how the representation of the character is in part distorted by the viewpoints of other characters, in particular Paul and Mrs. Morel; she states that "Miriam is a girl growing into womanhood and experiencing her first, long, painful relationship. She is in love with a boy growing into manhood who is not, finally, in love with her, and much of what we see of her is profoundly affected by this unrequited love. As she matures, much of the mist, romantic and otherwise, clears from her eyes" (p. 41).

37. During the adolescents' excursion to Wingfield Manor, Miriam "did not live till they came to the church" (*SL* 202). At the end of the novel, Paul meets her in a Nottingham church where "she looked as if she had got something, at any rate: some hope in heaven if not in earth" (*SL* 457).

38. An opposition later confirmed in the episode of the seaside vacation, when Paul "talked to her [Miriam] endlessly about his love of horizontals: how they ... meant to him the eternity of the will: just as the bowed Norman arches of the church, repeating themselves, meant the dogged leaping forward of the persistent human soul, ... in contradiction to the perpendicular lines and to the Gothic arch, which ... leapt up at heaven and touched the ecstasy and lost itself in the divine. Himself, he said, was Norman, Miriam was Gothic" (*SL* 215).

39. Miriam's awareness that the country life, its isolation and distance from cultural centers are causes of separation and interior impoverishment, is confirmed by her observations on Miss Limb's strangeness during the walk with Clara and Paul to Strelley Mill: "It's not the right sort of life for her [Miss Limb]. I [Miriam] think it's cruel to bury her there" (*SL* 277).

40. In reference to this episode, Colin Milton, *Lawrence and Nietzsche*, Aberdeen UP, Aberdeen 1987, p. 90, extends Miriam's gratification from the spiritual realm to the sensual one, emphasizing that "despite the fact that there is no 'inferior' physical contact in the experience, it is described in a way which suggests that her apparently 'exalted' feelings have their roots in a sensuality which, on a conscious level, she rejects and represses." A link between sensuality and desire for transcendence, together with a tendency towards an aesthetic transfiguration of reality which is constantly present in Miriam, is also noted by Holderness, *D. H. Lawrence: History, Ideology and Fiction*, cit., p. 154, who observes that "Miriam is constantly leading Paul towards experiences of a quasi-sexual, religious intensity, experiences which sometimes recall the aesthetic intensities of *The White Peacock* and *The Trespasser*." In reference to the rose bush episode, the critic observes that "flowers are being transformed into something 'holy,' 'immortal,' capable of worship; living things translated by Miriam's emotional intensity into transcendent objects." Black, *D. H. Lawrence: Sons and Lovers*, cit., p. 75, agrees on this point, stating that at the end of the episode, "we are left with the sense that this, for them, and especially for her, is a spiritual substitute for sexuality."

41. In this regard, Worthen, *D. H. Lawrence*, cit., p. 28, observes that "Paul finds Miriam's invitation imprisoning, because it leaves him and his body out of the count. There is no experience of the other as 'other' in such an offer, or such a sacrifice. Paul, young and vitally inexperienced, is helpless; he can do nothing except try and get away until next time, when he can be more guarded." According to Karen Z. Sproles, "D. H. Lawrence and the Pre-Raphaelites: Love Among the Ruins," *D. H. Lawrence Review* 22 (1990), pp. 299–305, Paul's discomfort is determined by his sexual immaturity, compared in this episode to Miriam's sexual maturity: "[Paul] cannot allow Miriam to have sexual desires when he is not yet sure he can cope with his own ... . The connection between Miriam's sensual pleasure in looking at the roses and her sexual desire for Paul is clearly established. She can look openly at the roses and at him ... . But Paul turns away. The only comfortable place he can find to locate emotion is in the rose bush" (p. 300).

42. Miriam's identification with the "victim" Mary Queen of Scots is confirmed several times during the novel: "She was wearing a new net blouse ... . It had a high collar with a tiny ruff, reminding her of Mary Queen of Scots, and making her ... look wonderfully a woman" (*SL* 255–56).

43. A similar situation is found at Annie's house, where Paul throws one of Mrs. Morel's grey hairs in the fire: an instinctive gesture which alludes to the imminent death of his mother and the end of their relationship.

44. "He noticed how her breasts swelled inside her blouse, and how her shoulder curved handsomely under the thin muslin at the top of her arm" (*SL* 270).

45. Paul and Miriam's space is in a certain sense violated by Clara's logic. Lotman, *Tipologia della cultura*, cit., p. 227, states: "the concept of limited space, of a frontier, has value insofar as it can be violated, and the violation is not always by a physical movement, but also by an act of will and by *liberation*." (translation mine).

46. Regarding the necessity of coming to terms with an Other reality with certain negative connotations, as an essential element of passage from the country to the city and therefore of the jump to a higher social level, David Newmarch, "'Death of a Young Man in London': Ernest Lawrence and William Morel in *Sons and Lovers*," *Durham University Journal* 76 (1983), pp. 73–79, observes that "the daily reality of William's work in the Port of London ... or of Paul's up the 'dismal stairs of Jordan's Surgical Appliance Factory,' seems far from heroic, but that does not mean that Mrs. Morel is simply deluded or naïve. Rather, it seems to me that we have ourselves to be able to adjust to a difference in the emotional perspectives of ambition, success, making our way in the world" (p. 74).

47. This is a parallel episode to George and Meg's supper in the Nottingham hotel in *The White Peacock*.

48. A reaction which emphasizes, on the one hand, how much the mines are imprinted on Paul's mind (who "reads" the place with the tools which he brings with him; cf. La Cecla, *Perdersi*, cit., pp. 26–30), and, on the other hand, how the world of urban industry (with its darkness and desolation) is not, after all, so very different from the mines.

49. Observe how entrance into another universe means to the protagonist the meeting of a challenge, an initiation to the laws of that place.

50. This experience, traumatic for Paul, who becomes aware of the impossibility of finding a companion in his mother — "*Why* can't you walk? *Why* can't you come with me to places?" (*SL* 282) — corresponds to the logic of development in the novel.

51. Just as Willey Farm was only partly Miriam's place, so Nottingham is only partly Clara's place, a place that she resists and from which she seeks to free herself.

52. "The parlour ... was a small, stuffy, defunct room..., the kitchen ... was a little, darkish room too, but it was smothered in white lace" (*SL* 301).

53. In fact, it is Clara who opens his eyes to the abnormality of his relationship with Miriam: "she [Miriam] doesn't want any of your soul communion. That's your own imagination. She wants you" (*SL* 321).

54. "'But the town's all right,' he [Paul] said. 'It's only temporary. This is the crude, clumsy make-shift we've practised on, till we find out what the idea is. The town will come all right'" (*SL* 314).

55. In reference to this episode, Doherty ("The Dialectic of Space in D. H. Lawrence's *Sons and Lovers*," cit., pp. 337–38) states that "disclosures of space may involve a specifically literal dimension, as the homely and familiar is exchanged for the remote and distant. Paul and Clara's search for a secret love-making site

Notes: Chapter 4

by the Trent river turns on such an exchange. Transformed into romantic explorers, they penetrate the unknown."

56. "Every step creaked, and his back was creeping, lest the old woman's door should open behind him, up *above*. He fumbled with the door at the *bottom*" (*SL* 382, emphasis mine).

57. "When he came to, he wondered what was near his eyes, curving and strong with life in the dark, and what voice it was speaking. Then he realised it was the grass, and the peewit was calling ... . What was she. A strong, strange, wild life, that breathed with his in the darkness through this hour" (*SL* 398). Francesco Gozzi, *La narrativa del primo Lawrence*, ETS, Pisa 1979, p. 118, points out how in this episode, Paul is able to "make Clara disappear" in the "immensity of passion," confirming his tendency to elude "every personal relation, enjoying the impersonality of their collaboration at work and their sexual relationships to make Clara a kind of *invisible woman*." (translation mine). Worthen, *D. H. Lawrence*, cit., pp. 30–1, after pointing out that the episode is the only occasion in which "Paul and Clara experience ... a revelation of each other," maintains that "this passage — which entered the novel in its last writing, around October 1912 — presents a radically new kind of bodily and sexual experience: something Lawrence wanted to write about when *Sons and Lovers* was at last completed." Kingsley Widmer, "Desire and Negation: the Dialectics of Passion in D. H. Lawrence," in Salgãdo and Das (eds), *The Spirit of D. H. Lawrence*, cit., pp. 125–43, notes how Paul's relationship with Miriam fails because of the "constricting provincial Protestant ethos" of which the girl is the very incarnation, and the relationship with Clara brings for the first time in the novel "the 'baptism of fire in passion,' the sexual realisation of 'impersonal desire'." For Widmer, "Paul and Clara's intercourse ... in a field at night, is not mere coitus but transformation ... . 'having known the immensity of passion,' they also 'know their own nothingness,' which is the desire-negation recognition of the true ultimate flow of life" (p. 134).

58. Wayne Templeton, "The Drift Towards Life: Paul Morel's Search for a Place," *D. H. Lawrence Review* 15 (1982), pp. 177–94, indicates in the fight with Baxter the culmination of Paul's growth, the moment in which he reaches harmony between body and soul: "He loses to Dawes when he stops to ponder his unknown and novel potential: the ability to be strong and unified, body and mind" (p. 188). Jeffrey Meyers, *D. H. Lawrence: A Biography*, Macmillan, London 1990, p. 115, in his psychoanalytical reading of *Sons and Lovers* as a therapeutic work, makes much of the Paul/Baxter relationship as the complement to the resolution of Paul's conflictual relationship with his parents: "Dawes is so similar in speech and temperament to Walter Morel, his fight with Paul signifies Paul's need to be punished by his symbolic father for usurping his real father's role as lover and for unconsciously desiring sex with his mother." The fight between Paul and Baxter is read Oedipally by Black, *D. H. Lawrence: Sons and Lovers*, cit., p. 61, who calls attention to the place where the fight occurs and to the significance which Clara and Baxter assume in light of the conflicting relationship between Paul's parents: "Paul and Dawes meet and fight at night ... in a place where three roads cross, where Oedipus, unknowing, killed his father... . In the Dawes affair Lawrence is very subtly rewriting the Oedipus legend. The novel has Paul fall in love with women in whom we can see something of his mother, and he half-wants to kill, but importantly is reconciled with, a man in whom he can almost see his father."

59. An important episode inasmuch as it represents, on the one hand, the sea as the place providing formative experiences that would be impossible in the everyday world, while on the other, it represents an attempt at liberation and detachment from the mother (to whom Paul suggests that she go to his sister's at Sheffield), an attempt which is suddenly interrupted by her sickness upon his return home.

60. This scene recalls what Bachelard, *The Poetics of Space*, cit. pp. 45–46, describes as "an image of concentrated being ... this house that "clings" to its inhabitant and becomes the cell of a body with its walls close together. The refuge shrinks in size. And with its protective qualities increased, it grows outwardly stronger. From having been a refuge, it has become a redoubt. The thatched cottage becomes a fortified castle for the recluse, who must learn to conquer fear within its walls."

61. This is another element linking him to Baxter: the lack of a center, of a place to which he may belong. Templeton, "The Drift Towards Life: Paul Morel's Search for a Place," cit., pp. 190–91, maintains that the protagonist's dilemma, once he has resolved his conflictual relationship with his mother, resides "not in his inclination towards death but in his feeling of homelessness, of being so alienated that, while he exists and can continue to survive, he has no place in which to exist." In light of these observations, the critic sees in Paul's final choice, his facing the phosphorescent lights of the city, the synthesis of his interior conflict, the discovery of a place of belonging: "he walks to the city (integration into the community) having found a place and knowing at last how to overcome the estrangement that has plagued him thus far in life." Holderness (*D. H. Lawrence: History, Ideology and Fiction*, cit., pp. 157–58) identifies Paul's self-destructive impulse with his isolation and separation from community: "Man cannot live by 'life' alone. And so *Sons and Lovers* ends with Paul facing the awful doom of isolation in its most poignant form, yet determined to resist it ... . From this limit of experience Paul walks back — towards the town; back towards relationship, interdependence, social connection; back towards the community in which alone human life can have meaning and reality."

Chapter 5

1. "I only care about what a woman *is*— what she *is*— inhumanly, physiologically, materially — according to the use of the word: but for me, what she *is* as a phenomenon..., instead of what she feels according to the human conception" (*Letters* ii. 183).

2. The destructive effects produced, at a psychic level, by the war emerge in the hallucinated monologue of Captain Herbertson in Lilly's room: "And on and on he talked..., it was ... the same hot, blind, anguished voice of a man who has seen too much, experienced too much, and doesn't know where to turn. None of the glamour of returned heroes, none of the romance of war: only a hot, blind, mesmerised voice, going on and on, mesmerised by a vision that the soul cannot bear" (*AR* 119). It is no coincidence that the confession occurs in the middle of the night,

symbolic of the dark state left by a war, "humanly quite false" (*AR* 119), and that it covers most of Chapter X, placed in the middle of the novel.

3. In reference to Lawrence and Frieda's persecution during their stay in Cornwall, rendered vividly in the chapter "The Nightmare" in *Kangaroo*, pp. 212–59, cf. Louise E. Wright, "D. H. Lawrence, Robert Mountsier and the Journalist Spy Controversy," *The Journal of the D. H. Lawrence Society* (1992–93), pp. 7–21. Particularly interesting, especially in reference to the sense of terror and the xenophobic attitude of the local population, is Helen Dunmore's novel, *Zennor in Darkness*, Penguin, London 1994.

4. Both novels signal a new start in Lawrence's artistic career and intellectual quest, as suggested also by the names of the characters Alvina and Aaron, which both start with "a."

5. "The whole morale of the house rested immediately on Miss Frost … . She was steering the poor domestic ship of Manchester House" (*LG* 7). Miss Frost is far from exercising a positive influence on Alvina, as suggested also by her name, Frost.

6. A Frenchman, two Swiss (respectively speaking French and German) and an Italian; at the outbreak of World War I some of them will be recalled to their countries and the company will have to disband. Even through such an event, the novel witnesses the disintegrating effect that the war has on human relationships.

7. In this regard, Hilary Simpson, *D. H. Lawrence and Feminism*, Crom Helm, London and Canberra 1982, p. 76, observes that "the pre-war Lawrence was intensely interested in the theme of a young woman breaking out from the conventional life prescribed for her … even though he was dissatisfied with the traditional methods of portraying such a rebellion and with its traditional fictional conclusions. Lawrence represents Alvina's revolt as the triumph of a kind of healthy vulgarity over an outdated, false refinement. She escapes from 'the beautiful, but unbearable tyranny' of 'purity and high-mindedness' as represented by Miss Frost, into the vulgarity of being a midwife, a cinema pianist and a member of a variety troupe."

8. Notwithstanding Madame's initial opposition to Alvina and Ciccio's union ("they live in a bad way, the Italians. They do not know the English home," *LG* 181), it is she who in a certain sense arranges the marriage, appreciating the value of Alvina's dowry and the use that she can make of it.

9. Gary A. Wiener, "Lawrence's 'Little Girl Lost,'" *D. H. Lawrence Review* 19 (1987), pp. 243–53, states that Italy, although unknown and primitive, presents characteristics of richness and vitality which, contrasted to England's sterility, signifies for Alvina a positive destination: "Inhabited by morally upright yet emotionally cold types such as Miss Frost and Miss Pinnegar, Alvina's England is barren as a desert. But once Alvina arrives in Italy … there are lush descriptions of narcissus, olives, irises, acorns, violets, almond blossoms, crocuses, hyacinths, plentiful corn, magenta anemones, and more. Even during the final scene describing Ciccio's imminent departure, the richness of the Italian milieu comes through" (p. 246).

10. In this regard, Michael Bell, *D. H. Lawrence: Language and Being*, CUP, Cambridge 1992, p. 143, observes that "Aaron's departure from the married home,

and the unfeeling manner of his leaving, reflect Lawrence's more radical project with respect to the whole social realm that marriage traditionally represents." On this subject see also Barbara Mensch, *D. H. Lawrence and the Authoritarian Personality*, Macmillan, London 1991, pp. 119–69.

11. "'Well!' cried Josephine to him. 'How do you come here?' 'I play the flute,' he [Aaron] answered" (*AR* 53–54). It is art which permits his passing through social barriers, offering the possibility of being admitted in Other environments, as for Gudrun in *Women in Love*: "Gudrun had already come to know a good many people of repute and standing ... . She was a *Kulturträger*, a medium for the culture of ideas" (*WL* 16).

12. Aaron and Lilly's intimacy helps to bring Aaron back to life, whereas it gives Lilly an unpleasant sense of surpassing a threshold, of exposing too much: "I wonder why I bother with him ... . As soon as this man's really better he'll punch me in the wind, metaphorically if not actually, for having interfered with him" (*AR* 96).

13. According to John Turner, "Comedy and Hysteria in *Aaron's Rod*," in Paul Eggert and John Worthen (eds), *D. H. Lawrence and Comedy*, CUP, Cambridge 1996, pp. 70–88, this episode confirms Aaron's desire to detach himself from a world which he no longer feels is his, maintaining his position as observer on the threshold, a position which he will keep during the entire novel: "from the security of his garden shed, the unseen Aaron surveys the home he has deserted. Yet this is the perspective that he needs in order to resist the impingements of family life, with all its insatiable demands upon him. Jealously the outsider must guard his inner space. Later on, in Italy, he finds a new perspective ... . Even when the expatriate community presses him close, the old defences still work ... . He has come abroad to safeguard the foreignness of his inner self" (p. 78).

14. John B. Humma, *Metaphor and Meaning in D. H. Lawrence's Later Novels*, University of Missouri Press, Columbia 1990, p. 13, sees in the scene of the meeting at Argyle's house a moment in which the correspondence between Aaron and the Giotto bell tower is highlighted, as "the tower, through its phallic suggestiveness, provokes natural associations with Aaron's rod — with Florence, too, through its name and through its identification with the lilies, since the flute is said in that earlier passage to blossom with red lilies." For Turner, "Comedy and Hysteria in *Aaron's Rod*," cit., p. 78, it represents the distance between Aaron and the rest of the world: "Aaron most typically looks out upon this new world from a hotel window in Milan ('XX Settembre') and from a high attic-terrace in Florence ('High Up over the Cathedral Square')."

15. According to Simpson, *D. H. Lawrence and Feminism*, cit., pp. 77–78, the arrival in Pescocalascio signals the turning point in the novel, a starting point for the protagonist's regeneration, as "the real hero of the book turns out to be not so much Ciccio as the primitive but breathtakingly beautiful landscape to which he transports her ... . It is in this remote part of Italy that Alvina is finally 'lost — lost — lost utterly,' possessed by a 'savage hardness' which issues in terrible despair and wild happiness"; for Simpson the landscape exercises a liberating effect on the protagonist and she perceives it as a necessary phase in her growth and passage to a new life.

16. "The railway would take her anywhere" (*LG* 331).

17. "She was happy in the quietness with Ciccio, now they had their own pleasant room.... She felt he was never very far away: that he was a good deal a stranger in Califano, as she was: that he clung to her presence as she to his ... . She was one with them. But she could never endure it for a life-time. It was only a test on her. Ciccio must take her to America, or England — to America preferably" (*LG* 331, 320). According to David Holbrook, *Where D. H. Lawrence Was Wrong about Women*, Associated University Presses, London and Toronto 1992, p. 271, nevertheless, at Pescocalascio "what we feel [Alvina] has achieved is a real, existential state of being, in touch with the natural world, and with her husband, who is both richly intimate and yet at times distant with that inscrutable, reserved distance of the rather primitive man, which Lawrence admired so much."

18. In both novels the train is a place of interaction between various social classes, of the first contact with an Other world where one finds habits and ways of life of various communities: "here, in the third class carriage, there was no tight string round every man ... . They had a sufficient amount of callousness and indifference and natural equanimity ... . But in the dining car were mostly middle-class, well-to-do Italians [looking] with some criticism, and some class-envy" (*AR* 199–200). "She [Alvina] loved the lounging carelessness of the train..., hearing the Italians round her though they were neither as beautiful nor as melodious as she expected" (*LG* 299).

19. The awakening to a new life through a foreigner, after the "death" brought about by the war, is present as well in the novella *The Ladybird* (1923).

20. Paradoxically, it is Alvina who "save[s] them [Ciccio and Pancrazio] from extinction" (*LG* 314), and represents to them the possibility of escape, a passage to elsewhere, the glamor of what is different, which permits them to defend themselves from the hostility of the place's inhabitants: "he loved serving her. He [Pancrazio] seemed to see a fairness, a luminousness in the northern soul, something free, touched with divinity such as 'these people here' lacked entirely" (*LG* 325).

21. According to Jill Franks, *Revisionist Resurrection Mythologies: A Study of D. H. Lawrence's Italian Works*, Peter Lang, New York 1994, p. 96, Aaron's lack of development is due to a failure to interact not only with characters but also with populations and cultures: "In *Aaron's Rod* there is no transformation of the main characters because they do not interact in the deep way symbolized by sexual intercourse...: there is virtually no exchange between the insouciant, vital Southerners and the sterile, frustrated Northerners."

22. In reference to the correspondence between the broken ball in the beginning of the novel and the loss of the flute due to the exploding bomb, Humma, *Metaphor and Meaning in D. H. Lawrence's Later Novels*, cit., p. 15, observes that "the breaking of the blue ball signifies in part the disintegration or perversion of time-honored traditional values, especially when we think of this scene in relation to the Christmas-tree scene at the Bricknell's. The broken rod, the shattered panpipe, signifies the triumph of mechanistic functionalism over 'the spontaneous life-ideal.' That is, the modern tendency to disintegration or fragmentation sweeps before it the ancient (including medieval: hence Giotto's tower) ideal of organic integration." According to Frank Kermode, *Lawrence*, Fontana/Collins, Suffolk 1973, p. 81, "the bombing of the flute is the end of an era, the sign that he must

move into a newer and harsher one, an epoch of power in which there will be 'deep, unfathomable, free submission,' especially by women."

23. Aaron's quest, which began with his flight from home with his flute and ends in failure with the loss of the flute, forms an analogy to the protagonist in *The Trespasser*. Siegmund too abandons his family in hopes of reaching, far from them and in an Other place, the Absolute of experience, a search which not only fails, but ends tragically after his return home. Unlike Siegmund, Aaron does not return home and does not stay for a long time in one place; he continues his quest, which, although evading death, does not seem to promise any fixed goal nor any experiential Absolute.

24. On this topic, Franks, *Revisionist Resurrection Mythologies*, cit., p. 104, observes: "Although Aaron felt that the Piazza della Signoria was the center of the world, its effect on him was much less than the effect that mountains, streams and donkeys had on Alvina. This comparison illustrates the fact that rural Italy was the place of places for Lawrence, from which he drew more creative inspiration than any other place." Bell, *D. H. Lawrence: Language and Being*, cit., pp. 138–39, has a different opinion; he states that in the "village in the Abruzzi mountains ... peasant life is not idealised and Alvina cannot truly join it. As in *Twilight in Italy*, Lawrence notes the peasants' recurrent desire to escape their claustrophobic life form. Indeed, Alvina is accepted by Ciccio's neighbours only because she continues to represent a superior form of life to them. Meanwhile, Alvina recognises that, despite her love of the place itself, she does not really wish to identify herself with its essentially alien human element."

Chapter 6

1. Some weeks after its publication in 1915, *The Rainbow* was condemned for obscenity, with a verdict from the Bow Street Magistrat Court. All copies were destroyed and for more than ten years (until 1926), the novel was unavailable in England. The consequences of this editorial catastrophe extended inevitably to the second part of the saga, *Women in Love*, already finished in 1916. For four years no publisher was willing to risk publishing it; the novel came out for the first time in 1920 in a private edition (a fate destined to repeat itself for others of the writer's works, especially *Lady Chatterley's Lover*).

2. It is enough to remember that Birkin's "sermon" on dissolution is taken directly from "The Crown," while echoes of "Study of Thomas Hardy" can be heard everywhere in *The Rainbow* and *Women in Love*.

3. On the predominance of the historical perspective in *The Rainbow*, see Mark Kinkead-Weekes, "The Sense of History in *The Rainbow*," in Peter Preston and Peter Hoare (eds), *D. H. Lawrence in the Modern World*, Macmillan, London 1989, pp. 121–38.

4. Regarding the harmony between man and nature that characterizes the beginning of *The Rainbow*, John Haegert, "Lawrence's World Elsewhere: Elegy and History in *The Rainbow*," *CLIO* 15 (1986), pp. 115–35, observes that "the pastoral world of this section is notable both for its peacefulness, secluded from the larger

world of time, and for its plentitude, grounded in a living 'exchange and interchange' with the fertile earth ... . The associated imagery of wave and seed and seasonal cycle, with their notion of rising and falling life, attests to the underlying and 'eternal stillness' of the old Brangwen world. From its elemental perspective all human effort and all human movement are circumscribed by a sense of cyclic fate in which all play their humble part" (p. 119).

5. In reference to the sense of disorientation linked to losing a familiar place, see Leonard Lutwack, *The Role of Place in Literature*, Syracuse UP, New York 1984, in particular the chapter "Placelessness," pp. 182–245, where the author states that "assaults on the certainties of place are reflected in literature by frequent expressions of loss and regret over the passing of old places and bitter disaffection with new places ... . The despair of deracination is countered with the hope of restoring attachments to remnant places, expatriation alternates with return to the impaired homeland, disaffection is answered with accommodation to the new places of our time" (p. 184). See also "La scomparsa dei punti familiari di riferimento" and "L'architettura moderna come lobotomia spaziale," in La Cecla, *Perdersi*, cit., pp. 33–34 and 37–40; and in relation to home, the chapter "I significati dell'abitare," in Corigliano, *Tempo spazio identità*, cit., pp. 33–52.

6. In his "Introduction" to *Donne innamorate*, Einaudi, Torino 1995, pp. v-xxvii, Giovanni Cianci notes in the anxiety that characterizes the Brangwens of succeeding generations the emergence of a "progressive erosion of the organic community, the loss of a sense of harmonic integration and of vital circularity," which he attributes to "the growing difficulty of personal and social relations." In *Women in Love*, says the critic, "the sense of unstoppable crisis that hits ... the third generation of Brangwens ... is due to the progressive loss of all fixed points, the dissolution of all anchors" (pp. ix-xi). (translation mine).

7. "'I wanted eternal union with a man too: another kind of love,' he [Birkin] said ... . 'You can't have it, because it's false, impossible,' she [Ursula] said. 'I don't believe that,' he answered" (*WL* 481); "'And whom shall I submit to?' he [Aaron] said. 'Your soul will tell you,' replied the other" (*AR* 299); "'I'll come back' he [Ciccio] said. 'Sure?' she [Alvina] whispered" (*LG* 339). These open endings are destined to repeat themselves in the well-known sentence that ends *The Plumed Serpent*, "'Then go! Oh certainly go!'.... 'You won't let me go!' she [Kate] said to him [Cipriano]" (*PS* 444).

8. In regard to Gudrun's longing for unreachable metropolis, Cianci, in the cited "Introduction," p. xii, states that she, "'anxious bird' ... is attracted to avant-garde capitals without limits, where destabilization and revolt are programmatic (Paris, Munich, Dresden, Vienna, Petersburg, Moscow): but more as an unattainable elsewhere, so that she can delay forever the possibility of finding a definite haven, than a place in which to settle down and eradicate the uncontrollable anxiety of evasion." (translation mine).

9. In regard to the characters' movements which paradoxically twist back upon themselves, Diane S. Bonds, "Going into the Abyss: Literarization in *Women in Love*," *Essays in Literature* 8 (1981), pp. 189–202, observes that "the metaphor of a journey is repeatedly transvalued, and the travels that literalize that metaphor are of equivocal meaning. Ceaseless journeying in a world that is round and that does not run off into space (as Birkin sometimes wishes he could do) is bound eventually

to take on the appearance of travelling in circles. When Birkin returns to the Tyrol to claim Gerald's body…, he questions his transitory mode of existence and the ideal of perpetual journeying into the unknown … . And the final, brief scene of the novel, which pictures Birkin and Ursula back at the Mill, 'both very quiet,' constitutes an implicit reconsideration of the idea of mobility" (p. 195).

10. In reference to Gudrun's problem of orienting herself in her place of origin, Bell (*D. H. Lawrence: Language and Being*, cit., p. 102) notes that "Gudrun has been living away from home and therefore provides the viewpoint for a defamiliarized vision which Lawrence clearly wishes to present as not merely hers. It has a normative force. She experiences it as an unnerving, vertiginous sense of unreality; a sense of living in a completely different 'world.'"

11. "Gudrun had already come to know a good many people of repute and standing … . It would be queer to meet again down here in the Midlands, where their social standing was so diverse, after they had known each other on terms of equality in the houses of sundry acquaintances in town" (*WL* 16). The suspicion is later confirmed when, during a walk, Ursula and Gudrun run into Hermione and Laura Crich at the garden gate and the latter pair "moved off, as if they [Ursula and Gudrun] had been dismissed like inferiors" (*WL* 50).

12. Lawrence uses this image of the imperial Road as a means of access to the heart of Europe in other works of this period. See the two versions of the essay "Christs in the Tyrol" and "The Crucifix Across the Mountains" in *Twilight in Italy and Other Essays*, ed. Paul Eggert, CUP, Cambridge 1994, pp. 43–47, 91–100 and 229–33.

13. According to Inez R. Morris, "African Sculpture Symbols in *Women in Love*," *D. H. Lawrence Review* 16 (1983), pp. 25–43, in the representation of the African statue and the reactions it elicits in the characters, "Lawrence makes an effort to capture the world of the unknown, which in his view, goes beyond the sensual and is not thwarted by the intellectual. He presents a paradoxical condition which the primitive culture of Africa has accomplished but of which the intellectual, civilized western world has no knowledge" (p. 33).

14. Holderness, *D. H. Lawrence: History, Ideology and Fiction*, cit., pp. 174–89, sees the representation of Marsh Farm as the result of Ursula's retrospective myth-making. According to the critic, "we should see the novel not as a record of historical process, with Wiggiston as the culmination of a real history of social decline, but as mythology, where the 'history' is deduced from the present and cast backwards into the past. Marsh Farm is a myth created to fill that blank space in the centre of Wiggiston, that human absence at the heart of the modern community" (p. 180). Although the description of Marsh Farm in the beginning of the novel contains nostalgic language charged with Biblical overtones, in my opinion Holderness' insistence on such myth making is a bit excessive and also ideologically incompatible with the tension towards the unknown (therefore towards the future) that characterizes all the characters of both *The Rainbow* and *Women in Love*.

15. "He [Tom] dreamed of foreign parts. But somehow he had no contact with them. And it was a very strong root which held him to the Marsh, to his own house and land" (*R* 27). Interesting, in this regard, is the reading of *The Rainbow* and *Women in Love* in the Gothic modernist mode offered by Pinkney, "Northernness and Modernism," in *D. H. Lawrence*, cit., pp. 54–99, where "Northernness,"

for all its qualities of "ruins, brokenness, changefulness and grotesqueness," is seen as a fertile alternative to arid, abstract classicism. Pinkney notes in Tom and Lydia's marriage an opening of the closed English Midlands to the cosmopolitism of European capitals, to the creative, regenerative influence of the German avant-garde: "Marrying the Midlands to modernism, the Erewash to Europe, Lydia kick-starts the whole narrative into motion" (p. 71).

16. Haegert, "Lawrence's World Elsewhere: Elegy and History in *The Rainbow*," cit., pp. 120–21, sees in the vital flux which animates the first generation of Brangwens "the drama of human beings struggling to adapt themselves to the rhythmic order of creation. In their mutual attraction both Tom and Lydia aspire toward a timeless condition, toward a return to life's original and unhurried rhythms; in which nature rules rather than social laws and customs; in which life begets life only to fall away in turn in one unalterable motion of existence." According to the critic this "'paradisal' Old World of the first generation is never completely lost or lost sight of in the book" insofar as "in some measure it is always being reasserted..., operative within every generation." See also Mark Kinkead-Weekes, "The Marriage of Opposites in *The Rainbow*," in Mara Kalnins (ed.), *D. H. Lawrence: Centenary Essays*, Classical Press, Bristol 1986, pp. 21–40.

17. Regarding this, Bell, *D. H. Lawrence: Language and Being*, cit., p. 107, observes that, unlike *The Rainbow* in which the passage through several generations "places everything within a temporal frame of understanding whether on a personal, a family, an historical or an evolutionary scale..., the spatial structure of [*Women in Love*] has an immediate dramatic appropriateness to the sensibility of his modern characters, whose freedom to range across so many inner and outer possibilities goes with their loss of rootedness in time." Anne Fernihough, *D. H. Lawrence: Aesthetics and Ideology*, Clarendon Press, Oxford 1993, pp. 151–52 states that "Gudrun and Gerald epitomize the ruthless, restless, errant humanity that peoples the novel as a whole."

18. It is interesting to note that even Gudrun is prey to a type of nostalgia for home which, however, in her is revealed as the desire to possess the place, feel herself part of the mechanism and suck out all of its vital fluids: "she hated it [the mining village], she knew how utterly cut off it was ... . And yet, she was overcome by the nostalgia. She struggled to get more and more into accord with the atmosphere of the place, she craved to get her satisfaction of it" (*WL* 116).

19. When Ursula attributes her anxiety to her place of origin: "I looked back at England, and thought I'd done with it," Birkin responds: "France is far worse" (*WL* 249).

20. Home (cf. Bachelard, *The Poetics of Space*, cit.; Corigliano, *Tempo, Spazio, Identità*, cit.) is the place where a person lives in harmony with the surrounding environment, rather than simply a lodging (cf. La Cecla, *Perdersi*, cit.), as occurs in modern industrial societies.

21. "Ursula sat black-souled and very bitter, hearing the two of them talk. There seemed something ghoulish even in their very deploring of the state of things ... . His [Tom's] real mistress was the machine, and the real mistress of Winifred was the machine. She too, Winifred, worshiped the impure abstraction, the mechanisms of matter" (*R* 324–25). Virginia Hyde, "Toward 'the Earth's New Architecture': Triads, Arches and Angles in *The Rainbow*," *Modernist Studies* 4

(1982), pp. 7–35, notes in the mining village the reversal of values represented by the cathedral; it is a monument which represents a true "blasphemy ... against life." "[Wiggiston's] colliery," emphasizes the critic, "is a formidable counterfeit cathedral, though inverting the values of the place of worship it replaces. There is even a 'swooning perverse satisfaction' in the structure, which is not even the sacred 'she' of Lincoln, but, nonetheless, 'the mistress' of the workers and of Tom Jr. and Winifred" (p. 27).

22. The image of the flood wiping out the house recurs in *The Virgin and the Gipsy* (1930).

23. The presence of an element of dissolution which gradually insinuates itself into the farm and eventually destroys it is perceived by Ursula even in the most lively of the Brangwen sons, her adored uncle Tom: "Tom came in out of the broiling sunshine, heated from walking ... . He too had something *marshy* about him — the succulent moistness and turgidity, and the same brackish, nauseating effect of a marsh, where life and decaying are one" (*R* 325, emphasis mine).

24. "Shortlands ... was a long, low old house, a sort of manor farm, that spread along the top of a slope just beyond the narrow little lake of Willey Water. Shortlands looked across a sloping meadow that might be a park..., at the wooded hill that successfully hid the colliery valley beyond..., the scene was rural and picturesque, very peaceful, and the house had a charm of its own" (*WL* 23).

25. Deaths at the Crich house are always connected with a certain cosmic element: fire, when Gerald kills his brother with a gun shot, water in the drowning of his sister and finally the freezing of Gerald himself.

26. "Then suddenly the father died. It happened one spring-time ... . Tom Brangwen drove off on a Saturday morning to the market in Nottingham, saying he might not be back till late, as there was a special show and then a meeting he had to attend. His family understood that he would enjoy himself" (*R* 226).

27. In a way that recalls the film *Metropolis* by Fritz Lang (1927), where the Edenic garden of the industrialist overlooks the crowd of workers laboring below.

28. In reference to this scene, Morris, "African Sculpture Symbols in *Women in Love*," cit., p. 34, observes that "[Birkin's] wandering into the woods and his lying among the primroses suggest his move from extreme spirituality to the other extreme of excessive, mindless sensuality."

29. The projection of a place of belonging, of a domesticity in conflict with the character's restlessness that in Gudrun's imagination corresponds more to a theatrical representation than to the idea of married life in a stable home, reveals the self-destructive conflict inherent in the character.

30. "He opened the doors, upper and lower, they [Tom and Anna] entered into the high, dry barn, that smelled warm even if it were not warm ... . They were in another world now ... . Outside there was the driving rain, inside, the softly-illuminated stillness and calmness of the barn" (*R* 75).

31. As seen in Chapter II, the transformation of a domestic place into a sacred place where one undergoes an initiation ritual is also present, in a different way, in the stories "The Christening" and "The Thorn in the Flesh."

32. In reference to the domestic conflict between Anna and Will, Kinkead-Weekes, "The Sense of History in *The Rainbow*," cit., p. 132, notes that "the creative conflict of opposites turns into a battle for domination which Anna, the more

self-assured articulate individual, is bound to win. But having conquered, she dances her own fertility to the Lord, against the shadowy man in the doorway. She builds a house for herself on Pisgah, but doesn't enter the Promised Land or open it for Will." Paul Poplawski, *Promptings of Desire: Creativity and the Religious Impulse in the Works of D. H. Lawrence*, Greenwood Press, Westport (Conn.), 1993, p. 111, finds in Anna's dance a moment in which "the 'unknown God,' the macrocosmic life-force, appears to manifest itself to and through the individual microcosm. The characters involved seem to lose their consciousness and individuality, as they are apparently 'possessed' by something beyond their conscious control."

33. "'There she is,' he [Will] said. The 'she' irritated her [Anna]. Why 'she'? It was 'it.' What was the cathedral, a big building, a thing of the past, obsolete, to excite him to such a pitch?... So she caught sight of the wicked, odd little faces carved in stone..., giving suggestion of the many things that had been left out of the great concept of the church" (*R* 186, 189). Regarding Anna's reaction to the cathedral, Pinkney, *D. H. Lawrence*, cit., p. 73, notes that "The Gothic deconstructs the rigid model of inside/outside that Anna erects here. Its outside is its inside; even the sly stone faces that denounce its incompletion are, after all, part of it. The Gothic contains its own 'negation,' which thereafter ceases to be its negative pure and simple, and is rather granted local validity within a more generous total system which exceeds it." Hyde, "Toward 'the Earth's New Architecture': Triads, Arches and Angles in *The Rainbow*," cit., p. 24, sees in the cathedral episode a revelatory moment about the real nature of Anna and Will's relationship, as "[Anna's] deliberate, and successful, attack on his [Will's] faith actually strikes out at the quality of her own marriage, which receives the repercussions of the change in him. It is his sense of the sacred which has previously conditioned his perception of his wife. Will's deepest feelings, as both artist and husband, have been integrally related to the cathedral culture ... . Losing his dynamic faith in it, Will becomes simply a voluptuary at home and an ineffectual figure in the world."

34. In reference to the closed/open binary opposition, see Fernando Ferrara's analysis of *Lady Chatterley's Lover* in *Romanzo e profezia. L'amante di Lady Chatterley di D. H. Lawrence come mito e predicazione*, Officina, Roma 1982, in particular the chapter "Spazio e tempo," pp. 170–81, where the enclosure of the shed and the female womb become, with respect to the squalid external environment, a refuge overflowing with riches for rebirth. I maintain, however, that the enclosure to which the critic refers is only apparent, inasmuch as it lacks definite boundaries and is in direct communication with the surrounding environment (the woods), from which it draws stimulus and nourishment for the life inside, thus representing the idea of the perfect home (cf. Bachelard, *The Poetics of Space*, cit.; Emmanuel Lévinas, "The Dwelling," in *Totality and Infinity: An Essay on Exteriority* (1961), trans. by Alphonso Lingis, Duquesne UP, Pittsburgh 1969, pp. 152–74; and Norberg-Schulz, "*The concept of dwelling*, cit., pp. 89–110) and keeping intact at the same time its own identity (cf. Remotti, *Luoghi e corpi*, cit.; Lotman and Uspenskij, *Tipologia della cultura*, cit.).

35. In regard to the ritualistic nature of Birkin and Ursula's encounter in Sherwood Forest, Virginia Hyde, *The Risen Adam: D. H. Lawrence's Revisionist Typology*, Pennsylvania State UP, University Park 1992, p. 112, notes that "if the location is not precisely a church, yet it is clearly one of the rare places that

Lawrence elsewhere designates as 'quick' spots of the earth, sacred centers adapting themselves age after age to successive expressions of religious feeling." For Bonds, "Going into the Abyss: Literarization in *Women in Love*," cit., p. 194, the place of their encounter is like "a place not to be perceived as a place, a 'nowhere.' In this non-place, the language of the chapter insists, they achieve a transcendent, liberating union." It is an encounter in which, observes Jack F. Stewart, "Dialectics of Knowing in *Women in Love*," *Twentieth Century Literature* 37 (1991), pp. 59–75, "[their] unspeakable knowledge is mediated by a tactile language, and there is no translation of this 'dark, subtle reality' into mental images or concepts" (p. 69).

36. Stewart, "Dialectics of Knowing in *Women in Love*," cit., pp. 63–65, states that "[Gudrun's] characteristic mode of seeing is to enclose within a frame, and this is the link between her self-contained being and her nearly perfect art of miniatures ... . In reducing the human flux, with all its unseen potential, to precisely delineated forms, Gudrun's perception reduces process to product and character to caricature ... . Gudrun regards others with 'objective curiosity,' as material for her art, just as Gerald regards men and matter as instruments of his will."

37. "Gudrun ... went in a strange, palpitating dance towards the cattle..., her throat exposed as in some voluptuous ecstasy towards them..., ebbing in strange fluctuations upon the cattle ... . She could feel them just in front of her, it was as if she had the electric pulse from their breasts running into her hands. Soon she would touch them, actually touch them. A terrible shiver of fear and pleasure went through her" (*WL* 167–68).

38. Stephen Rowley, "Gerald's White Light — A Modern metaphor: The Meaning of Whiteness in D. H. Lawrence's *Women in Love*," *The Journal of the D.H. Lawrence Society* 4 (1988–89), pp. 20–30, points out that the mountain landscape is the catalyst for Gerald's metamorphosis, accelerating his process of dissolution: "there is nothing surprising about the visual changes he undergoes — from his impressive sartorial elegance (which is no more than a contrived diversion), to the metamorphosis into a weird, white world, and finally into the white ghost (notably devoid of all substance) which confronts Gudrun and Loerke at the end" (p. 28). Cianci, in the above-cited "Introduction," p. xviii, sees in "Gerald's final death in the snow..., in the objective correlative of the ghostly, abstract, dazzling landscape of the Tyrol," a symbolic confirmation of the destructive effect of the process of modernization that Gerald himself began in the mines.

39. The alpine landscape is used as catalyst for a reversal in a couple's relationship in *The Captain's Doll* as well.

40. Analyzing the opposition between "rapture and despair: communion and isolation" which characterizes the effect of the alpine landscape upon the characters, Eric P. Levy, "Lawrence's Psychology of Void and Center in *Women in Love*," *D.H. Lawrence Review* 23 (1991) pp. 5–19, states that Gudrun and Gerald "are far too threatened by their own inner emptiness ever to trust an experience that will overwhelm their sense of identity altogether. At bottom, love for them resolves into fear and anger: fear of absorption or complete rejection by another and anger at such an outrage" (pp. 15–16).

41. In reference to Ursula's metamorphosis elicited by the moonlight, Poplawski, *Promptings of Desire*, cit., p. 104, observes that "she experiences an actual communion, a co-mingling, with nature that enables her to take a step forward in her development, and this literal communion symbolically predicates a

reintegration with her 'other ego' and the life force it represents. Dramatically, of course, it precipitates the final sundering clash between the incompatible egos of the two characters and the collapse of their relationship." Jack F. Stewart, "Expressionism in *The Rainbow*," *Novel* 13 (1980), pp. 296–315, notes that "exposure to moonlight — a symbol of female anima — becomes more devastating in successive phases, culminating in Anton's destruction as a sexual being. It is space, rhythm, and the unknown, rather than personal psychology, that make the dynamics of such scenes" (p. 304). According to Jan Verleun, "The Inadequate Male in D. H. Lawrence's *The Rainbow*," *Neophilologus* 72 (1988), pp. 116–35, "herself afraid of what she has become…, Ursula must seek, in spite of her fear, the maximum expansion of the sexual self which both the moon and the subjection in Skrebensky provoke her to seek" (p. 129).

42. Worthen, *D. H. Lawrence*, cit., p. 48, notes that in Ursula and Anton's relationship, "discovery" leads to "exploitation" and self-gratification: "She turns the final relationship with Skrebensky into an exercise in control and dominance; and that makes the relationship one of the most destructive and frightening relationships in all Lawrence's writing — not, for once, narrated from the point of view of man, but of the woman."

43. Kinkead-Weekes, "The Sense of History in *The Rainbow*," cit., p. 128, observes that "[Winifred's] lesbian relation with Ursula is finally rejected by the girl, yet she [Winifred] had been a liberating and enriching influence." Peter G. Christensen, "Problems of Characterization in D. H. Lawrence's *The Rainbow*," *AUMLA* 77 (1992), pp. 78–96, states that "Lawrence wishes to insist that Winifred introduces Ursula to chaos, but instead of indicating the real chaos, the possibility of a lesbian relationship in a homophobic society, he declares chaos to be in the split personalities of Ursula and her friends, which are never described … . To many people, lesbianism can only be understood as deviance, something at the border and probably sinister. With Lawrence, it gives up this position and enters a form of 'non-existence.' In this metaphysical twilight zone it cannot be called into being. Thus, Ursula's unnamable attraction to Winifred takes place outside all the social givens" (pp. 82–84).

44. Rowley, "Gerald's White Light — A Modern Metaphor: The Meaning of Whiteness in D. H. Lawrence's *Women in Love*," cit., pp. 21–24, reads Gerald's rituals, especially that of dress, as a means to hide the unstoppable process of dissolution occurring in his soul, which manifests in that white aura which always distinguishes his person. "Gerald is always dressed 'comme il faut,' for appearance is crucial to him as it is a means of asserting his presence, and of giving him the impression of 'being.'"

45. See, in this regard, the above-cited "Introduction" by Cianci, p. XXIII, in particular his interpretation of Gerald's presence in the alpine landscape: "Both expression and champion of an industrial-technological culture that annihilates…, Gerald, 'perfect instrument,' who functions 'like a watch' and whose 'luminous' aspect and 'crystalline and remote aura' is constantly remarked upon, is figured, while skiing, in the guise of a crazy machine, to exemplify the 'multiplied man' postulated by the famous Futurist manifesto and as if he were putting into practice one of Loerke's axioms: to masochistically enjoy the mechanical movement of his own body." (translation mine). Bonds, "Going into the Abyss: Literarization

in *Women in Love,*" cit., p. 197, notes that Gerald's abandonment to the ecstasy of velocity in the freezing snow "implies no life-giving release of energy, but rather moves in the direction of 'snow-abstract annihilation.'"

46. Cf. Chapter x of *The Rainbow,* entitled "The Widening Circle," dedicated to Ursula's growth, to her gradual discovery of the outside world that foreshadows her entry into adult life.

47. On the gradual process of "crystallization" occurring in the novel, characterized by the increase of "geometrical surfaces which impede free flow" (p. 193), see John B. Foster, Jr., "Crystal and Star: Nietzsche and the Symbolic Action of *Women in Love,*" in *Heirs to Dionysus: A Nietzschean Current in Literary Modernism,* Princeton UP, Princeton 1981, pp. 185–206.

48. "To remain faithful to the nature of *Women in Love,* which is without conclusion, and intentionally exempt from a soothing ending, we must guard against the entrenchment of those same negative values with which the novel is marked. The epochal dimension of the text is true to all of the radical agitation caused by modernist disruption, and to its exasperatingly experimental character. Its unmistakable testimony, its *Stimmung,* is that which, far from positing a resolved and finished universe, concedes maximum space to the plurality of instances and aspirations, leaving them open and free to offer all of their urgency, conflict and dissonance, while at the same time it explores profound historical necessity." (Cf. Cianci, "Introduction" to *Donne innamorate,* cit., p. xxv, translation mine).

Chapter 7

1. Tzvetan Todorov, *On Human Diversity: Nationalism, Racism, and Exoticism in French Thought* (1989), trans. by Catherine Porter, Harvard UP, Cambridge (Mass.) 1993, analyzing the conflict between the universal and the particular, observes that "the universalist pretention has turned out, over the centuries, to be nothing but a mask worn by ethnocentrism. Thus, the universalist ideology is responsible for events that number among the most unfortunate in recent European history — namely, the colonial conquests. Under the pretext of spreading 'civilization' (a universal value if there is one), a few western European countries have helped themselves to the wealth of all the others and have exploited numerous faraway peoples to their advantage" (pp. 387–88). On Lawrence's condemnation of Roman imperialism in *Sketches of Etruscan Places,* see Stefania Michelucci, "D. H. Lawrence's Discovery of the Etruscans: A Pacific Challenge Against Imperialism," in Marialuisa Bignami and Caroline Patey (eds), *Moving the Borders,* Unicopli, Milano 1996, pp. 374–81. See also, in reference to the opposition between the Romans' abstract will to power and the serene, pagan acceptance of Etruscan life, Simonetta de Filippis, "Lawrence of Etruria," in Preston and Hoare, *D. H. Lawrence in the Modern World,* cit., pp. 104–20, and Carla Comellini, "The Influence of the Mediterranean and Aztec Myth and the Utopian Quest," in *D. H. Lawrence: A Study on Mutual and Cross References and Interferences,* CLUEB, Bologna 1995, pp. 59–88.

2. Mark Kinkead-Weekes, "D. H. Lawrence and the Dance," *The Journal of the D. H. Lawrence Society* (1992–93), pp. 44–62, notes that his extraordinary rendering

Notes: Chapter 7

of Indian dance reflects Lawrence's problematic attempt to "decolonize" his own mind: "to get inside the communal culture and the religious feelings embodied in the dancing of Indians in New Mexico [is] an effort of imagination very unlike the 'tradition' of English writing, which tends to be richly but also narrowly provincial ... as an evocation of dance that embodies a culture utterly different from the observer's, the three essays now to be found in *Mornings in Mexico* are extraordinary" (p. 57).

3. Cf. The description of the work of Franciscan Bernardino de Sahagún by Tzvetan Todorov, *The Conquest of America: the Question of the Other* (1982), trans. by Richard Howard, Harper & Row, New York 1984, pp. 219–41. Unlike other evangelical missionaries, Sahagún neither demonized nor idealized the Indians, who "have virtues and defects, just like the Spaniards, but in a different distribution. He complains on occasion of various features of their character which seem to him regrettable; he accounts for these, however, not by a natural inferiority ... but by the different conditions in which they live, notably climatic conditions" (p. 239).

4. The story's protagonist locates in the "exotic" and "primitive" which she idealizes, a possibility of escape from her misery, from her death-in-life state. That which she seeks and convinces herself she has found is assessed from her perspective upon the point of departure. Todorov (*On Human Diversity*, cit, p. 264) notes that "ideally, exoticism is a form of relativism, just as nationalism is. However, the two forms are diametrically opposed. In each case, what is valorized is not a stable content but a country and a culture defined exclusively by their relation to the observer ... . in both cases what is at issue is a relativism overtaken at the last minute by a value judgment (we are better than the others, the others are better than we are), but in which the definition of the entities compared, 'ourselves' and 'the others', remains purely relative." In reference to the construction of the primitive on the part of modernist writers as a means of redefining their own identity, see Marianna Torgovnick, *Gone Primitive: Savage Intellects, Modern Lives*, University of Chicago Press, Chicago 1990; and, with particular attention to the North American situation, and the paradox of the recovery and the political destruction of a tradition (and of the races which are its mouthpiece), Helen Carr, *Inventing the American Primitive: Politics, Gender and the Representation of Native American Literary Tradition, 1789–1935*, Cork UP, Cork 1996.

5. Norberg-Schulz, *The concept of dwelling*, cit., p. 13, states that "to dwell implies the establishment of a meaningful relationship between man and a given environment." This is what is missing in the "princess's" life, as her wandering existence and especially her two houses on different continents, reflect the interior disintegration of her personality, the unsurpassable distance between the surface — her stubborn, willful character — and the depths of her self which she is not able to bring to the light.

6. Peter Balbert, *D. H. Lawrence and the Phallic Imagination: Essays on Sexual Identity and Feminist Misreading*, Macmillan, London 1989, pp. 109–32, states that the protagonist's desire to reach the Indian tribe is not the fruit of a conscious choice, but of the instinctive desire towards "the only 'unknown' she can possibly enter at this time; she correctly senses her relation to the tribe as part of some fabled, irresistible fate — an alternative, at least, to the death-in-life she now experiences" (p. 118).

7. Cf. La Cecla, *Perdersi*, cit., pp. 26–30. In a way which recalls Aaron's departure from home on Christmas Eve in *Aaron's Rod*, the protagonist in "The Woman Who Rode Away" leaves the ranch, once her husband is gone, saying that she is going to visit her daughter in a nearby convent school and does not turn back even to wave to her son after she has started out, while the "princess" tells her host family that she is going to stay for a few days in a well-known and often-visited canyon.

8. Mark Kinkead-Weekes, "The Gringo Señora Who Rode Away," *D. H. Lawrence Review* 22 (1990), pp. 251–65, observes that the identity of the woman is based not so much on her individuality as on her being white and belonging to the dominating class: "she thinks of herself as 'a beautiful white woman' and a 'lady' whom men ought to serve; as sexually desirable, and as powerful both because she is a rich American and because she is female." Her power fails once she reaches the crack in the rock which leads to the village, a passage which, says the critic, is presented as a "crossing over into a different, uncolonized world … . To look down on the brilliant whiteness of the pueblo, in that other world, is both to be frightened by a sense of a whiteness quite different from hers and to judge her deathliness by it" (pp. 252–56).

9. When the woman arrives at the village, "all the doors of the windowless houses gave on to this blank square, but all the doors were closed" (*WRA* 53). The window, by virtue of its position with respect to the door, is comparable to a type of "higher" awareness, of a purely intellectual nature. The door, on the other hand, because it is located at a lower place and because of the immediate access it gives to the outside, is comparable to an instinctive, physical knowledge, to immediate interaction between inside and outside.

10. John Worthen, "The Woman Who Rode Away," in Aa.Vv., *Miroirs de la femme dans la litterature d'expression anglaise*, Université de Bretagne Occidentale, Brest 1992, pp. 205–20, shows how the protagonist is in part responsible for her own tragedy because of the superficiality with which she relates to the Indian community: "her reaction to a primitive society, and to another kind of consciousness, is blank incomprehension." The woman's response to the question of the wise old man ('Yes, she does … . She would like to serve the gods of the Chilchui'), the critic justly emphasizes, "is wholly, though also terribly, superficial … . She has … absolutely no conception of what might be meant by God" (p. 214). In his analysis of the distinction between a society of sacrifice (the Aztecs) and a society of massacre (the Spanish colonizers), Todorov, *The Conquest of America*, cit., p. 144, observes that "once captured [the sacrificial victims], they are kept in prison for some time, thereby partially — but never completely — assimilated." An extremely rigid code regulates sacrifice, which Todorov calls a "religious murder," which "testifies to the power of the social fabric, to its mastery over the individual," as opposed to the massacre, "an atheistic murder," which "reveals the weakness of this same social fabric, the desuetude of the moral principles that once assured the group's coherence."

11. On the symbolic values of this scene, cf. Mario Domenichelli, "Lawrence, l'inconscio, Freud: il limite e la ripetizione," in Comellini and Fortunati (eds), *D. H. Lawrence cent'anni dopo*, cit., pp. 85–100.

12. In reference to the origins of the three characters, L. D. Clark, "Reading

Lawrence's American Novel: *The Plumed Serpent*" (1976), in Dennis Jackson and Fleda Brown Jackson (eds), *Critical Essays on D. H. Lawrence*, G. K. Hall, Boston 1988, pp. 118–28, observes that "in the first and still unpublished version of his American novel, Lawrence betrayed some indecision as to which race was to dominate ... . The first Ramón and the first Cipriano both possess a large strain of American Indian blood, and both identify strongly with the aboriginal America. In the definitive *Plumed Serpent* Lawrence took his final stand: the European must lead. Don Ramón Carrasco has scarcely any Indian blood — in Kate's eyes, he belongs to aboriginal Europe — while Don Cipriano Viedma is nearly pure Indian, and Ramón is unquestionably the leader" (pp. 121–22). Even if Don Ramón is unquestionably the leader of the new movement, the European component in his personality reflects Kate's point of view and Lawrence's only in part. Peter Fjågesund, *The Apocalyptic World of D. H. Lawrence*, Norwegian UP, Oslo 1991, p. 137, emphasizes the western education of the three protagonists and states that "the Mexicanness of *The Plumed Serpent* ... is a cleverly constructed facade which, to some extent, successfully conceals the European structure behind it."

13. See Silvia Albertazzi, "L'uomo che amava (a modo suo) le donne: appunti di una 'lettrice arpia,'" in Comellini and Fortunati (eds.), *D. H. Lawrence cent'anni dopo*, cit., pp. 13–27.

14. It is a physical relationship which recalls Birkin and Gerald's in *Women in Love*, but without its violence: "Ramón bound the ankles ... holding Cipriano's feet to his own abdomen. And both men passed into perfect unconsciousness, Cipriano within the womb of undisturbed creation, Ramón in the death sleep" (*PS* 369).

15. "'It is a strange darkness, the Mexican darkness! ... Perhaps the night here scares me,' she [Kate] laughed. 'Yes. But why not? The smell of the flowers at night may make one feel afraid, but it is a good fear'" (*PS* 68).

16. The idea of home as an extension of the self seems to represent a characteristic element of the western heritage (Ramón and Kate both have European origins), in which home is seen as a protector of privacy, whereas for the Indians (Cipriano) it is identified with one's own land, with the open instead of the closed.

17. See Remotti, *Luoghi e corpi*, cit., pp. 76–89.

18. In a Biblical reading of the novel's two versions, Hyde, "The New World Schema, New Eve and the Aztec Patriarchs in *Quetzalcoatl* and *The Plumed Serpent*," in *The Risen Adam*, cit., pp. 173–206, notes the correspondence between Sayula's lake and the center of the world: "while this setting is literally — and memorably — one in Mexico, it has a symbolic relationship with the *axis mundi*. From the matrix of creation, 'the heart of the world,' the various saviors of mankind cycle forth: in this 'infinite room,' where 'even the trees come and go,' Christ and Quetzalcoatl pass each other in their cycling" (p. 181). The lake is also a catalyst for epiphanic revelations, as when, towards the end of the novel, Kate perceives, in a man who is delicately convincing a bull to board a boat, a fullness of life not present elsewhere. In reference to these small episodes which provide background for the main events, Sarah Urang, *Kindled in the Flame: The Apocalyptic Scene in D. H. Lawrence*, UMI Research Press, Ann Arbor 1983, p. 85, notes that "the symbolic scene, and the transmutation of the ordinary into the important, carries the validation for the reader of Lawrence's belief in the living cosmos. Much of the

time this validation is found in *The Plumed Serpent* not at crucial points in the plot, but in what might be called the 'negative spaces' of the narrative…, the so-called 'background,' including minor plot elements, is given sufficient figure quality so that these negative spaces stand in clear relation to the major events of the plot itself; they are, as in the case of a painting, an important element in our reception of the whole novel."

19. Norberg-Schulz, *The concept of dwelling*, cit., p. 13, states that "dwelling … also comprises that withdrawal which is necessary to define and develop one's own identity. We may call this mode *private dwelling*, intending those actions which are secluded from the intrusion of others."

20. Cf. Corigliano, *Tempo spazio identità*, cit., pp. 93–107; and Bachelard, "Drawers, Chests and Wardrobes," *The Poetics of Space*, cit., pp. 74–89.

21. "Kate felt that the cry: *Niña — Child*! by which she was addressed, held in it a slight note of malevolent mockery" (*PS* 110).

22. In regard to the microcosm represented by Don Ramón's home, Fjågesund, *The Apocalyptic World of D. H. Lawrence*, cit., p. 132–33, observes that "taking the reader on a guided tour of the hacienda, Lawrence portrays it as a closed but happy community with an old-fashioned William Morris-like reverence for quality handicrafts … . The hacienda is almost like a medieval village."

23. Marianna Torgovnick, "'Oh, Mexico!': D. H. Lawrence's *The Plumed Serpent*," in *Gone Primitive*, cit., pp. 159–74, observes how Lawrence manages in *The Plumed Serpent* to go beyond two visions of the primitive typical of western thought: "in the Mexican dance, sexual divisions meld, with male and female reenvisioned as two halves of a cosmic whole. Similarly, the novel collapses together the ideas of the primitive as the dangerous and the primitive as the idyllic. Violence seems different once it is seen as loosing the essential stream of 'blood' which unifies existence, even death can be 'naturalized' as part of this cosmic system … . If we take Kate's dance in *The Plumed Serpent* seriously," observes the critic, "Lawrence yearns for what Kate achieves here — a state of cosmic oneness, beyond words because beyond humanity, an utter mixing of things antipodal to language" (pp. 168–79). Bell, *D. H. Lawrence: Language and Being*, cit., p. 180, shows that Kate (like the author) lacks the means for transformation, which she would have undergone if she had completely surrendered to the dance: "The experience is a glimpse of something outside Kate's world. That Kate should look on the dance with sympathy, and even participate in it, is not unconvincing, but the profound transformation she would need to undergo to become part of its 'world' cannot be communicated in this way … . There is a gap here which, although Lawrence often tries to override it by force of rhetoric, he yet recognizes to be a real gap for Kate."

24. Quetzalcoatl, described in the novel as "Lord of the Two Ways" (*PS* 341), is contrasted to the Christian God "of the one way."

25. Cf. Remotti, *Luoghi e corpi*, cit., pp. 96–107.

26. See Lawrence's observations in the essay "Market Day," where the flux of inhabitants in the town plaza is seen as the result of the irrepressible desire to participate in "the great stream of men flowing to a centre, to the vortex of the market-place" (*MM* 49).

27. The *auto da fé* on the island acquires also another meaning in relation to

the colonial past; while the *conquistadors* made it the site of a penitentiary, it is there that *their* God is sacrificed and "imprisoned."

28. Ramón's idea corresponds to what Todorov, *The Conquest of America*, cit., p. 189, defines, describing the work of Bartolomé de Las Casas, as the introduction of "perspectivism" in religion: "What then remains common and universal [between the Spaniards and the Aztecs] is no longer the God of the Christian religion, to whom all should accede, but the very idea of divinity, of what is above us; the religious rather than religion." Torgovnick, "'Oh, Mexico!': D. H. Lawrence's *The Plumed Serpent*," in *Gone Primitive,* cit., p. 164, shows that Don Ramón's ideal mirrors Lawrence's idea of the rebirth of western society expressed in *Fantasia of the Unconscious*: "these ancient gods would meet together as emanations of the male and female principles to make the world a unified, harmonious place quite different from the modern West. The new order would reproduce the global unity Lawrence postulated in *Fantasia of the Unconscious* as existing before the flood through a new understanding of sex as the instrument of spirituality."

29. In the same way as other charismatic figures who characterize Lawrence's later work, Lilly in *Aaron's Rod*, Count Dionys Psanek in *The Ladybird*, Kangaroo in *Kangaroo*, and finally Mellors in *Lady Chatterley's Lover*.

30. According to Debra A. Castillo, "Postmodern Indigenism: 'Quetzalcoatl and all that,'" *Modern Fiction Studies* 41 (1995), pp. 35–73, Kate, with her origins, "provides the connection to European high culture that the educated mestizos, Ramón and Cipriano, are unable to make alone. At the same time, Ramón reminds her, the common people's animal resentment will eventually bring her down. To the degree that her difference from them cannot be internalized (her orientation is modern/spiritual to their primitive/corporal), she becomes the obvious sacrificial victim, both the unwanted element that must be cast out, as well as the representative of the best that can be achieved through miscegenation" (p. 46).

31. "Montes declared the old Church illegal in Mexico, and caused a law to be passed, making the religion of Quetzalcoatl the national religion of the Republic" (*PS* 420).

32. For Clark, "Reading Lawrence's American Novel: *The Plumed Serpent*," cit., p. 126, the violent execution of the traitors signals a turning-point in the novel, a degeneration of the religious movement towards bloody Aztec sacrifices, a degeneration which brings out the central dilemma of the novel: "If some kind of return to the primitive lies in the future of the continent, does the concomitant violence belong to a temporary, restorative phase, or would it be permanent and crippling to a revived primitivism, even one inspired by the best of human instincts? If men confess that the blood as well as the spirit belongs to the gods, then how does a blood-worshipping society avoid the brutal excesses to which such societies have been prone in the past? Recognizing that the Aztecs had made this fatal error and drowned in their own gory rites, Lawrence foresaw a recurrence, and he often blamed this disaster of the Aztecs on the inability of man to cope with the fierce spirit of the continent itself."

33. "I can't understand that people want to have everything, all life, no? so safe and ready-made as in England and America. It is good to be *awake*. On the *qui vive*, no?" (*PS* 203).

34. Kate's tendency to maintain a certain distance from the surrounding world is due, in Urang's opinion, *Kindled in the Flame*, cit., p. 78, to the fact that in the novel, "Lawrence is less sure of the implications of that new world that he begins to envision … . Kate realizes that he [Ramón] is at the end of a road she has not yet herself finished traveling. It seems as though here, as elsewhere in his characterization of Kate, Lawrence is writing of his own position; he senses a new call in the air, but is unsure of the particulars of its utterance, as they will work out in the specifics of action. There is, therefore, a continual repudiation of the apocalyptic event in Kate's consciousness." In reference to the protagonist's continuous oscillation between two worlds, Bibhu Padhi, "Familiar and Unfamiliar World: The Fabular Mode in Lawrence's Late Narratives," *Philological Quarterly* 64 (1985), pp. 239–55, observes that "Kate is held between the primitive gods and everyday realities, between mystic rituals carried out in a magic language and the conscious meditations of an Irish woman on the value of such rituals." For the critic, it is the "'over-explicitness' of the details of the rituals and hymns in the novel that … is really the structural equivalent of the natural and difficult search of Kate (as well as of her creator) toward making the Quetzalcoatl cult a comprehensible and meaningful phenomenon" (pp. 245–46).

35. See Remotti, *Luoghi e corpi*, cit., pp. 113–24.

Conclusion

1. While the Mexican experience finds expression in a novel, some short stories, and a travel book, the Australian environment is the center of two novels, *Kangaroo* and *The Boy in the Bush*, the second of which is the rewriting of "The House of Ellis" by Mollie L. Skinner.

2. Another element common to both is the heroines' relationships with their respective partners. It is no coincidence that both Connie Chatterley and Kate Leslie come from England's neighbor countries (Scotland and Ireland), and that both are attracted to people foreign to their own origins and cultural conditioning, who are completely immersed in the "spirit of place" where they live, the gamekeeper Mellors for Connie, Cipriano and Don Ramón for Kate.

3. "The changeless bush … . Nothing was hidden. It was all open and fair. And yet it was haunted with a malevolent mystery. You felt yourself so small, so tiny, so absolutely insignificant in the still, eternal glade. And this again is the malevolence of the bush, that it reduces you to your own absolute insignificance, go where you will" (*BB* 286).

4. It is true that modern England places a restricting net over the regenerating relationship between Connie and Mellors and indeed they plan to move to the New World at the end of the novel, but the vital core of the novel concerns Connie's regeneration, which takes place in the intimate closeness of the gamekeeper's home.

5. Bachelard, *The Poetics of Space*, cit., p. 65, notes that "the dream house must possess every virtue. However spacious, it must also be a cottage, a dove-cote, a nest, a chrysalis. Intimacy needs the heart of a nest."

6. In the chapter "Savages, Barbarians, Civilized Men," Gilles Deleuze and Félix Guattari, *Anti-Oedipus: Capitalism and Schizophrenia* (1972), trans. by Robert Hurley, Mark Seem and Helen R. Lane, Viking, New York 1977, pp. 139–271, state: "Savage formations are oral, are vocal, but not because they lack a graphic system: a dance on the earth, a drawing on a wall, a mark on the body are a graphic system, a geo-graphism, a geography. These formations are oral precisely because they possess a graphic system that is independent of the voice, a system that is not aligned on the voice and not subordinate to it, but connected to it, co-ordinated 'in an organization that is radiating, as it were,' and multidimensional." (p. 188).

Bibliography

(D. H. Lawrence's works appear in the section "Abbreviations" on pages xi–xii)

Space / Place / Home

Abram, David, *The Spell of the Sensuous: Perception and Language in a More-Than-Human World*, Pantheon Books, New York 1996.
Amendolagine, Francesco and Cacciari, Massimo, *Oikos. Da Loos a Wittgenstein*, Officina, Roma 1975.
Arnheim, Rudolf, *The Power of the Center: a Study of Composition in the Visual Arts*, University of California Press, Berkeley 1982.
Assunto, Rosario, "Le due città," *Rivista di Estetica* 4 (1980), pp. 1–16.
Augé, Marc, *Non-Places: Introduction to an Anthropology of Supermodernity* (1992) trans. by John Howe, Verso, London 1995.
Bachelard, Gaston, *The Poetics of Space* (1957), trans. by Maria Jolas, Beacon Press, Boston 1969.
Bammer, Angelika (ed.), *Displacements: Cultural Identities in Question*, Indiana UP, Bloomington 1994.
Bartkowski, Frances, *Travelers, Immigrants, Inmates: Essays in Estrangement*, University of Minnesota Press, Minneapolis 1995.
Bhabha, Homi K., *The Location of Culture*, Routledge, London 1994.
Bonfiglioli, Sandra, *L'architettura del tempo. La città multimediale*, Liguori, Napoli 1990.
Buchanan, Ian, "Lefebvre and the Space of Everyday Life," *Southern Review* 27 (1994), pp. 127–35.
Buttimer, Anne and Seamon, David (eds), *The Human Experience of Space and Place*, St. Martin's Press, New York 1980.

Cacciari, Massimo, *Metropolis*, Officina, Roma 1973.
_____, "Eupalinos o l'architettura," *Nuova Corrente* 76/77 (1978), pp. 422–42.
_____, *Dallo Steinhof*, Adelphi, Milano 1980.
Carr, Helen, *Inventing the American Primitive: Gender, and the Representation of Native American Literary Traditions, 1789–1936*, Cork UP, Cork 1996.
Casey, Edward S., *Getting back into Place: Toward a Renewed Understanding of the Place-World*, Indiana UP, Bloomington 1993.
_____, *The Fate of Place: A Philosophical History*, University of California Press, Berkeley 1997.
Choay Françoise, *L'urbanisme, utopies et réalités, une anthologie*, Editions du Seuil, Paris 1965.
Consonni, Giancarlo, *L'internità dell'esterno. Scritti sull'abitare e il costruire*, Clup, Milano 1989.
Corigliano, Emma, *Tempo spazio identità. No place like home*, Angeli, Milano 1991.
Crang, Mike, *Cultural Geography*, Routledge, London 1998.
Deleuze, Gilles and Guattari, Félix, *Anti-Oedipus: Capitalism and Schizophrenia* (1972), trans. by Robert Hurley, Mark Seem and Helen R. Lane, Viking, New York 1977.
Dorfles, Gillo, "'Innen' e 'Aussen' nell'architettura e nella psicanalisi," *Rivista di Estetica* 1 (1979), pp. 30–39.
Entrikin, Nicholas J., *The Betweenness of Place: Towards a Geography of Modernity*, Johns Hopkins UP, Baltimore 1991.
Faré, Ida (ed.), *Il discorso dei luoghi: genesi e avventure dell'ordine moderno*, Liguori, Napoli 1992.
Flavell, John H., *The Developmental Psychology of Jean Piaget*. With a foreword by Jean Piaget, Van Nostrand, Princeton (N.J.) 1963.
Formaggio, Dino, *Estetica, tempo, progetto*, Clup, Milano 1990.
Foucault, Michel, "Of Other Spaces" (1984), trans. by Jay Miskowiec, *Diacritics* 16 (1986), pp. 22–27.
Gale, Stephen and Olsson, Gunnar (eds), *Philosophy in Geography*, D. Reidel, Dordrecht 1979.
Geertz, Clifford, *Local Knowledge: Further Essays in Interpretive Anthropology*, Basic Books, New York 1983.
Gehlen, Arnold, *Man in the age of technology* (1957), trans. by Patricia Lipscomb; with a foreword by Peter L. Berger, Columbia UP, New York 1980.
_____, *Man, his nature and place in the world* (1962), trans. by Clare McMillan and Karl Pillemer, with an introduction by Karl-Siegbert Rehberg, Columbia UP, New York 1988.
Giannone, Roberto, *Abitare la frontiera. Il moderno e lo spazio dei possibili*, CLUVA, Venezia 1985.
Goffman, Erving, *The Presentation of Self in Everyday Life* (1959), Penguin, London 1990.
Gottdiener, Mark and Lagopoulos, Alexandros (eds), *The City and the Sign: An Introduction to Urban Semiotics*, Columbia UP, New York 1986.
Greenblatt, Stephen, *Marvelous Possessions: the Wonder of the New World*, University of Chicago Press, Chicago 1991.
Gregory, Derek, *Geographical Imaginations*, Blackwell, Cambridge 1994.
_____, Martin, Ron and Smith, Graham (eds), *Human Geography: Society, Space and Social Science*, University of Minnesota Press, Minneapolis 1994.

Halbwachs, Maurice, *On collective memory* (1968), ed., trans., and with an introduction by Lewis A. Coser, University of Chicago Press, Chicago 1992.
Heidegger, Martin, *Being and Time* (1929), trans. by Joan Stambaugh, State University of New York Press, Albany (NY) 1996.
_____, "Art and Space" (1969), trans. by Charles H. Seibert, *Man and World* 6 (1973), pp. 3–8.
Jarris, Brian, *Postmodern Cartographies: The Geographical Imagination in Contemporary American Culture*, Pluto Press, London 1998.
Kern, Stephen, *The Culture of Time and Space 1880–1918*, Harvard UP, Cambridge (Mass.) 1983.
La Cecla, Franco, *Perdersi. L'uomo senza ambiente*, Laterza, Bari 1988.
Lefebvre, Henri, *The Production of Space* (1974), Blackwell, Oxford 1994.
Lévinas, Emmanuel, *Totality and Infinity: An Essay on Exteriority* (1961), trans. by Alphonso Lingis, Duquesne UP, Pittsburgh 1969.
Lévi-Strauss, Claude, *Tristes tropiques* (1955), trans. by John and Doreen Weightman, Penguin, New York 1992.
Lotman Jurij M. and Uspenskij, Boris A., *Tipologia della cultura* (1965–73), ed. Remo Faccani and Marzio Marzaduri, Bompiani, Milano 1987.
Löwith, Karl, *Das Verhältnis von Gott, Mensch und Welt in der Metaphysik von Descartes und Kant*, C. Winter, Heidelberg 1964.
Maldonado, Tomás, *Il futuro della modernità*, Feltrinelli, Milano 1992.
Milton, Kay (ed.), *Environmentalism: The View from Anthropology*, Routledge, London 1993.
_____, *Environmentalism and Cultural Theory: Exploring the Role of Anthropology in Environmental Discourse*, Routledge, London 1996.
Murphy, Patrick D., *Literature, Nature and Other: Ecofeminist Critiques*, State University of New York Press, Albany 1995.
Norberg-Schulz, Christian, *Existence, Space and Architecture*, Studio Vista, London 1971.
_____, *Genius loci: towards a phenomenology of architecture*, Rizzoli, New York 1980
_____, *The concept of dwelling: On the way of figurative architecture* (1984), Rizzoli, New York 1985.
Perniola, Mario, "Ars e Urbs," *Rivista di Estetica* 4 (1980), pp. 27–34.
Pile, Stephen and David, Keith, *Place and Politics of Identity*, Routledge, London 1993.
Reed, Christopher (ed.), *Not at Home: The Suppression of Domesticity in Modern Art and Architecture*, Thames and Hudson, London 1993.
Rella, Franco, *Miti e figure del moderno*, Feltrinelli, Milano 1993.
_____, *The myth of the other: Lacan, Deleuze, Foucault, Bataille*, Maisonneuve Press, Washington, D.C. 1994.
_____, *Confini: la visibilità del mondo e l'enigma dell'autorappresentazione*, Pendragon, Bologna, 1996.
Remotti, Francesco, *Noi primitivi. Lo specchio dell'antropologia*, Bollati Boringhieri, Torino 1990.
_____, *Luoghi e corpi. Antropologia dello spazio, del tempo e del potere*, Bollati Boringhieri, Torino 1993.

—, Pietro Scardelli and Ugo Fiabetti, *Centri, ritualità, potere. Significati antropologici dello spazio*, Il Mulino, Bologna 1989.
Sack, Robert D., *Human Territoriality: Its Theory and History*, CUP, Cambridge 1986.
Said, Edward, *Orientalism*, Vintage Books, New York 1978.
—, *Culture and Imperialism*, Vingate, London 1994.
Scheler, Max, *Die Stellung des Menschen in Kosmos*, A. Francke Verlag, Bern 1962.
Seamon, David and Mugerauer, Robert (eds.), *Dwelling, Place and Environment: Towards a Phenomenology of Person and World*, Martinus Nijhoff, Dordrecht 1985.
Sennet, Richard, *The Coscience of the Eye: The Design and Social Life of Cities*, Alfred A. Knopf, New York 1990.
Thrift, Nigel, *Spatial Formations*, Sage Publications, London 1996.
Todorov, Tzvetan, *The Conquest of America: the Question of the Other* (1982), trans. by Richard Howard, Harper & Row, New York 1984.
—, *On Human Diversity: Nationalism, Racism, and Exoticism in French Thought* (1989), trans. by Catherine Porter, Harvard UP, Cambridge (Mass.) 1993.
Tuan, Yi-Fu, *Topophilia: A Study of Environmental Perception, Attitudes, and Values*, Prentice-Hall, Englewood Cliffs 1974.
Vattimo, Gianni, *La fine della modernità*, Garzanti, Milano 1985.
Walmsley, D.J and Lewis, G.J., *Human Geography: Behavioural Approaches*, Longman, London 1984.
—, *Urban living: the Individual in the City*, Wiley, New York 1988.
Zumthor, Paul, *La mesure du monde: représentation de l'espace au Moyen Age*, Éditions du Seuil, Paris 1993.

Space and Place in Literature

Aa.Vv., "Ecrire le paysage," *Revue des Sciences Humaines*, No. 209 (1988).
—, "Le città immaginarie," *L'asino d'oro* 7 (1993).
Appleton, Jay, *The Experience of Landscape*, Wiley, London 1975.
Armstrong, Frances, *Dickens and the Concept of Home*, UMI Research Press, Ann Arbor 1990.
Bachtin, Michail, *Estetica e romanzo* (1975), trans. by Clara Strada Janovic, Einaudi, Torino 1997.
Barrell, John, *The Idea of Landscape and the Sense of Place 1730–1840: An Approach to the Poetry of John Clare*, CUP, Cambridge 1972.
Blanchot, Maurice, *L'espace littéraire*, Gallimard, Paris 1955.
Butler, Christopher, *Early Modernism*, Clarendon Press, Oxford 1994.
Cabibbo, Paola (ed.), *Sulla soglia. Questioni di liminalità in letteratura*, Il Calamo, Roma 1993.
—, (ed.), *Lo spazio e le sue rappresentazioni: stati, modelli, passaggi*, Edizioni Scientifiche Italiane, Napoli 1993.
Ceserani, Remo, "Su alcuni simboli della tradizione e della modernità in Thomas Hardy: la cattedrale e la stazione ferroviaria," in Paolo Amalfitano (ed.), *Il romanzo tra i due secoli (1880–1918)*, Bulzoni, Roma 1993, pp. 23–38.

Bibliography

_____, *Treni di carta*, Marietti, Genova 1993.
Chambers, Iain, *Migrancy, Culture, Identity*, Routledge, London and New York 1994.
Chialant Maria Teresa, and Eleonora Rao (eds.), *Per una topografia dell'altrove. Spazi altri nell'immaginario letterario e culturale di lingua inglese*, Liguori, Napoli 1995.
Cianci, Giovanni (ed.), *Modernismo/Modernismi*, Principato, Milano 1991.
_____, and Maria Rita Cifarelli (eds.), "La città (1830–1930)," *Quaderni del Dipartimento di Lingue e Letterature Straniere Moderne* 4 (1991).
Colley, Ann C., *The Search for Synthesis in Literature and Art*, University of Georgia Press, Athens (Ga.) 1990.
Dainotto, Roberto M., *Place in Literature: Regions, Cultures, Communities*, Cornell UP, Ithaca and London 2000.
Daiches, David, and John Flower *Literary Landscapes of the British Isles: A Narrative Atlas*, Paddington Press, New York and London 1979.
Darian-Smith, Kate, Liz Gunner, and Sarah Nuttal (eds), *Text, Theory, Space: Land, Literature and History in South Africa and Australia*, Routledge, London 1996.
Fiorentino, Francesco (ed.), *Raccontare e descrivere. Lo spazio nel romanzo dell'Ottocento*, Bulzoni, Roma 1997.
Frank, Ellen E., *Literary Architecture*, University of California Press, Berkeley 1979.
Frank, Joseph, *The Idea of Spatial Form*, Rutgers UP, New Brunswick 1991.
Gurr, Andrew, *Writers in Exile: The Identity of Home in Modern Literature*, Harvester, Brighton 1981.
Hefferman, James A.W., "Space and Time in Literature and the Visual Arts," *Soundings*, 7 (1987), pp. 95–119.
_____, (ed.), *Space, Time, Image, Sign: Essays on Literature and the Visual Arts*, Peter Lang, New York 1987.
Holtz, William, "Spatial Form in Modern Literature: A Reconsideration," *Critical Inquiry* 4 (1977), pp. 271–83.
Ibsch, Elrud, "Historical Changes of the Function of Spatial Description in Literary Texts," *Poetics Today* 3 (1982), pp. 97–113.
Iengo, Francesco, *La grande città dei letterati*, Unicopli, Milano 1988.
Innocenti, Loretta (ed.), *Scene, itinerari, dimore. Lo spazio nella narrativa del '700*, Bulzoni, Roma 1995.
Isaak, Jo A., *The Ruin of Representation in Modernist Art and Texts*, UMI Research Press, Ann Arbor 1986.
Kestner, Joseph, *The Spatiality of the Novel*, Wayne State UP, Detroit 1978.
King, Russel, Connel, John and White, Paul (eds), *Writing Across Worlds: Literature and Migration*, Routledge, London 1995.
Loriggio, Francesco, "The Dynamics of Space: The Literary Voyage and Narratology," in Roger Bauer *et al.* (eds), *Proceedings of the XIIth Congress of the International Comparative Literature Association*, Vol. II: *Space and Boundaries in Literature*, Iudicium, Munich 1990, pp. 355–61.
Loxley, Diana, *Problematic Shores: The Literature of Islands*, Macmillan, London 1990.
Lutwack, Leonard, *The Role of Place in Literature*, Syracuse UP, New York 1984.
Marenco, Franco (ed.), *Nuovo Mondo. Gli Inglesi 1496–1640*, Einaudi, Torino 1990.

McLuhan, Marshall, and Harley Parker, *Through the Vanishing Point: Space in Poetry and Painting*, Harper and Row, New York 1968.
Mester, Terri A., *Movement and Modernism: Yeats, Eliot, Lawrence, Williams, and Early Twentieth-Century Dance*, University of Arkansas Press, Fayetteville 1997.
Miller, Hillis J., *Topographies*, Stanford UP, Stanford 1995.
Mitchell, W.J.T., "Spatial Form in Literature: Toward a General Theory," in W.J.T. Mitchell (ed.), *The Language of Images*, University of Chicago Press, Chicago 1974, pp. 271–99.
———, "The Politics of Genre: Space and Time in Lessing's *Laocoon*," *Representations* 6 (1984), pp. 98–115.
———, *Iconology, Image, Text, Ideology*, University of Chicago Press, Chicago 1986.
———, (ed.), *Landscape and Power*, University of Chicago Press, Chicago 1994.
Modenesi, Marco, "Verso una definizione del romanzo decadente," in Paolo Amalfitano (ed.), *Il romanzo tra i due secoli (1880–1918)*, Bulzoni, Roma 1993, pp. 5–19.
Moretti, Franco, *Atlante del Romanzo Europeo 1800–1900*, Einaudi, Torino 1997.
Orlando, Francesco, *Gli oggetti desueti nelle immagini della letteratura*, Einaudi, Torino 1993.
Page, Norman, and Peter Preston, (eds), *The Literature of Place*, Macmillan, London 1993.
Pagetti, Carlo (ed.), *La città senza confini. Studi sull'immaginario urbano nelle letterature di lingua inglese*, Bulzoni, Roma 1995.
Peck, Daniel H., "An American Poetics of Space: Applying the Work of Gaston Bachelard," *Missouri Review* 3 (1980), pp. 77–91.
Perosa, Sergio, *From Islands to Portraits: Four Literary Variations* (1996), 10$ Press, Amsterdam 2000.
Pocock, Douglas C.D. (ed.), *Humanistic Geography and Literature: Essays on the Experience of Place*, Croom Helm, London 1981.
Pratt, Mary L., *Imperial Eyes: Travel Writing and Transculturation*, Routledge, London 1992.
Rabkin, Eric S., "Spatial Form and Plot," *Critical Inquiry* 4 (1977), pp. 253–70.
Reichel, Norbert, *Der Erzählte Raum*, Wissenschaftliche Buchgesellschaft, Darmstadt 1987.
Ritter, Alexander (ed.), *Landschaft und Raum in der Erzählkunst*, Wissenschaftliche Buchgesellschaft, Darmstadt 1975.
Robertson, George et al. (eds), *Travellers's Tales: Narratives of Home and Displacement*, Routledge, London 1994.
Robinson, Alan, "Towards Abstraction," in *Poetry, Painting and Ideas, 1885–1914*, Macmillan, London 1985, pp. 119–49.
Ronen, Ruth, "Space in Fiction," *Poetics Today* 7 (1986), pp. 421–38.
Rubino, Gianfranco, and Carlo Pagetti, (eds.), *Dimore narrate. Spazio e immaginario nel romanzo contemporaneo*, Bulzoni, Roma 1988.
Schenkel, Elmar, *Sense of Place*, Max Niemeyer Verlag, Tübingen 1993.
Sertoli, Giuseppe, *Le immagini e la realtà. Saggio su Gaston Bachelard*, La Nuova Italia, Firenze 1972.
———, *La strada e il desiderio. The Woodlanders di Thomas Hardy*, Annali della Facoltà di Lettere e Filosofia dell'Università di Perugia, 13 (1975–76).

Skulj, Jola, "The Modern Novel: The Concept of Spatialization (Frank) and the Dialogic Principle," in Roger Bauer et al. (eds), *Proceedings of the XIIth Congress of the International Comparative Literature Association*, Vol. V: *Space and Boundaries in Literary Theory and Criticism*, Iudicium, Munich 1990, pp. 43–50.

Smitten, Jeffrey R. and Daghistany, Ann (eds), *Spatial Form in Narrative*, Cornell UP, Ithaca and London 1981.

Soja, Edward W., *Postmodern Geographies: The Reassertion of Space in Critical Social Theory*, Verso, London 1989.

Spanos, William W., "Modern Literary Criticism and the Spatialization of Time: An Existential Critique," *Journal of Aesthetics and Art Criticism* 29 (1970), pp. 87–104.

Sternberg, Meir, "Ordering the Unordered: Time, Space, and Descriptive Coherence," *Yale French Studies* 61 (1981), pp. 60–88.

Tindall, Gillian, *Countries of the Mind: The Meaning of Places to Writers*, The Hogarth Press, London 1991.

Varey, Simon, *Space and the Eighteenth-Century English Novel*, CUP, Cambridge 1990.

Williams, Raymond, *The Country and the City*, Chatto and Windus, London 1973.

Zoran, Gabriel, "Towards a Theory of Space in Narrative," *Poetics Today* 5 (1984), pp. 309–35.

D.H. Lawrence — Criticism

The following is a list of works cited. D. H. Lawrence is abbreviated DHL. For a more extensive bibliography on the writer see Paul Poplawski, *DHL: A Reference Companion*, Greenwood Press, Westport (Conn.) 1996, which is organized in sections, each one treating single works of the writer and various critical approaches. In this volume, there are no essays in languages other than English.

See also Warren Roberts and Paul Poplawski, *A Bibliography of D.H. Lawrence*, 3rd ed., CUP, Cambridge 2001. Among the most recent studies, not covered by Roberts' and Poplawski's books and not included in the Works Cited, see the following volumes: Robert Burden, *Radicalizing Lawrence: Critical Interventions in the Reading and Reception of DHL's Narrative Fiction*, Rodopi, Amsterdam 2000; Terry R. Wright, *DHL and the Bible*, CUP, Cambridge 2000; Nicholas Marsh, *DHL: The Novels*, St. Martin's Press, New York 2000; Anne Fernihough (ed.), *The Cambridge Companion to DHL*, CUP, Cambridge 2001; Anne Odenbring Ehlert, *"There's a bad time coming": Ecological Vision in the Fiction of DHL*, Uppsala UP, Uppsala 2001; Louis K. Greiff, *DHL: Fifty Years on Film*, Southern Illinois UP, Carbondale and Edwardsville 2001; Earl G. Ingersoll, *DHL, Desire, and Narrative*, UP of Florida, Gainesville 2001; Paul Poplawski (ed.), *Writing the Body in DHL: Essays on Language, Representation, and Sexuality*, Greenwood Press, Westport (Conn.) 2001; and Elizabeth M. Sargent (ed.), *Approaches to Teaching the Works of DHL*, MLA, New York 2001.

For DHL's biography see the three volumes published by Cambridge UP: John Worthen, *DHL: The Early Years 1885–1912* (1991); Mark Kinkead-Weekes, *DHL: Triumph to Exile 1912–1922* (1996); and David Ellis, *DHL: Dying Game*

1922-1930 (1998). For information on the writer's stay in Cornwall, see also the novel by Helen Dunmore, *Zennor in Darkness*, Penguin, London 1994.

Monographs

Alcorn, John, *The Nature Novel from Hardy to Lawrence*, Macmillan, London 1977.
Alldritt, Keith, *The Visual Imagination of DHL*, Edward Arnold, London 1971.
Balbert, Peter, *DHL and the Phallic Imagination: Essays on Sexual Identity and Feminist Misreading*, Macmillan, London 1989.
Beal, Anthony, *DHL*, Oliver and Boyd, Edinburgh 1961.
Bell, Michael, *DHL: Language and Being*, CUP, Cambridge 1992.
Björkén, Cecilia, *Into the Isle of Self: Nietzschean Patterns and Contrasts in DHL's The Trespasser*, Lund UP, Lund 1996.
Black, Michael, *DHL: The Early Fiction*, Macmillan, London 1986.
____, *DHL: Sons and Lovers*, CUP, Cambridge 1992.
Comellini, Carla, *DHL: A Study on Mutual and Cross References and Interferences*, CLUEB, Bologna 1995.
Cushman, Keith, *DHL at Work: The Emergence of the 'Prussian Officer' Stories*, Harvester, Sussex 1978.
De Zordo, Ornella, *The Parable of Transition: A Study of DHL and Modernism*, ETS, Pisa 1987.
Doman, Akos, *Die andere Moderne: Knut Hamsun, DHL und die lebensphilosophische Stromung des literarischen Modernismus*, Bouvier, Bonn 1995.
Ebbatson, Roger, *Lawrence and the Nature Tradition*, Harvester Press, Brighton 1980.
____, *The Evolutionary Self: Hardy, Forster, Lawrence*, Harvester Press, Brighton 1982.
Fernihough, Anne, *DHL: Aesthetics and Ideology*, Clarendon Press, Oxford 1993.
Ferrara, Fernando, *Romanzo e profezia. L'amante di Lady Chatterley di DHL come mito e predicazione*, Officina, Roma 1982.
Fjågesund, Peter, *The Apocalyptic World of DHL*, Norwegian UP, Oslo 1991.
Franks, Jill, *Revisionist Resurrection Mythologies: A Study of DHL's Italian Works*, Peter Lang, New York 1994.
Gozzi, Francesco, *La narrativa del primo Lawrence*, ETS, Pisa 1979.
Harris, Janice H., *The Short Fiction of DHL*, Rutgers UP, New Brunswick 1984.
Herzinger, Kim A., *DHL in His Time: 1908-1915*, Associated University Presses, London and Toronto 1982.
Holbrook, David, *Where DHL Was Wrong about Women*, Associated University Presses, London and Toronto 1992.
Holderness, Graham, *DHL: History, Ideology and Fiction*, Gill and Macmillan, Dublin 1982.
Humma, John B., *Metaphor and Meaning in DHL's Later Novels*, University of Missouri Press, Columbia 1990.
Hyde, Virginia, *The Risen Adam: DHL's Revisionist Typology*, Pennsylvania State UP, University Park 1992.
Kelsey, Nigel, *DHL: Sexual Crisis*, Macmillan, London 1991.
Kermode, Frank, *Lawrence*, Fontana/Collins, Suffolk 1973.

Kushigan, Nancy, *Pictures and Fictions: Visual Modernism and the Pre-War Novels of DHL*, Peter Lang, New York 1990.
Mensch, Barbara, *DHL and the Authoritarian Personality*, Macmillan, London 1991.
Meyers, Jeffrey, *DHL: A Biography*, Macmillan, London 1990.
Milton, Colin, *Lawrence and Nietzsche: A Study in Influence*, Aberdeen UP, Aberdeen 1987.
Niven, Alastair, *DHL: The Novels*, CUP, Cambridge 1978.
Pinkney, Tony, *DHL*, Harvester Wheatsheaf, Hemel Hempstead 1990.
Poplawski, Paul, *Promptings of Desire: Creativity and the Religious Impulse in the Works of DHL*, Greenwood Press, Westport (Conn.) 1993.
Sagar, Keith, *The Art of DHL*, CUP, Cambridge 1966.
Simpson, Hilary, *DHL and Feminism*, Crom Helm, London and Canberra 1982.
Sinzelle, Claude M., *The Geographical Background of the Early Works of DHL*, Didier, Paris 1964.
Stewart, Jack, *The Vital Art of D.H. Lawrence: Vision and Expression*, Southern Illinois UP, Carbondale and Edwardsville 1999.
Swigg, Richard, *Lawrence, Hardy and American Literature*, OUP, New York 1972.
Torgovnick, Marianna, *The Visual Arts, Pictorialism and the Novel: James, Lawrence and Woolf*, Princeton UP, Princeton 1985.
Urang, Sarah, *Kindled in the Flame: The Apocalyptic Scene in DHL*, UMI Research Press, Ann Arbor 1983.
Worthen, John, *DHL*, Edward Arnold, London 1991.

Essays

Adamowski, T.H., "The Father of All Things: The Oral and the Oedipal in *Sons and Lovers*," *Mosaic* 14 (1981), pp. 69–88.
Adelman, Gary, "Beyond the Pleasure Principle: An Analysis of DHL's 'The Prussian Officer'," *Studies in Short Fiction* 1 (1963), pp. 8–15.
Albertazzi, Silvia, "L'uomo che amava (a modo suo) le donne: appunti di una 'lettrice arpia'," in Carla Comellini and Vita Fortunati (eds.), *DHL cent'anni dopo, Nuove prospettive della critica lawrenciana*, Pàtron, Bologna 1991, pp. 13–27.
Atkins, A.R., "Recognizing the 'Stranger' in DHL's *The Trespasser*," *Cambridge Quarterly* 20 (1991), pp. 1–20.
_____, "Textual Influences on DHL's 'The Saga of Siegmund'," *DHL Review* 24 (1992), pp. 7–26.
Baron, Helen, and Carl Baron, "Introduction" to *Sons and Lovers*, CUP, Cambridge 1992, pp. XXI-LXXXI.
Black, Michael, "A Bit of Both: George Eliot and DHL," *Critical Review* (Canberra) 29 (1989), pp. 89–109.
_____, "A Kind of Bristling in the Darkness: Memory and Metaphor in Lawrence," *Critical Review* (Melbourne) 32 (1992), pp. 29–44.
Bonds, Diane S., "Going into the Abyss: Literarization in *Women in Love*," *Essays in Literature* 8 (1981), pp. 189–202.
Brown, Christopher, "As Cyril Likes It: Pastoral Reality and Illusion in *The White Peacock*," *Essays in Literature* 6 (1979), pp. 187–93.

Burden, Robert, "Libidinal Structure and the Representation of Desire in *Sons and Lovers*," *The Journal of the DHL Society* (1994–95), pp. 21–38.

Castillo, Debra A., "Postmodern Indigenism: 'Quetzalcoatl and all that'," *Modern Fiction Studies* 41 (1995), pp. 35–73.

Cenni, Serena, "Psico-narrazione e monologo interiore in 'The Prussian Officer' e 'The Fox'," in Carla Comellini and Vita Fortunati (eds.), *DHL cent'anni dopo. Nuove prospettive della critica lawrenciana*, Pàtron, Bologna 1991, pp. 29–46.

Christensen, Peter G., "Problems of Characterization in DHL's *The Rainbow*," *AUMLA* 77 (1992), pp. 78–96.

Cianci, Giovanni, "D.H. Lawrence and Futurism/Vorticism," *Arbeiten zur Anglistik und Amerikanistik* 8 (1983), pp. 41–53.

———, "Introduction" to *Donne innamorate*, Einaudi, Torino 1995, pp. v–xxvii.

Clark, L.D., "Reading Lawrence's American Novel: *The Plumed Serpent*," in Dennis Jackson and Fleda Brown Jackson (eds), *Critical Essays on DHL*, G.K. Hall, Boston 1988, pp. 118–28.

Cushman, Keith, "The Young Lawrence and the Short Story," *Modern British Literature* 3 (1978), pp. 101–12.

Daleski, H.M., "Lawrence and George Eliot: The Genesis of *The White Peacock*," in Jeffrey Meyers (ed.), *DHL and Tradition*, Athlone, London 1985, pp. 51–68.

de Filippis, Simonetta, "Lawrence of Etruria," in Peter Preston and Peter Hoare, *DHL in the Modern World*, Macmillan, London 1989, pp. 104–20.

Delany, Paul, "*Sons and Lovers*: The Morel Marriage as a War of Position," *DHL Review* 21 (1989), pp. 153–65.

Delavenay, Emile, "Lawrence and the Futurists," in Lawrence B. Gamache and Ian S. MacNiven (eds), *The Modernists: Studies in a Literary Phenomenon*, Associated University Presses, London and Toronto 1987, pp. 140–62.

Digaetani, John L., "Situational Myths: Richard Wagner and DHL," in *Richard Wagner and the Modern British Novel*, Associated University Presses, London 1978, pp. 58–89.

Doherty, Gerald, "The Dialectic of Space in DHL's *Sons and Lovers*," *Modern Fiction Studies* 39 (1993), pp. 327–43.

Domenichelli, Mario, "Lawrence, l'inconscio, Freud: il limite e la ripetizione," in Carla Comellini and Vita Fortunati (eds.), *DHL cent'anni dopo. Nuove prospettive della critica lawrenciana*, Pàtron, Bologna 1991, pp. 85–100.

Eagleton, Terry, *Exiles and Emigrés: Studies in Modern Literature*, Chatto and Windus, London 1970, pp. 192–200.

———, "Psychoanalysis (*Sons and Lovers*)" (1983), in Peter Widdowson (ed.), *DHL*, Longman, London 1992, pp. 62–66.

Eggert, Paul, "Lawrence and the Futurists: The Breakthrough in His Art," *Meridian* 1 (1982), pp. 21–32.

———, "Opening Up the Text: The Case of *Sons and Lovers*," in Keith Brown (ed.), *Rethinking Lawrence*, Open UP, Milton Keynes and Philadelphia 1990, pp. 38–52.

Englander, Ann, "'The Prussian Officer': The Self Divided," *Sewanee Review* 71 (1963), pp. 605–19.

Finney, Brian H., "DHL's Progress to Maturity: From Holograph Manuscript to Final Publication of *The Prussian Officer and Other Stories*," *Studies in Bibliography* 28 (1975), pp. 321–32.

Fortunati, Vita, "'The word unsaid': il tema dell'omosessualità nella narrativa di DHL," in Carla Comellini and Vita Fortunati (eds.), *DHL cent'anni dopo. Nuove prospettive della critica lawrenciana*, Pàtron, Bologna 1991, pp. 117–28.

———, "The Visual Arts and the Novel: The Contrasting Cases of Ford Madox Ford and DHL," *Etudes Lawrenciennes* 10 (1994), pp. 129–43.

Foster, John B. Jr., "Crystal and Star: Nietzsche and the Symbolic Action of *Women in Love*," in *Heirs to Dionysus: A Nietzschean Current in Literary Modernism*, Princeton UP, Princeton 1981, pp. 185–206.

Furness, Raymond, "Wagner and Myth," in *Wagner and Literature*, Manchester UP, Manchester 1982, pp. 79–107.

Gavin, Adrienne E., "Miriam's Mirror: Reflections on the Labelling of Miriam Leivers," *DHL Review* 24 (1992), pp. 27–41.

Gorlier, Claudio, "Uccidere il porcospino. Ipotesi sui racconti di Lawrence," *Il Verri* 17 (1980), pp. 37–49.

Gouirand, Jacqueline, "*The Trespasser*: aspects génétiques," *Etudes Lawrenciennes* 1 (1986), pp. 41–57.

Haegert, John, "Lawrence's World Elsewhere: Elegy and History in *The Rainbow*," *CLIO* 15 (1986), pp. 115–35.

Heath, Jane, "Helen Corke and DHL: Sexual Identity and Literary Relations," *Feminist Studies* 11 (1985), pp. 317–42.

Hinz, Evelyn J., "*Sons and Lovers*: The Archetypal Dimensions of Lawrence's Oedipal Tragedy," *DHL Review* 5 (1972), pp. 26–53.

Hyde, Virginia, "Toward 'the Earth's New Architecture': Triads, Arches, and Angles in *The Rainbow*," *Modernist Studies* 4 (1982), pp. 7–35.

Jones, Lawrence, "Imagery and the 'Idiosyncratic Mode of Regard': Eliot, Hardy, and Lawrence," *Ariel* 12 (1981), pp. 29–49.

Kazin, Alfred, "Sons, Lovers and Mothers," *Partisan Review* 29 (1962), pp. 373–85.

Kinkead-Weekes, Mark, "The Marriage of Opposites in *The Rainbow*," in Mara Kalnins (ed.), *DHL: Centenary Essays*, Bristol Classical Press, Bristol 1986, pp. 21–40.

———, "The Sense of History in *The Rainbow*," in Peter Preston and Peter Hoare (eds), *DHL in the Modern World*, Macmillan, London 1989, pp. 121–38.

———, "The Gringo Señora Who Rode Away," *DHL Review* 22 (1990), pp. 251–65.

———, "DHL and the Dance," *The Journal of the DHL Society* (1992–93), pp. 44–62.

Kuttner, Alfred B., "*Sons and Lovers*: A Freudian Appreciation," *Psychoanalytic Review* 3 (1916), pp. 295–317.

Langbaum, Robert, "Lawrence and Hardy," in Jeffrey Meyers (ed.), *DHL and Tradition*, Athlone, London 1985, pp. 69–90.

Levy, Eric P., "Lawrence's Psychology of Void and Center in *Women in Love*," *DHL Review* 23 (1991), pp. 5–19.

Lindsay, Jack, "The Impact of Modernism on Lawrence," in Mervyn Levy (ed.), *Paintings of DHL*, Cory, Adams, and MacKay, London 1964, pp. 35–53.

Mansfield, Elizabeth, "Introduction" to *The Trespasser*, CUP, Cambridge 1981, pp. 3–37.

Meisel, Perry, "Hardy, Lawrence, and the Disruptions of Nature," in *The Myth of the Modern: A Study in British Literature and Criticism after 1850*, Yale UP, New Haven 1987, pp. 11–36.

Meyers, Jeffrey, "Maurice Greiffenhagen and *The White Peacock*," in *Painting and the Novel*, Manchester UP, Manchester 1975, pp. 46–52.

Michelucci, Stefania, "DHL's Discovery of the Etruscans: A Pacific Challenge Against Imperialism," in Marialuisa Bignami and Caroline Patey (eds.), *Moving the Borders*, Unicopli, Milano 1996, pp. 374–81.

Mitchell, Giles R., "*Sons and Lovers* and the Oedipal Project," *DHL Review* 13 (1980), pp. 209–19.

Morris, Inez R., "African Sculpture Symbols in *Women in Love*," *DHL Review* 16 (1983), pp. 25–43.

Newmarch, David, "'Death of a Young Man in London': Ernest Lawrence and William Morel in *Sons and Lovers*," *Durham University Journal* 76 (1983), pp. 73–79.

Nielsen, Inge P., and Karsten H. Nielsen, "The Modernism of DHL and the Discourses of Decadence: Sexuality and Tradition in *The Trespasser, Fantasia of the Unconscious* and *Aaron's Rod*," *Arcadia* 25 (1990), pp. 270–86.

Padhi, Bibhu, "Familiar and Unfamiliar Worlds: The Fabular Mode in Lawrence's Late Narratives," *Philological Quarterly* 64 (1985), pp. 239–55.

Panken, Shirley, "Some Psychodynamics in *Sons and Lovers*: A New Look at the Oedipal Theme," *Psychoanalytic Review* 16 (1974–75), pp. 571–89.

Rowley, Stephen, "Gerald's White Light — A Modern Metaphor: The Meaning of Whiteness in DHL's *Women in Love*," *The Journal of the DHL Society* 4 (1988–89), pp. 20–30.

Sproles, Karen Z., "DHL and the Pre-Raphaelites: Love Among the Ruins," *DHL Review* 22 (1990), pp. 290–305.

Stanford, Raney, "Thomas Hardy and Lawrence's *The White Peacock*," *Modern Fiction Studies* 5 (1959), pp. 19–28.

Stewart, Jack F., "Expressionism in *The Rainbow*," *Novel* 13 (1980), pp. 296–315.

———, "Expressionism in 'The Prussian Officer'," *DHL Review* 18 (1985–86), pp. 275–89.

———, "Dialectics of Knowing in *Women in Love*," *Twentieth Century Literature* 37 (1991), pp. 59–75.

———, "Landscape Painting and Pre-Raphaelitism in *The White Peacock*," *DHL Review* 27 (1997–98), pp. 3–25.

Storch, Margaret, "The Lacerated Male: Ambivalent Images of Women in *The White Peacock*," *DHL Review* 21 (1989), pp. 117–36.

Templeton, Wayne, "The Drift Towards Life: Paul Morel's Search for a Place," *DHL Review* 15 (1982), pp. 177–94.

Torgovnick, Marianna, "'Oh, Mexico!': DHL's *The Plumed Serpent*," in *Gone Primitive: Savage Intellects, Modern Lives*, University of Chicago Press, Chicago 1990, pp. 159–74.

Turner, John, "Comedy and Hysteria in *Aaron's Rod*," in Paul Eggert and John Worthen (eds), *DHL and Comedy*, CUP, Cambridge 1996, pp. 70–88.

Ulmer, Gregory L., "DHL, Wilhelm Worringer, and the Aesthetics of Modernism," *DHL Review* 10 (1977), pp. 165–81.

Verhoeven, W.M., "DHL's Duality Concept in *The White Peacock*," *Neophilologus* 69 (1985), pp. 294–317.

Verleun, Jan, "The Inadequate Male in DHL's *The Rainbow*," *Neophilologus* 72 (1988), pp. 116–35.

Bibliography

Vickery, John B., "Myth and Ritual in the Shorter Fiction of DHL," *Modern Fiction Studies* 5 (1959), pp. 65–82.
Watson, J.R., "'The country of my heart': DHL and the East Midlands Landscape," in Gāmini Salgādo and G.K. Das (eds), *The Spirit of DHL*, Macmillan, London 1988, pp. 16–31.
Weiss, Daniel, "Oedipus in Nottinghamshire," *Literature and Psychology* 7 (1957), pp. 33–42.
Widmer, Kingsley, "Desire and Negation: the Dialectics of Passion in DHL," in Gāmini Salgādo and G.K. Das (eds), *The Spirit of DHL*, Macmillan, London 1988, pp. 125–43.
Wiener, Gary A., "Lawrence's 'Little Girl Lost'," *DHL Review* 19 (1987), pp. 243–53.
Worthen, John, "Introduction" to *The Prussian Officer and Other Stories*, CUP, Cambridge 1983, pp. XIX-LI.
_____, "Short Story and Autobiography: Kinds of Detachment in DHL's Early Fiction," *Renaissance and Modern Studies* 29 (1985), pp. 1–15.
_____, "The Woman Who Rode Away," in Aa.Vv., *Miroirs de la femme dans la litterature d'expression anglaise*, Université de Bretagne Occidentale, Brest 1992, pp. 205–20.
Wright, Louise E.,"DHL, Robert Mountsier and the Journalist Spy Controversy," *The Journal of the DHL Society* (1992–93), pp. 7–21.

Index

Aaron's Rod 55–57, 60, 62–63, 67, 88, 126, 138–41, 143, 152, 155, 170
Abram, David 159
Adamowski, T.H. 129, 167
Adelman, Gary 122, 167
Albertazzi, Silvia 153, 167
Alcorn, John 118, 166
Alldritt, Keith 119, 166
Amalfitano, Paolo 118, 120, 162, 164
Amendolagine, Francesco 159
Amstrong, Frances 162
Appleton, Jay 162
Arnheim, Rudolf 159
Assunto, Rosario 159
Atkins, A.R. 125, 167
Augé, Mark 159

Bachelard, Gaston 131, 138, 145, 147, 154, 159, 164
Bachtin, Michail 162
Bacigalupo, Massimo 117
Balbert, Peter 151, 166
Bammer, Angelika 159
Baron, Carl 132, 167
Baron, Helen 132, 167
Barrell, John 162
Bartkowski, Frances 159
Bataille, Georges 161
Bauer, Roger 163, 165
Beal, Anthony 125, 166

Beethoven, Ludwig van 27
Bell, Michael 139, 142, 144–45, 154, 166
Berger, Peter L. 160
Bhabha, Homi K. 159
Bianchi, Ruggero 117
Bignami, Marialuisa 117, 150, 169
Birds, Beasts and Flowers 10
Bizet, Georges 122
Björkén, Cecilia 125, 166
Black, Michael 121–23, 125, 132–33, 135, 137, 166–67
Blanchot, Maurice 162
Boccioni, Umberto 85
Bonds, Diane S. 143, 148–49, 167
Bonfiglioli, Sandra 159
The Boy in the Bush 89, 107–09, 112, 156
Brown, Christopher 120, 167
Brown, Fleda 153, 168
Brown, Keith 132, 168
Buchanan, Ian 159
Burden, Robert 129, 165, 168
Butler, Christopher 115, 162
Buttimer, Anne 159

Cabibbo, Paola 162
Cacciari, Massimo 159–60
The Captain's Doll 148
Carr, Helen 151, 160
Casey, Edward S. 160

Index

Castillo, Debra A. 155, 168
Cenni, Serena 123, 168
Ceserani, Remo 120, 128, 162
Chambers, Iain 163
Chialant, Maria Teresa 163
Choay, Françoise 160
"The Christening" 20, 98, 132, 146
Christensen, Peter G. 149, 168
"Christs in the Tyrol" 144
Cianci, Giovanni 87, 115, 117, 129, 143, 148–50, 163, 167
Cifarelli, Maria Rita 163
Clare, John 162
Clark, L.D. 152, 155, 168
Clausen, George 8
Colley, Ann C. 163
Comellini, Carla 121, 123, 150, 152–53, 166–68
Connel, John 163
Consonni, Giancarlo 160
Corigliano, Emma 133, 143, 145, 154, 160
Corke, Helen 125, 169
Coser, Lewis A. 161
Crang, Mike 160
Crivelli, Renzo S. 117
"The Crown" 64, 142
"The Crucifix Across the Mountains" 144
Cushman, Keith 122, 166, 168

Daghistany, Ann 117, 165
Daiches, David 163
Dainotto, Roberto M. 163
Daleski, H.M. 121, 168
Darian-Smith, Kate 163
Darwin, Charles 4, 33, 38, 40–41
Das, G.K. 130, 137, 170
"Daughters of the Vicar" 20, 22, 126, 130
David, Keith 161
de Filippis, Simonetta 150, 168
Delany, Paul 131, 168
Delavenay, Emile 115, 168
Deleuze, Gilles 157, 160–61
Descartes, René 161
De Zordo, Ornella 116, 166
Dickens, Charles 162
Digaetani, John L. 125, 168
Doherty, Gerald 130, 133, 136, 168
Doman, Akos 116, 166

Domenichelli, Mario 152, 168
Dorfles, Gillo 160
Dunmore, Helen 139, 166

Eagleton, Terry 129, 131, 168
Ebbatson, Roger 118, 121, 126–27, 166
Eggert, Paul 115, 132, 140, 168, 170
Eliot, George 118, 121, 167–69
Eliot, T.S. 112, 116, 164
Ellis, David 165
Englander, Ann 122, 168
Entrikin, Nicholas J. 160

Faccani, Remo 117, 161
Fantasia of the Unconscious 126, 134, 155, 170
Faré, Ida 160
Fernihough, Anne 145, 165–66
Ferrara, Fernando 147, 166
Fiabetti Ugo 162
Finney, Brian H. 122, 168
Fiorentino, Francesco 163
Fjågesund, Peter 153–54, 166
Flavell, John H. 116, 160
Flower, John 163
Ford, Ford Madox 115, 124, 168
Formaggio, Dino 160
Forster, E.M. 118, 166
Fortunati, Vita 115, 121, 123, 152–53, 167, 169
Foster, John B., Jr. 150, 169
Foucault, Michel 117, 160–61
The Fox 123, 167
"A Fragment of Stained Glass" 23, 124
Frank, Ellen E. 163
Frank, Joseph 115, 117, 163, 165
Franks, Jill 141–42, 166
Frazer, James G. 122
Freud, Sigmund 32, 129, 152, 168–69
Furness, Raymond 125, 169

Gale, Stephen 160
Galsworthy, John 65
Gamache, Lawrence B. 115, 168
Garnett, Edward 129, 132
Gavin, Adrienne E. 134, 169
Geertz, Clifford 127, 160
Gehlen, Arnold 160
Giannone, Roberto 160
Giotto 141
Goffman, Erving 127, 160

Index

"Goose Fair" 19, 98
Gorlier, Claudio 123, 169
Gottdiener, Mark 160
Gouirand, Jacqueline 125, 169
Gozzi, Francesco 137, 166
Greenblatt, Stephen 160
Gregory, Derek 161
Greiff, Louis K. 165
Greiffenhagen, Maurice 8, 119, 169
Guattari, Félix 157, 160
Gunner, Liz 163,
Gurr, Andrew 163

Haeckel, Ernst H. 128
Haegert, John 142, 145, 169
Halbwachs, Maurice 161
Hamsun, Knut 116, 166
Hardy, Thomas 110, 118, 120, 162, 164, 167, 169-70
Harris, Janice H. 122, 166
Heath, Jane 125, 169
Hefferman, James A.W. 163
Heidegger, Martin 1, 116, 161
Herzinger, Kim A. 115, 166
Hinz, Evelyn J. 129, 169
Hoare, Peter 142, 150, 168-69
Holbrook, David 141, 166
Holderness, Graham 132-33, 135, 138, 144, 166
Holtz, William 117, 163
Howard, Richard 151, 162
Howe, John 159
Humma, John B. 140-41, 166
Hurley, Robert 157, 160
Hyde, Virginia 145, 147, 153, 166, 169

Ibsch, Elrud 163
Iengo, Francesco 163
"Indians and Entertainment" 89
Ingersoll, Earl G. 165
Innocenti, Loretta 163
Isaak, Jo A. 115, 117, 163

Jackson, Dennis 153, 168
James, Henry 115, 167
Jarris, Brian 161
Jolas, Maria 131, 159
Jones, Lawrence 118, 169
Joyce, James 1, 115

Kafka, Franz 87
Kalnins, Mara 145, 169

Kangaroo 89, 108-09, 111-12, 139, 155-56
Kant, Immanuel 161
Kazin, Alfred 129, 169
Keats, John 47
Kelsey, Nigel 131-32, 166
Kermode, Frank 141, 166
Kern, Stephen 117, 161
Kestner, Joseph 117, 163
King, Russel 163
Kinkead-Weekes, Mark 142, 145-46, 149-50, 152, 165, 169
Kushigan, Nancy 116, 167
Kuttner, Alfred B. 129, 169

Lacan, Jacques 161
La Cecla, Franco 116-17, 122, 136, 143, 145, 152, 161
Lady Chatterley's Lover 64, 67, 89, 91, 107-08, 111-13, 120, 142, 147, 155, 166
The Ladybird 141, 155
Lagopoulos, Alexandros 160
Lane, Helen R. 157, 160
Lang, Fritz 146
Langbaum, Robert 118, 169
Las Casas, Bartolomé de 155
Lawrence, Ernest 136, 169
Lawrence, Frieda 77, 139
Lefebvre, Henri 159, 161
Lessing, Gotthold E. 164
Lévinas, Emmanuel 32, 147, 161
Lévi-Strauss, Claude 161
Levy, Eric P. 148, 169
Levy, Mervyn 115, 169
Lewis, G.J. 162
Lindsay, Jack 115, 169
Lingis, Alphonso 147, 161
Lipscomb, Patricia 160
Loos, Adolf 159
Loriggio, Francesco 163
The Lost Girl 5, 55-57, 59, 61-62, 67, 85, 88, 138-40, 143, 170
Lotman, Jurij M. 116-17, 121, 130, 136, 147, 161
Löwith, Karl 161
Loxley, Diana 163
Lutwack, Leonard 143, 163

MacNiven, Ian S. 116, 168
Maldonado, Tomás 161
Mallarmé, Stéphane 55
Mann, Thomas 65

Mansfield, Elizabeth 125, 169
Marenco, Franco 163
"Market Day" 154
Marsh, Nicholas 165
Martin, Ron 160
Marvell, Andrew 7
Marx, Karl 129
Mary, Queen of Scots 47, 135
Marzaduri, Marzio 117, 161
McLuhan, Marshall 164
McMillan, Clare 160
Meisel, Perry 118, 169
Mensch, Barbara 140, 167
Mester, Terry A. 116, 164
Meyers, Jeffrey 118–19, 121, 137, 167, 168, 170
Michelucci, Stefania 150, 170
Millais, John E. 8
Miller, Hillis J. 164
Milton, Colin 135, 167
Milton, Kay 161
Miskowiec, Jay 117, 160
Mitchell, Giles R. 129, 170
Mitchell, W.J.T. 164
Modenesi, Marco 118, 164
Moretti, Franco 164
Mornings in Mexico 89–91, 151, 154
Morris, Inez R. 144, 146, 170
Morris, William 154
Mountsier, Robert 139, 171
Movements in European History 64
Mugerauer, Robert 162
Murphy, Patrick D. 161

Newmarch, David 136, 170
Nielsen, Inge P. 126, 170
Nielsen, Karsten H. 126, 170
Nietzsche, Friedrich 24, 60, 84, 125, 135, 150, 166, 168
Niven, Alastair 121, 125, 126, 167
Norberg-Schulz, Christian 116, 133, 147, 151, 154, 161
"Nottingham and the Mining Countryside" 119
Nuttal, Sarah 163

Odenbring Ehlert, Anne 165
"Odour of Chrysanthemums" 21, 123–24
Olsson, Gunnar 160
Orlando, Francesco 164

Padhi, Bibhu 156, 170
Page, Norman 164
Pagetti, Carlo 117, 164
Panken, Shirley 129, 170
Parker, Harley 164
Pascal, Blaise 107
Pater, Walter 7
Patey, Caroline 150, 169
Peck, Daniel H. 164
Perniola, Mario 161
Perosa, Sergio 164
Piaget, Jean 116, 160
Pile, Stephen 161
Pillemer, Karl 160
Pinkney, Tony 116, 121, 125, 144–45, 147, 167
The Plumed Serpent 6, 63, 91, 93, 95–102, 104–08, 112, 143, 153–55, 167, 170
Pocock, Douglas C.D. 164
Poplawski, Paul 147, 148, 165, 167
Porter, Catherine 150, 162
Pratt, Mary L. 164
Preston, Peter 142, 150, 164, 168–69
"The Princess" 6, 63, 91–93, 95, 97, 151
"The Prussian Officer" 19, 22–23, 122–24, 127, 167–68, 170
The Prussian Officer and Other Stories 4, 18–23, 122–24, 126, 129, 166, 168, 171

Quetzalcoatl 153

Rabkin, Eric S. 117, 164
The Rainbow 1, 5, 30–32, 63–78, 81–86, 88–89, 96, 98, 102, 106, 125, 142, 144–47, 149–50, 167, 169–70
Rao, Eleonora 163
Reed, Christopher 161
Rehberg, Karl-Siegbert 160
Reichel, Norbert 164
Rella, Franco 161
Remotti, Francesco 116–18, 127, 134, 147, 153–54, 156, 161
"The Return Journey" 89
Ritter, Alexander 164
Roberts, Warren 165
Robertson, George 164
Robinson, Alan 164
Ronen, Ruth 117, 164

Rowley, Stephen 148–49, 170
Rubino, Gianfranco 164

Sack, Robert D. 162
"The Saga of Siegmund" 125, 167
Sagar, Keith 123, 167
Sahagún, Bernardino de 151
Said, Edward 162
St. Mawr 89, 108, 110–11
Salgādo, Gāmini 130, 137, 170
"San Gaudenzio" 91
Sargent, Elizabeth M. 165
Saussure, Ferdinand de 3
Scardelli, Pietro 162
Scheler, Max 162
Schenkel, Elmar 164
Schopenhauer, Arthur 30
Scott, Walter 44, 46
Seamon, David 159, 162
"Second Best" 22, 126, 130
Seem, Mark 157, 160
Seibert, Charles H. 116, 161
Sennet, Richard 162
Sertoli, Giuseppe 164
"The Shades of Spring" 20–22, 123, 126
"The Shadow in the Rose Garden" 21–22
Shakespeare, William 125
Simpson, Hilary 139–40, 167
Sinzelle, Claude M. 119, 167
"The Sisters" 65
Sketches of Etruscan Places 90, 112, 150
Skinner, Mollie L. 156
Skulj, Jola 165
Smith, Graham 160
Smitten, Jeffrey R. 117, 165,
Soja, Edward W. 165
Sons and Lovers 9, 10, 16, 18, 31–42, 44–48, 50–51, 53–54, 56–57, 63, 67, 70, 72, 82, 110, 129–38, 166–70
Spanos, William W. 165
Spengler, Oswald 64, 89
"The Spirit of Place" 88, 90, 101
Sproles, Karen Z. 135, 170
Stambaugh, Joan 161
Stanford, Raney 118, 170
Sternberg, Meir 165
Stevens, Wallace 64
Stewart, Jack F. 115, 119, 124, 148–49, 167, 170
Storch, Margaret 120, 170

Strada, Clara Janovic 162
Studies in Classic American Literature 5, 90
"Study of Thomas Hardy" 64, 118, 134, 142
Swigg, Richard 118, 167
The Symbolic Meaning 90, 101

Templeton, Wayne 137–38, 170
"The Theatre" 91
Theocritus 128
Thoreau, Henry D. 18
"The Thorn in the Flesh" 22–23, 98, 124, 146
Thrift, Nigel 162
Tindall, Gillian 165
Todorov, Tzvetan 150–52, 155, 162
Torgovnick, Marianna 115, 151, 154–55, 167, 170
The Trespasser 4, 23–26, 28–31, 44, 67, 110, 124–28, 135, 142, 166–67, 169–70
Tuan, Yi-Fu 162
Turner, John 140, 170
Turner, Victor W. 127
Twilight in Italy 89–90, 134, 142, 144

Ulmer, Gregory L. 115, 170
Urang, Sarah 153, 156, 167
Uspenskij, Boris A. 117, 147, 161

Varey, Simon 165
Vattimo, Gianni 162
Verhoeven, W.M. 122, 170
Verleun, Jan 149, 170
Vickery, John B. 122, 171
Villa, Luisa 117
The Virgin and the Gispy 6, 146

Wagner, Richard 24–25, 27, 125, 127, 168
Walmsley, D.J. 162
Watson, J.R. 130, 171
"The Wedding Ring" 65
Weightman, Doreen 161
Weightman, John 161
Weiss, Daniel 129, 171
White, Paul 163
The White Peacock 4, 7–8, 10–13, 15–16, 18–21, 23–25, 28–29, 31, 33–34, 44, 108, 110, 118–22, 124–25, 129, 134–36, 167–70

Widdowson, Peter 131, 168
Widmer, Kingsley 137, 171
Wiener, Gary A. 139, 171
Williams, Raymond 165
Williams, William Carlos 116, 164
Wittgenstein, Ludwig 159
"The Woman Who Rode Away" 6, 63
    91–95, 97, 102, 109, 152, 169, 171
Women in Love 1, 5, 30–32, 64–69,
    71–81, 84–86, 88–89, 96, 98, 102, 106,
    112, 120, 125–26, 134, 140, 142–46,
    148–50, 153, 167, 168–70

Woolf, Virginia 115, 167
Worringer, Wilhelm 115, 170
Worthen, John 122, 124–25, 129, 135,
    137, 140, 149, 152, 165, 167, 170–71
Wright, Louise E. 139, 171
Wright, Terry R. 165

Yeats, W.B. 116, 164

Zola, Émile 65
Zoran, Gabriel 117, 165
Zumthor, Paul 16

www.ingramcontent.com/pod-product-compliance
Lightning Source LLC
Chambersburg PA
CBHW032103300426
44116CB00007B/867